Teaching Guide

Book Seven of *A History of US*:

Reconstructing America

a program of Johns Hopkins University
School of Education

© Copyright, 2010. The Johns Hopkins University. All Rights Reserved.

Talent Development Secondary
Center for the Social Organization of Schools
Johns Hopkins University
School of Education
2701 N. Charles Street
Baltimore, MD 21218
410-516-8800 telephone
410-516-8890 fax
www.TalentDevelopmentSecondary.com

All rights reserved. Student assessments, activity sheets, handouts, and transparencies may be duplicated for classroom use only; the number is not to exceed the number of students in each class. No other part of this document may be reproduced, in any form or by any means, without permission in writing from the publisher. This manual may contain Internet website IP (Internet Protocol) addresses. At the time this manual was printed, any website and/or email addresses were checked for both validity and content as it relates to this manual's corresponding topic. The Johns Hopkins University, and its licensors, is not responsible for any changes in content, IP addresses changes, pop advertisements, or redirects. It is further recommended that teachers confirm the validity of the listed addresses if they intend to share such addresses with students.

Teaching Guide

Reconstructing America

Susan Dangel

Editors: Cora Teter and Maria Garriott
Desktop Publishing: Jennifer Svara & Sharon J. Allen

**TALENT DEVELOPMENT SECONDARY
UNITED STATES HISTORY CURRICULUM**
© The Johns Hopkins University, 2010

Acknowledgements

The authors would like to thank the following individuals and organizations who helped make this curriculum possible:
- the Carnegie Corporation of New York and the United States Department of Education
- our colleagues at the Center for Social Organization of Schools: Doug MacIver, Director, and Robert Balfanz, Co-Director, Talent Development Secondary; Allen Ruby; Leslie Jones; Alta Shaw; Christine Snee; Bob Petza; and Andrew Dangel
- our pilot teachers in Philadelphia: Dawn Davis, Cecelia Johnson, Aaron Moore and Felix Muniz at Central East Middle School; Joan Brooks, Julie Buschel and Carol Heinsdorf at Clemente Middle School
- Betsey Useem and Amy Cohen at the Philadelphia Education Fund
- Kathleen DeBoer and Brad Andrews at Oxford Press
- Dan Taylor at Oxford University Press for his helpful suggestions and the generous use of his personal library
- Byron Hollinshead of American Historical Publications for his friendship, advice, and support
- special thanks to Joy Hakim for her continued support and encouragement; and
- personal thanks to Timothy Dangel and Craig Garriott for believing in us.

This curriculum development was supported by grants from the Office of Educational Research and Improvement, United States Department of Education. The contents or opinions expressed herein do not necessarily reflect the views of the U.S. Department of Education or any other agency of the U.S. government.

Permission is granted to copy and distribute all materials contained herein for a teacher's use in individual classrooms. Other reproductions without permission are prohibited. Copyright © 1999, 2010. The Johns Hopkins University. All rights reserved.

TALENT DEVELOPMENT SECONDARY
UNITED STATES HISTORY CURRICULUM

ABOUT US

The Center for Social Organization of Schools (CSOS) was established in 1966 as an educational research and development center at Johns Hopkins University. The Center maintains a staff of sociologists, psychologists, social psychologists, and educators who conduct programmatic research to improve education, as well as support staff engaged in developing curricula and providing technical assistance to help schools use the Center's research.

The Johns Hopkins Talent Development Secondary (TDS) program has decades of experience developing challenging, engaging curriculum to foster achievement and love of learning in middle and high schools. TDS offers research-based, practice-validated materials in history, science, mathematics, and language arts. The TDS English language arts curriculum pairs significant literary works for middle and high school students with Discussion Guides for engaging, text-based learning. Discussion Guides for dozens of nonfiction titles, most notably in the memoir and biography genres, offer multiple opportunities for teachers to expand the use of nonfiction text to fulfill the Common Core State Standards. In addition, TDS Discussion Guides for novels, plays, and poetry include significant nonfiction and informational connections. Ordering information can be found on the TDS website.

TRAINING WORKSHOPS AVAILABLE

Talent Development Secondary offers training, consultation, and support services in the use of its United States history curriculum to teachers, social studies and history specialists, and administrators. The training is designed to meet the individual needs of participants and can be tailored to upper elementary, middle school, or high school educators.

Initial training provides workshops in using the *Teaching Guide* and *Resource Book*, implementing the lessons in the classroom, and tailoring the curriculum to meet local needs. Participants engage in activities that demonstrate effective instructional strategies and techniques for vocabulary development, reading for a purpose, student team learning, and reflection and review, among others.

Additional training is also available in using primary sources and incorporating historical thinking strategies and techniques in the classroom.

For more information about scheduling workshops and consultation services, contact Talent Development Secondary at 410-516-8800 or visit our website at http://www.talentdevelopmentsecondary.com.

TABLE OF CONTENTS

USING THE TEACHING GUIDE AND RESOURCE BOOK

- Curriculum Standards
- Lesson Format
- Student Team Learning
- Lesson Techniques and Strategies
- Modifying the Lessons
- Materials List

THE LESSONS

Section 1—Rise and Fall of Reconstruction

Lesson 1	Are We Equal?	1
Lesson 2	Reconstruction	12
Lesson 3	Reconstruction	22
Lesson 4	Reconstruction	35
Lesson 5	Collapse of Reconstruction	46
Lesson 6	A Failed Revolution	58
Review Lesson		67

Section 2—The West

Lesson 7	Out West	71
Lesson 8	The Cowboy	82
Lesson 9	The Railroads	92
Lesson 10	The Homesteaders	101
Lesson 11	The Indians	112
Lesson 12	Chief Joseph	123
Lesson 13	Tweed, Beach, and Nast	132
Lesson 14	Barnum and Twain	144
Review Lesson		154

Section 3—Immigration and Suffrage

Lesson 15	Immigrant Voices	157
Lesson 16	Backlash	167
Lesson 17	Lee Yick Goes to Court	176
Lesson 18	The American Dream	187
Lesson 19	A Tea Party	196
Lesson 20	Anthony Goes to Trial	206
Review Lesson		217

Section 4—Unfinished Journey

Lesson 21	Happy Birthday!	221
Lesson 22	The Wizard of Electricity	229
Lesson 23	Jim Crow	237
Lesson 24	Ida B. Wells	245
Lesson 25	Booker T. and W.E.B.	254
Lesson 26	End Words	264
Review Lesson		272

RESOURCE Book includes:
Student Sheets, Team Sheets, Transparencies, and Documents
Game Cards, Assessments, and Library and Media Resources

USING THE TEACHING GUIDE AND RESOURCE BOOK

This *Teaching Guide* (and the accompanying *Resource Book*) for *Reconstructing America* (Book Seven of *A History of US* by Joy Hakim) contains twenty-six lessons; four review lessons; and four assessments. The lessons correspond with chapters in *Reconstructing America* and use a wide variety of primary sources and supplemental resources.

Each lesson in the *Teaching Guide* includes background information and instructional guidance for the teacher, including strategies and techniques for interactive teaching and student activities. In addition, the lessons contain suggestions for simulations and role playing, focus activities, review and reflection activities, writing about history, ways to connect history to other disciplines, homework assignments, and supplemental library and media resources. A review lesson in a game format and an assessment follow each section of five or six lessons.

The accompanying *Resource Book* provides duplication masters for Student Sheets, Team Sheets, and Documents, Game Cards, and Assessments.

History/Social Studies Curriculum Standards

These Talent Development United States history lessons and curriculum materials meet the national standards as set by the National Center for History in the Schools and the National Council for the Social Studies. This United States history curriculum:

- is intellectually demanding for all students
- promotes sound historical reasoning and thinking skills
- extends students' reading and writing skills
- contributes to citizen education
- is supported by interactive teaching and learning techniques and strategies
- follows a cohesive and chronological order
- uses a wide variety of written, visual, and auditory materials
- reflects the nation's diversity and commonalties of backgrounds, points of view, and experiences

Common Core State Standards

A History of US (*HOFUS*) is an excellent resource both for its strong, literary nonfiction voice and its extensive use of primary sources. *A History of US* has been recommended by CCSS as exemplary nonfiction text, and the nation's most influential reading experts—Lucy Calkins, Stephanie Harvey, and Janet Allen—are all *HOFUS* fans.

Although this curriculum was written before the adoption of the Common Core State Standards, it supports these standards. CCSS encourages students to:

- closely read and analyze increasingly complex texts, including primary source documents;
- tackle more nonfiction and informational material[1];
- engage in significant collaborative text-based discussions;
- use evidence to support an argument or defend a position;
- write across the curriculum[2];
- understand historical context; and
- read multiple accounts and perspectives.

These strategies for close analysis of informational text are embedded in nearly every single lesson in the TDS *HOFUS* curriculum.

The Common Core also calls for a significant pedagogical shift: that teachers facilitate a "create-and-learn versus sit-and-get" environment. Students are not to be passive recipients of lectures but must "be actively interacting with the teacher and other students relative to the content of the lesson... Students will be expected to collaborate and engage in meaningful, productive classroom discussions centered on worthwhile content."[3]

This curriculum provides multiple opportunities to fulfill these mandates with challenging, engaging lesson plans. These lessons also support CCSS ELA Reading Standards for Informational Text 6-12 and Reading Standards for Literacy in History/Social Studies for grades 6-12.

---

[1] In keeping with recommendations of the National Assessment of Educational Progress (NAEP), CCSS recommends that by 12th grade, 70% of student reading across the grade (i.e., across all content areas) should be nonfiction.

[2] In grades 9-12, the CCSS recommends that 40% of student writing be argumentative, 20% informative and 20% narrative.

[3] *Implementing the Common Core State Standards: The Role of the Secondary School Leader.* MetLife, p. 18

Lesson Format

Each Talent Development history lesson includes the following sections.

Before Teaching the Lesson

THEME: The theme briefly summarizes the main historical focus of the lesson.

OVERVIEW: The overview discusses the content and historical importance of the lesson and provides background information for the teacher.

STANDARDS: This section identifies Content and Historical Thinking Standards for the lesson from the National Standards for United States History.

RESOURCES: The resources section lists student and teacher materials needed for the lesson and related web sites to help the teacher use computers as research tools for the students.

VOCABULARY: The vocabulary includes important words, names, and places in the lesson. The most essential words are starred (*).

Teaching the Lesson

FOCUS ACTIVITY: A brief Focus Activity introduces the lesson, engages the students, and draws upon their prior knowledge. The *Focus Activity* might ask students to make predictions based on a historical quotation, interpret a photograph or a video clip, brainstorm with teammates, or react to a short anecdote or an intriguing question. The *Focus Activity* usually incorporates partner or team interaction.

TEACHING ACTIVITY: This component features interactive instruction through teacher-directed questions, discussion, and modeling to teach content and employ historical thinking processes. The Teaching Activity usually includes the guided reading of historical narratives, especially the text, for a specific purpose. In addition, the teacher prepares students for the team learning activity, giving instructions and setting standards for the teamwork product.

STUDENT TEAM LEARNING ACTIVITY: Working in small teams, students actively investigate the lesson content, solve problems, use information for a purpose, and apply the tools of the historian. Whenever possible, the task or problem is authentic and structured so that each student has an identified individual responsibility or product to contribute to the team effort. Student Team Learning activities include simulation and role playing, analyzing primary documents (written and visual), jigsaw and group investigation, using web sites, reading primary and secondary historical materials, and problem solving. The activity is usually completed in one class session but may be a long-range assignment.

REFLECTION AND REVIEW ACTIVITY: In this brief conclusion activity, the students review, thoughtfully consider, and respond to a lesson's concepts or meaning. For example, students make connections to other historical events or ideas, respond with their own ideas or actions, consider ethical or moral implications, think and write about history, or judge the historical significance of events and individuals.

HOMEWORK: Suggestions for homework include preparation activities for the next class session, reports, projects, or journal entries. Teachers whose students have personal copies of the text may assign chapter reading in addition to or instead of the suggested homework assignment.

LIBRARY/MEDIA RESOURCES: This section lists supplemental materials (fiction and non-fiction books, magazines, videos, and CD ROMs) that support but are not essential to the lesson. The teacher works closely with the librarian/media specialist to provide these resources whenever possible and to teach and support student research, research skills, and use of the library.

CONNECTIONS: Some brief suggestions to connect history with other disciplines are offered.

Student Team Learning

Student Team Learning is an essential feature of each Talent Development history lesson. Lessons incorporate both a specific *Student Team Learning Activity* and many other opportunities for formal and informal teamwork. These team activities are more than just students working together; they clearly indicate learning structures that guide students to respond to and interact with each other in specific ways and to process information in their teams in a variety of ways.

Team activities encourage students to work together in an atmosphere of positive interdependence and to contribute to their own and their teammates' understanding of historical content and processes. As students work in learning teams, they begin to see their classmates as important and valuable sources of knowledge. Students sharpen their own historical thinking skills and benefit academically because in a cooperative learning team atmosphere they have more chances to understand the material through oral rehearsal, thinking out loud, and discussing their views with others. Essential *Student Team Learning* skills—acquired step by step and reinforced in every lesson—make the classroom climate more positive and nurturing as students learn to give each other encouragement and praise.

Each student participates in the *Student Team Learning Activity* with a specific responsibility or task within the overall team assignment. Each student is individually evaluated for his or her contribution: assessment does not include group grades. Although the team helps individuals to learn, ultimately each student is personally responsible for his or her own achievement.

The teacher not only instructs the students but also guides and facilitates individual learning. During all teamwork activities, the teacher constantly circulates among the teams, interacts with the students, guides their learning, and monitors their progress.

The students work in teams of four (or five, if necessary) with each student paired with a learning partner on the team. The teams should be heterogeneous and reflect the composition of the classroom. In assigning students to their teams, the teacher balances gender, ethnicity, and ability. Once the teams are formed, the teacher provides opportunities for the students to learn to work together. Instead of breaking up teams that have problems, the teacher emphasizes the social skills that the students need to learn to work together. Teams remain together throughout the study of each book. Team composition changes whenever a new text is introduced.

Lesson Techniques and Strategies

Assessments

The assessments focus on multiple choice factual information, short answer, and essay questions, but teachers are strongly encouraged to create their own evaluations that more closely fit the progress and abilities of their students or include other forms of assessment, such as performance-based evaluations.

Brainstorming

Brainstorming is an oral or written technique that encourages students to generate as many ideas as possible within a short, specific time period, such as one minute. Students discuss and evaluate responses only after the brainstorming time has ended.

Circulate and Monitor

For the *Student Team Learning Activity* (and all other team interactions) to succeed, the teacher must circulate among the teams and monitor their progress while students work. Besides encouraging the students to stay on task and complete the assignment, the teacher troubleshoots potential difficulties before they become large problems. During *Circulate and Monitor,* the teacher assists students with the task; asks stimulating, thought-provoking, and guiding questions; answers student queries; reinforces concepts and provides content information; checks assignments; and records grades. This interaction between the teacher and the teams provides the key to productive teamwork.

Graphic Organizers

Graphic organizers such as webs, Venn diagrams, charts, cause and effect, and other diagrams help students visualize, organize, and record ideas and information. Encourage students to create their own *graphic organizers* whenever helpful.

Introduce the Vocabulary

When *introducing the vocabulary*, the teacher pronounces the words and the names of people and places in the lesson with which the students are unfamiliar and provides a very brief definition of the terms as they are used in the lesson. This introduction is fast paced, and may include student generated definitions and the use of the term in a meaningful sentence. The teacher writes the vocabulary words with brief definitions on chart paper that is displayed in the classroom. Students do not copy the words or their definitions, as the purpose of *introducing the vocabulary* is to prepare the students to read the text or other historical materials.

Jigsaw

During *Jigsaw,* students research specific questions and become experts on their question. Experts from the different teams meet to discuss their common topics and then return to teach their topics to their teammates. *Jigsaw* has three steps:

- **Reading:** Each team member is assigned or chooses his or her expert topic or question. The student reads about and investigates that topic or question to prepare for meeting with his or her expert group.

- **Expert Group Discussion:** All students with the same topic or question meet together in an *expert group* to further investigate the topic and share information. Students may use a study guide, graphic organizer, or question sheet to guide this *expert group* research and discussion. If any *expert group* has more than six students, the teacher splits that group into two smaller groups so that each student has a better opportunity to participate. The teacher or *expert group* may appoint a discussion leader for each group. The leader moderates the discussion, making sure that everyone has an equal opportunity to participate. Note taking or secretarial tasks should be shared so that each student participates. Usually each student records information to share with his or her original teammates.

- **Team Report:** Students return to their respective teams and share information about their specific topic or question. Team members take notes and question the expert so that all team members understand the topic information or are able to answer the topic question. Usually each team member has a limited amount of time to make his or her presentation to the team, so that each team member has an equal opportunity to report information.

Notebooks

Notebooks encourage students to record, store, and organize information, handouts, and assignments in useful ways. Loose-leaf, three-ring binders allow students to organize information and practice how to keep a notebook.

Numbered Heads

In *Numbered Heads*, each student in the team has a number—1, 2, 3, or 4. During instruction or another learning activity, the teacher asks a question or gives a thinking prompt. Given. Team members put their heads together and discuss the question or prompt (*Think-Team-Share*). This gives the students an opportunity to immediately discuss the information and determine the right response together. Since the team does not know who will represent them in sharing their response with the class, all members of the team must be prepared to do so. After a set time for discussion, the teacher signals for attention. The teacher calls one of the numbers. All students with that number stand and are prepared to give their team's response or answer the question. *Numbered Heads* is a good technique for an oral quiz or to check understanding when all students need to know the information. For simultaneous responses, team members write a response on the chalkboard. Teachers may choose numbers by rolling a die or choosing a number stick or number card.

Partner Read

In *Partner Read* students share a reading assignment with their team partners. The students read the assignment to each other, paragraph by paragraph, and afterward usually discuss questions about the reading. This technique often assists students who are struggling readers. Consider the reading ability of individual students when assigning team partners. Although a stronger reader can help a weaker reader, the partnership often suffers if the two reading abilities diverge widely.

Predict

Much like speculation, *prediction* requires students to use information, their own knowledge, or other clues to make an educated guess about the unknown. When they *predict* students must explain their reasoning or cite evidence to support their opinions.

Reading for a Purpose

When reading both primary and secondary history materials, provide students with a clearly stated reason for reading the information.

Round Robin

Round Robin, an oral counterpart to *Roundtable,* is an excellent method for brainstorming, problem solving, divergent thinking, or creating a list. It is also effective with students who have limited writing skills or who need to verbalize their thinking.

Roundtable

Roundtable is a *Brainstorming* activity during which all team members contribute ideas on one sheet of paper. Each team member writes or draws an answer and passes the paper to the student on the right. Usually teams have a specific time limitation, such as one minute, to generate as many responses as possible.

Simultaneous Roundtable

During *Simultaneous Roundtable* more than one sheet of paper circulates within the team. Team members start with one sheet each and pass it on to the team member on the right. With four sheets of paper in constant motion, teams use this technique only after they become proficient with *Roundtable.*

Speculate

Students consider a question or idea in order to make inferences, express opinions or personal viewpoints, and predict consequences or effects. Although *speculations* are personal opinions, students must explain their reasoning or cite evidence to support their opinions.

Team Investigation

Following teacher instruction, students engage in a *Student Team Learning Activity* that reinforces, expands upon, requires the use of, or tests their knowledge. During the *Team Investigation,* team members search and analyze the text, primary sources, or other materials; draw conclusions and make connections; or complete a task that applies their learning and the tools of the historian. Students may share the results of their *Team Investigation* with other teams or the class.

Think-Pair-Share

Sometimes called *Turn to Your Partner, Think-Pair–Share* provides an opportunity for students to actively respond to a question, make a prediction, or state an opinion. Students reflect on the content or ideas just presented or consider a question or another prompt. They share their responses with team partners. Partners may exchange similar or different responses and ideas. This is usually a quick way—if the teacher sets a time limit—for students to share ideas, information, or opinions, but it also works when two students engage in a longer task. *Think-Pair–Share* is more time-efficient than *Think-Team–Share* and can be used in its place; however, whole team discussion usually elicits a greater number and a wider range of student responses.

Think-Team-Share

Think-Team-Share is the same as *Think-Pair-Share* except that the entire team does the sharing. *Think-Team-Share* allows for more diversity and a greater exchange of ideas, but it takes more time for all team members to respond. Always set a time limit for the exchange of ideas.

Think-Write-Pair-Share

Think-Write-Pair-Share is similar to *Think-Pair-Share* but requires more time for the written response. However, when students write their answers before sharing they won't be swayed by the opinions of others or lose direction. *Think-Write-Pair-Share* may be used in place of *Think-Pair-Share* or *Think-Team-Share.*

Timed Telling

During *Timed Telling* a student or team has a specific amount of time to share information, opinions, or results of an investigation with other students. The time limitation assists students with summarizing information, choosing main ideas, and organizing their responses to make the best use of the allotted time. Using a timer, rather than a clock or a watch, helps ensure the fair and accurate use of time limitations.

Modifying the Lessons

Teachers should modify the lessons to meet individual time constraints, the needs of students, or local and state requirements. Consider the following general guidelines when making adaptations.

First, as a general rule, do not eliminate any of the four sections of the lesson—that is the *Focus, Teaching, Student Team Learning*, and *Reflection and Review Activities*. These four lesson sections are vital to the structure and pace of the lesson and student learning. Instead, modify or shorten activity within the four lesson sections.

Modifying Reading

- The teacher reads the first page of the chapter to the students. This has four benefits: it saves time, models good reading skills, provides an active listening activity, and puts the students into the text immediately.
- Use *Partner Reading* to pair slower readers with faster readers. Avoid a wide gap in the partners' reading abilities, which often frustrates both students. Each partner reads every other paragraph, as this reading increment helps keep readers focused and on task.
- If each student has a personal copy of the text, both the reading and the *Reading for a Purpose* task may be assigned as homework.

Modifying Questions

- Eliminate some of the discussion questions in a multi-question task, particularly if the students already know the information or if the questions require lower level thinking.
- Students discuss the questions instead of writing answers.
- Assign one question to each team member in a multi-question task.
- To discuss questions, students use *Think-Pair-Share,* which takes less time than *Think-Team-Share.*

Introducing Vocabulary

- Before the lesson, write the vocabulary words and their brief definitions on chart paper.
- During the lesson, briefly review only terms, pronunciations, and definitions that are unfamiliar to the students.
- Students do not copy the terms and definitions, but instead refer to the words on the displayed chart. If students require additional vocabulary work, provide them with a study sheet after the lesson.

Modifying Activities

- Shorten a selected activity or an explanation if students are familiar with the information or if it is not essential to their understanding.
- Assign specific tasks within the larger activity to individual students.
- If students understand and fully share the results of their reading or a *Student Team Learning Activity*, eliminate a general class discussion of the same material.

- Use *Numbered Heads* for students to report information. This is a more time efficient technique than choosing students at random and keeps the discussion moving without lost time.

Management

- Use a timer to limit discussion and sharing periods. Better than a wall clock or watch, a timer is an efficient and accurate third-person time keeper. The timer also eliminates the possibility of distractions and or losing track of time.
- Constantly and consistently Circulate and Monitor to help students begin a task immediately, keep teams on task, encourage students to remain focused, and pace the activity.
- Immediately begin class with the Focus Activity, so that students enter into the lesson without lost time. Display the focusing task when the students enter the classroom.
- Establish efficient management patterns for the distribution and collection of all needed materials, documents, and work sheets and for the transition of students from task to task.
- Move the lesson along as rapidly as possible by eliminating pauses and times of inactivity.

Materials List

Student Materials and Equipment
- Markers or crayons
- Loose-leaf notebook
- Index Cards, 5 by 7 inches
- Chart paper
- Materials for a presentation
- Time Capsule
- Photograph or drawing of self
- Yarn
- Push-pins
- Scissors

Teacher Materials and Equipment
- Markers
- Chart paper
- LCD or overhead slides/ transparencies
- LCD or overhead projector
- Timer
- World map
- Examples of business cards

Optional Materials and Equipment
- CD: "Good Ol' Rebel Soldier"
- CD player
- Dictionaries

The Lessons

**TALENT DEVELOPMENT SECONDARY
UNITED STATES HISTORY CURRICULUM**

© The Johns Hopkins University
School of Education, 2010

Lesson 1
Are We Equal?
Preface

Theme

The end of the Civil War propelled the reunited states into an era of great turmoil and change. As the nation grew even more diverse, it struggled to extend justice and its democratic principles of life, liberty and the pursuit of happiness to all Americans.

Overview

The tangled problems of Reconstruction and reform were as important—and often as traumatic—as the Civil War itself. The Thirteenth, Fourteenth, and Fifteenth Amendments—fundamental revisions of the Constitution—led African Americans and many white lawmakers to hope that full equality had finally been achieved for blacks. Various plans to reconstruct the South, including Lincoln's legacy of forgiveness and harmony, were contested passionately by citizens and lawmakers.

The retreat from radical Reconstruction—the first attempt to establish a biracial democracy—vividly demonstrated how values shared by both the North and South sharply limited support for a social and racial democracy. The ubiquitous American belief in local control made direction from the federal government unpopular. Both Northerners and Southerners believed "the Negro" to be basically inferior, and so could not truly redistribute land, wealth, political power, or social opportunity to embrace the African American. Within a decade after the Civil War, the bright promise of radical reform fell victim to white Southern resistance, the termination of federal supervision, and the withdrawal of the military presence in the South. This led to the disenfranchisement of African Americans, the end of their involvement in Reconstruction state legislatures, greater racial separation, the rise of white intimidation and violence, and the birth of a desperately impoverished black rural working class. Not until the 1960s would the nation revisit the unfinished agenda of social and political justice for black Americans.

New goals and movements brought about by social change diverted most white Americans from Reconstruction. With the South in financial and political chaos and the North crowded by rapid urbanization and industrialization, national attention turned to a new frontier—the West. Here was an unspoiled land with the "Indian problem" under control and thousands of acres ready to be broken by the plow or encased by the newly invented barbed wire. Here was a fresh start for southern blacks, Civil War veterans, northern immigrants, and adventurers. Here economic opportunities and more open social and political systems beckoned. As agriculture, mining, and ranching transformed the land, they were in turn transformed into large-scale enterprises that employed engineering and technological advances. However, the West had its social stresses as African Americans, Chinese and Mexican immigrants, Native Americans, the old Spanish hierarchy, and women struggled for social and political equality.

Meanwhile, in the Northeast, rapid industrialization, the advent of big business, and the rise of the American corporation concentrated great wealth and power into the hands of a few entrepreneurs. The distance between the "haves" and the "have nots" steadily grew as large trusts and monopolies were built on an unskilled immigrant labor force that included women and children. And although wealth-producing industrial development raised the standard of living for a rapidly expanding middle class, an insurmountable chasm grew between the palatial mansions of the very rich and the teeming city tenements of the very poor.

The late 1800s also witnessed unprecedented immigration and urbanization. American society—always diverse—became even more so as immigrants from southern and eastern Europe, Asia, Mexico, and Central America joined the ever-growing, ever-changing American mosaic. Most settled in big cities where they could find jobs and other immigrants with the same county of origin, religion, customs, and language. Often the immigrant vision of the United States as the Promised Land bumped up against such anti-immigrant sentiments as racism, nativism, prejudice, and discrimination. Still, Americans searched for national unity amid expanding cultural diversity, and a growing system of free public education that promoted the assimilation of newcomers as it taught them to read and speak English and become naturalized citizens.

Women reformers, seeking to build on the success of their involvement in the war effort and antislavery movements, reached for an unprecedented public presence, but instead suffered an era of retrenchment on economic and political issues. Despite the committed effort of a number of gifted and hard-working leaders, the temperance, suffrage and women's rights movements made few significant gains. Temperance laws and restrictions were not passed, woman suffrage was not granted, and women and children still worked under inhumane conditions in factories and mills with little political, legal, or social recourse. Although women reformers had helped to secure the enfranchisement of black men and the passage of the Thirteenth, Fourteenth, and Fifteenth Amendments, they would not achieve universal woman suffrage for another generation.

The possibilities and problems, cross-currents and contradictions of the Reconstruction and reform period in some part resemble those our society faces today. The beginning strands of many of our modern problems are tangled in the fabric of the late 1800s. The themes of that era—change, diversity, and justice—continue as part of our nation's ongoing experiment in democratic government that promises life, liberty, and the pursuit of happiness to all of its people.

References

The Annals of America, 1858-1865: The Crisis of the Union. 1976. Chicago: Encyclopedia Britannica, Inc.

Bailey, Thomas A. and David M. Kennedy. 1998. *The American Spirit.* "The Ordeal of Reconstruction, 1865-1877." Boston: Houghton Mifflin Company.

Benedict, Michael Les. "Ulysses S. Grant: 18th President: 1869-1877." McPherson, James M. ed. 2000. *"To the Best of My Ability": The American Presidents.* Society of American Historians. New York: A Dorling Kindersley Book.

Dick, Everett. 1993 (1948 Reprint). *The Dixie Frontier: A Social History.* Norman: University of Oklahoma Press.

Douglass, Frederick. "Reconstruction." *Atlantic Monthly.* http://www.theatlantic.com/unbound/flashbks/black/douglas.htm. Access date October 1998.

"Finding Precedent: The Impeachment of Andrew Johnson." *HarpWeek, LLC.* http://www.impeach-andrewjohnson.com/. Access date October 1998

Foner, Eric. "June 13, 1866 Equality Before the Law." McPherson, James M. ed. 2001. *Days of Destiny: Crossroads in American History.* Society of American Historians. New York: A Dorling Kindersley Book.

Foner, Eric. 1999. *The Story of American Freedom.* New York: W. W. Norton & Company.

Foner, Eric. 1988. *Reconstruction: America's Unfinished Revolution, 1863-1877.* New York: Perennial.

Frankel, Noralee. 1996. *Break Those Chains at Last: African Americans, 1860-1880.* New York: Oxford University Press.

Grob, Gerald N. and George Athan Billias, ed. 1992. *Interpretations of American History: Patterns and Perspectives.* "The Reconstruction Era: Constructive or Destructive?" New York: The Free Press.

McCutcheon, Marc. *Everyday Life in the 1800s: A Guide for Writers, Students and Historians.* Cincinnati, Ohio: Writer's Digest Books.

Marcus, Robert D. and David Burner. 2001. *America Firsthand.* Caleb G. Forshey and Reverend James Sinclair. "White Southerners' Reactions to Reconstruction." Boston: Bedford/St. Martin's.

Meyer, Howard. 2000.*The Amendment that Refused to Die: Equality and Justice Deferred. The History of the 14th Amendment.* New York: Madison Books.

Murphy, Richard W. 1987. *The Nation Reunited: War's Aftermath.* Alexandria, Virginia: Time-Life Books.

Rawley, James A. "Rutherford B. Hayes: 19th President: 1877-1881." McPherson, James M. ed. 2000. *"To the Best of My Ability": The American Presidents.* Society of American Historians. New York: A Dorling Kindersley Book.

"Reconstruction and Its Aftermath." *American Memory.* Library of Congress. http://memory.loc.gov/ammem/aaohtml/exhibit/aopart5b.html, http://memory.loc.gov/ammem/aaohtml/exhibit/aopart5.html#05a. Access date October 1998.

Sutherland, Daniel E. 1989. *The Expansion of Everyday Life 1860-1876.* New York: Harper & Row.

Trefousse, Hans L. "Andrew Johnson: 17th President: 1865-1869." McPherson, James M. ed. 2000. *"To the Best of My Ability": The American Presidents.* Society of American Historians. New York: A Dorling Kindersley Book.

Standards

Historical Thinking

The student will

Historical Comprehension

- identify the central question(s) the historical narrative addresses
- read historical narratives imaginatively
- evidence historical perspectives

Historical Analysis and Interpretation

- compare or contrast differing sets of ideas, values, personalities, behaviors, and institutions
- consider multiple perspectives
- analyze cause and effect relationships and multiple causation, including the importance of the individual, the influence of ideas, and the role of chance
- hypothesize the influence of the past

Historical Research Capabilities

- obtain historical data
- support interpretation with historical evidence

Analysis and Decision-Making

- identify issues and problems in the past
- identify relevant historical antecedents

Content

The student will demonstrate understanding of

How various reconstruction plans succeeded or failed

- The political controversy over Reconstruction
    - contrast the Reconstruction policies advocated by Lincoln, Andrew Johnson, and sharply divided Congressional leaders, while assessing these policies as responses to changing events
- The Reconstruction programs to transform social relations in the South
    - explain the economic and social problems facing the South and appraise their impact on different groups of people

Resources

For each student
Reconstructing America by Joy Hakim: Preface, "Are We Equal? Are We Kidding?"
Notebook

For each team
Sentence strip

For the teacher
Chart paper
Markers

For the classroom
Vocabulary words written on chart paper
Optional: Dictionaries or definitions of words in the quotation on pages 10 and 11 of *Reconstructing America*

Web sites
US History Sources @ http://www.cl.ais.net/jkasper/1870.html

Gilded Age and Progressive Era
U.S. History

Internet Resources @ http://www.tntech.edu/www/acad/hist/gilprog.html

Timeline @ http://www.hfmgv.org/smartfun/timeline/timeline.html

Freedom: A History of US @ http://www.pbs.org/wnet/historyofus/ menu.html

Vocabulary

Words to Remember
self-evident — obvious, automatically apparent

endowed — naturally furnished

*unalienable — cannot be surrendered or taken away

*reconstruction — the act of rebuilding

*reform — to make better or improve what is corrupt or defective

*justice — fair and right treatment under the law

change — to make or become different

diversity — being different or having differences

People to Remember
*Abraham Lincoln — president of the United States during the Civil War who was assassinated days after the end of that war; Lincoln advocated a Reconstruction policy of harmony and forgiveness

Lesson 1   Are We Equal?

The Lesson

Focus Activity – 5 minutes

Notes

1. Teams use **Roundtable** to **Brainstorm**:

   • What problems did the South have at the end of the Civil War?

   • What problems did the North have at the end of the Civil War?

2. Use **Numbered Heads** for teams to share their responses. Record the information on two sheets of chart paper, one labeled Problems of the South and the other, Problems of the North. Guide the students to the following possible responses:

Problems of the South

- Devastated landscape
- Ruin of agriculture
- Destruction of property, farms, towns, cities
- Wrecked transportation systems
- Poverty of people
- Destruction of plantation system and economy
- Political disenfranchisement of white voter
- Freed slave population with few resources to care for themselves
- War casualties
- Physically and emotionally scarred populace

Problems of the North

- The ways and means to help the South recover
- Treatment of former Confederate soldiers and government leaders
- Providing for a freed black population

- Dealing with Southern refugee population
- Physically rebuilding the South
- Recovering from the assassination of President Lincoln and the reshuffling of political power
- Providing justice without vindictiveness

3. Briefly discuss the confusion and trauma of the North and South following the Civil War and lead the students into a discussion of the new period of Reconstruction and reform.

Teaching Activity – 10 minutes

1. Distribute copies of *Reconstructing America*. Discuss the title of the book. Help the students define *reconstruction* (the act of rebuilding) and *reform* (to make better or improve what is corrupt or defective). Write the words and their definitions on the vocabulary chart.

2. Ask the students to **Think-Team-Share**:
   - What needs rebuilding?
   - What needs reform?

   Help students to connect the problems of the North and South (refer to the lists from the Focus Activity) with:
   - the rebuilding and reform of the social, political, and economic systems of the South.
   - the role of the North as military victor in designing and implementing plans and systems to extend justice to former slaves and deal with the South fairly.

3. Ask the teams to review the table of contents of *Reconstructing America* to identify major events and trends (in addition to Reconstruction) in the United States in the late 1800s.

- Impeachment of a president
- Settlement of the West
- Relations with the Native Americans
- Immigration
- Woman suffrage

Lesson 1   Are We Equal?

> - Jim Crow and segregation
> - Urbanization of the North
> - Industrialization

4. Connect the preceding events and topics of *Reconstructing America* with its major themes of *change, diversity*, and *justice*. Ask the students to **Speculate**: How do you think each of these topics reflect change? Diversity? Justice?

5. Introduce the Vocabulary *Words and People to Remember*.

Student Team Learning Activity – 35 minutes

1. Begin the study of Reconstruction by posing the questions:
   - Are we equal?
   - Who is included in "we"?

2. **Reading for a Purpose:** Students read "Preface", pages 9 and 10 of *Reconstructing America,* and then **Think-Team-Share** to discuss the questions written on chart paper:

> - With what radical new idea did America begin? (All people are created equal.)
> - What do we as Americans mean when we say that "we are created equal?" (All people have certain rights that we hold equally. No one has more rights than anyone else, and no one can take our rights from us.)
> - In what important document are these rights listed? (Declaration of Independence)
> - What are those rights? (Life, liberty, and the pursuit of happiness)
> - Why is America still an experiment? (Our nation has wonderful goals of life, liberty, and the pursuit of happiness for all people, but has not achieved them yet. Americans are still striving and struggling to ensure *equal* rights to all, including minorities, immigrants, and women; to define the right to life in issues such as capital punishment and abortion; to ensure liberty and freedom to all people; and to protect the right of all to pursue happiness.)

3. **Circulate and Monitor**: Visit each team to help students read the text and discuss the questions.

4. Use **Numbered Heads** for the teams to share their answers with the class. If necessary, clarify the concepts concerning America as an experiment in democracy and its goals to secure justice and equality for all people.

5. Read the passage from the Declaration of Independence on pages 10 and 11 of *Reconstructing America* to the students.

    Distribute a sentence strip to each team on which the students paraphrase the quotation in their own words. **Note to the Teacher**: If necessary, provide dictionaries or definitions of the difficult words in the quotation.

    Use **Numbered Heads** for each team to read its paraphrase to the class.

    Display the sentence strips in the classroom.

6. **Reading for a Purpose:** Students read "A Water Bird and a Sparrow: Or, How Would Abraham Lincoln Reconstruct?" on page 11 of *Reconstructing America*.

    Help students identify Lincoln's Goals for Reconstruction. Write the goals on a chart to display during Lessons 1 through 6.

Lincoln's Goals for Reconstruction
• Reunite the North and the South
• Re-establish harmony
• Erase hatred
• Reconstruct into a harmonious whole
• All Americans are "entitled to . . . the right to life, liberty, and the pursuit of happiness" as guaranteed by the Declaration of Independence

    Urge the students to keep Lincoln's goals in mind as they discover what actually happened during Reconstruction.

Reflection and Review Activity – 10 minutes

1. Teams use **Think-Team-Share** to respond to the following questions (written on chart paper) about Lincoln's goals for Reconstruction:

> - Do you think Lincoln's goals are too generous toward people who kept others enslaved and fought a terrible war against loyal Americans?
> - In your opinion, were the Southern people traitors?
> - In your opinion, should the Southern people be punished? And if so, how?
> - Do you think the Southern people should have to earn their way back into the Union? And if so, how?

Be sure students explain or defend their opinions.

2. Explain that many Northern lawmakers and ordinary citizens were not as forgiving as Lincoln. Differing opinions on exactly how to rebuild the South and on how punitive to be split the nation and caused a turbulent Reconstruction period.

Note to the Teacher: An additional resource for this lesson is the video series *Freedom: A History of US,* Episode Seven—Part One: A Wounded Nation, Kunhardt Productions and Thirteen/WNET for PBS. Also explore the accompanying PBS Website: Freedom: A History of US @ http://www.pbs.org/wnet/historyofus/menu.html, especially the section for teachers.

Homework

Write an explanation of what this passage from the Declaration of Independence means to you personally. **Note to the Teacher:** Collect students' explanations for safe keeping to use in Lesson 26.

"We hold these Truths to be self-evident, that all Men are created equal, that they are endowed by their Creator with certain unalienable Rights, that among these are Life, Liberty and the Pursuit of Happiness . . ."

Library/Media Resources

Fiction

Freedom Road by Howard Fast, M.E. Sharpe

Out From This Place by Joyce Hansen, Camelot

Cold Sassy Tree by Olive A. Burns, Delta

Gone With the Wind by Margaret Mitchell, Warner Books

Nonfiction

Reconstruction: America After the Civil War by Zak Mettger, Lodestar Books

Reconstruction: The Great Experiment by Allen W. Trelease, Harper and Row

The Era of Reconstruction by Kenneth M. Stampp, Alfred Knopf

Up From Slavery by Booker T. Washington, Doubleday

Worth Fighting For by Agnes McCarthy and Lawrence Reddick, Zenith Books

Cobblestone Magazine

Civil War: Reconstruction

Black History Month: The Struggle for Rights

Old-Time Schools in America (establishment of free schools)

Video

The Civil War, Episode Nine: 1865—The Better Angels of Our Nature by Ken Burns

Reconstruction (Changing a Nation: 1865–1880), Film Rental Center at Syracuse University

Civil War: Postwar Period, Film Rental Center at Syracuse University

Freedom: A History of US, Episode Seven—Part One, Kunhardt Productions and Thirteen/WNET for PBS

CD Rom

Story of America 2: The Civil War, National Geographic Society

Reconstruction, Clearvue and ZCI Publishing, Inc.

Connections

Science — Students conduct experiments to measure differing reaction times, strength, and eyesight of individual students. Discuss whether differences in physical abilities should affect political rights.

Technology/Library — Students use websites (such as the Library of Congress, the National archives, or the Freedmen's Bureau) to locate photographs of the South and freed blacks. Students organize and display the photographs as a photo essay.

Writing/Library — Students research conditions in the South immediately after the Civil War. Students imagine they are traveling through the South at that time and, based on their research, write a diary or a series of postcards home describing their journey.

Science/Library — Many new practical inventions changed daily life after the Civil War. Students investigate these inventions and their impact.

Drama — Students write a play or perform skits that pose the problems of the North and the South following the Civil War.

Research/Library — Students research the lives of children after the Civil War. One excellent source is *American Childhoods*, edited by David Willis McCullough. Students write poems or present a reader's theater production.

Lesson 2
Reconstruction
Chapters 1 through 7

Theme

During Reconstruction—the twelve-year period of readjustment following the Civil War—the nation faced problems of rebuilding the South, reuniting the states, and ensuring the rights and protection of the newly freed African Americans.

Overview

The Civil War left the South in ruins both economically and ideologically. Newly freed slaves struggled to adjust to their liberation. Refugees wandered the devastated streets and towns, unsure of how to earn a living and make their way in the world. Plantation owners whose estates formerly epitomized grandeur, luxury, and gentility now faced the reality of their plundered land, which had been completely ravaged by the war. The hope and promise of Reconstruction quickly faded as the North became distracted by social changes, political factions, government corruption, urban industrialization, and the settlement of Western lands. In the South, African Americans lost their best hope of equality as former Confederate states passed laws that took freedom from blacks, imposed social segregation, and reestablished white supremacy.

Historians divide the twelve years of Reconstruction into two stages: Presidential Reconstruction (1865-1866) and Congressional (or Radical) Reconstruction (1867-1877). Even before the war's end, Abraham Lincoln had set policies for reconstructing the South. After Lincoln's untimely death, Andrew Johnson advanced pro-southern policies until his fall from power and the rise of the Radical Republicans in Congress.

Presidential Reconstruction began in 1865 with the ratification of the Thirteenth Amendment, freeing the slaves, and continued with Lincoln's signature of the bill that created the Freedmen's Bureau. The bureau was to feed both blacks and whites in the South, establish schools to teach former slaves to read and write, help them find paying jobs, and shield them from discrimination. To further protect African Americans, the Civil Rights Act of 1866 declared that all persons born in the United States were citizens.

After Lincoln was assassinated, his vice president, the Tennessee Democrat Andrew Johnson, became president. Johnson disagreed with Congressional Republicans about how to bring the Confederate states back into the Union and how to treat their leaders. Johnson pardoned most Southerners, including Confederate officials and military officers, an act which permitted former Confederates to vote and hold office. Johnson even pardoned Alexander Stevens, the former vice president of the Confederacy. In 1865, seventy former Confederate generals, cabinet officials, and congressmen were elected as representatives to the United States Congress. Meanwhile, black codes kept former slaves from voting, testifying against whites in court, serving on juries, and joining the militia.

Johnson so infuriated the Radical Republicans with his stubbornness, inability to compromise, and use of veto powers that in 1868 the House of Representatives voted to impeach him. Johnson's primary offense was his opposition to congressional policies and the violent language he used in criticizing them. The most serious charge against him was that he had removed from his cabinet the secretary of war, a staunch supporter of the Congress. The Senate held a trial but lacked one vote of the necessary two-thirds majority to convict. The trial proved Johnson was technically within his rights in removing a cabinet member, but even more significant, it set a dangerous precedent to remove a president just because he disagreed with the majority of the members of Congress.

The second stage of Reconstruction (from 1867 through 1877) began when Congress required each Southern state to ratify the Fourteenth Amendment (granting all citizens including the freed slaves the right to due process of law) to reenter the Union. Only Tennessee complied, so Congress divided the South—except for Tennessee—into five military districts. An army general and federal troops were sent to each district. Southern states were required to hold conventions with both black and white delegates to rewrite their state constitutions and bring them into compliance with the United States Constitution.

Led by Radical Republicans Thaddeus Stevens and Charles Sumner, Congress passed two amendments to the Constitution and several laws to protect the rights of former slaves. The Fourteenth Amendment made all former slaves United States citizens, and the Fifteenth Amendment gave African American men the right to vote. The Force Acts in 1870 and 1871 tried to protect blacks from acts of terrorism precipitated by white supremacy hate groups such as the Ku Klux Klan. The Civil Rights Act of 1875 was aimed at ending Jim Crow laws that legalized segregation, but it was overturned by the Supreme Court in 1883.

In spite of the antagonism of white supremacists, African American men established a beachhead on the political front. Between 1869 and 1876, fourteen black men were elected to the House of Representatives. Two others, Hiram R. Revels and Blanche K. Bruce, were elected to the Senate. During Reconstruction, more than six hundred African Americans served in state legislatures. The records of these men showed them to be competent and, in many cases, noteworthy legislators. But this promising beginning in interracial government did not last. The Compromise of 1877 settled a contested presidential election and ended Reconstruction. In exchange for supporting Republican Rutherford B. Hayes for president, Southern Democrats were promised that federal troops would be removed from the South. So it was, and so ended the social and political revolution of Reconstruction.

References

The Annals of America, 1858-1865: The Crisis of the Union. 1976. Chicago: Encyclopedia Britannica, Inc.

Bailey, Thomas A. and David M. Kennedy. 1998. *The American Spirit.* "The Ordeal of Reconstruction, 1865-1877." Boston: Houghton Mifflin Company.

Benedict, Michael Les. "Ulysses S. Grant: 18th President: 1869-1877." McPherson, James M. ed. 2000. *"To the Best of My Ability": The American Presidents*. Society of American Historians. New York: A Dorling Kindersley Book.

Dick, Everett. 1993 (1948 Reprint). *The Dixie Frontier: A Social History*. Norman: University of Oklahoma Press.

Douglass, Frederick. "Reconstruction." *Atlantic Monthly.* http://www.theatlantic.com/unbound/flashbks/black/douglas.htm. Access date October 1998.

"Finding Precedent: The Impeachment of Andrew Johnson." *HarpWeek, LLC.* http://www.impeach-andrewjohnson.com/. Access date October 1998.

Foner, Eric. "June 13, 1866 Equality Before the Law." McPherson, James M. ed. 2001. *Days of Destiny: Crossroads in American History.* Society of American Historians. New York: A Dorling Kindersley Book.

Foner, Eric. 1999. *The Story of American Freedom.* New York: W.W. Norton & Company.

Foner, Eric. 1988. *Reconstruction: America's Unfinished Revolution, 1863-1877.* New York: Perennial.

Frankel, Noralee. 1996. *Break Those Chains at Last: African Americans, 1860-1880.* New York: Oxford University Press.

Grob, Gerald N. and George Athan Billias, ed. 1992. *Interpretations of American History: Patterns and Perspectives.* "The Reconstruction Era: Constructive or Destructive?" New York: The Free Press.

McCutcheon, Marc. *Everyday Life in the 1800s: A Guide for Writers, Students and Historians.* Cincinnati, Ohio: Writer's Digest Books.

Marcus, Robert D. and David Burner. 2001. *America Firsthand.* Caleb G. Forshey and Reverend James Sinclair. "White Southerners' Reactions to Reconstruction." Boston: Bedford/St. Martin's.

Meyer, Howard. 2000.*The Amendment that Refused to Die: Equality and Justice Deferred. The History of the 14th Amendment.* New York: Madison Books.

Murphy, Richard W. 1987. *The Nation Reunited: War's Aftermath.* Alexandria, Virginia: Time-Life Books.

Rawley, James A. "Rutherford B. Hayes: 19th President: 1877-1881." McPherson, James M. ed. 2000. *"To the Best of My Ability": The American Presidents.* Society of American Historians. New York: A Dorling Kindersley Book.

"Reconstruction and Its Aftermath." *American Memory.* Library of Congress. http://memory.loc.gov/ammem/aaohtml/exhibit/ aopart5b.html, http://memory.loc.gov/ammem/aaohtml/exhibit/aopart5.html#05a. Access date October 1998.

Sutherland, Daniel E. 1989. *The Expansion of Everyday Life 1860-1876.* New York: Harper & Row.

Trefousse, Hans L. "Andrew Johnson: 17th President: 1865-1869." McPherson, James M. ed. 2000. *"To the Best of My Ability": The American Presidents.* Society of American Historians. New York: A Dorling Kindersley Book.

Standards

Historical Thinking

The student will

Chronological Thinking

- identify in historical narratives the temporal structure of a historical narrative or story
- create time lines

Historical Comprehension

- reconstruct the literal meaning of a historical passage
- identify the central question(s) the historical narrative addresses
- read historical narratives imaginatively
- utilize visual and mathematical data presented in charts, Venn diagrams, and other graphic organizers

Historical Analysis and Interpretation

- compare or contrast differing sets of ideas, values, personalities, behaviors, and institutions
- consider multiple perspectives
- analyze cause and effect relationships and multiple causation, including the importance of the individual, the influence of ideas, and the role of chance
- hypothesize the influence of the past

Historical Research Capabilities

- obtain historical data
- support interpretations with historical evidence

Lesson 2   Reconstruction

Analysis and Decision-Making

- identify issues and problems in the past
- marshal evidence of antecedent circumstances and contemporary factors contributing to problems and alternative courses of action

Content

The student will demonstrate understanding of

How various reconstruction plans succeeded or failed

- The political controversy over Reconstruction
  - contrast the Reconstruction policies advocated by Lincoln, Andrew Johnson, and sharply divided Congressional leaders, while assessing these policies as responses to changing events
  - analyze the escalating conflict between President Johnson and Republican legislators, and explain the reasons for and consequences of Johnson's impeachment and trial
  - explain the provisions of the Fourteenth and Fifteenth Amendments and the political forces supporting and opposing each
- The Reconstruction programs to transform social relations in the South
  - explain the economic and social problems facing the South and appraise their impact on different groups of people
  - evaluate the goals and accomplishments of the Freedman's Bureau
  - analyze how African Americans attempted to improve their economic position during Reconstruction and explain factors involved in their quest for land ownership
- The successes and failures of Reconstruction in the South, North, and West
  - examine the progress of "Black Reconstruction" and legislative reform programs promoted by reconstructed state governments
  - assess how the political and economic position of African Americans in the northern and western states changed during Reconstruction

Resources

For each student

Reconstructing America by Joy Hakim: one of Chapters 1 through 7

Student Sheets:
  Chapter Summary
  Evaluation Form

For the teacher

Chart paper

Markers

Transparency: *"Good Ol' Rebel Soldier"*

Optional recording of *"Good Ol' Rebel Soldier"*

For the classroom

Overhead projector

Web sites

Civil War and Reconstruction Hot Links @ http://www.sinc.sunysb.edu/Class/is265/hotlinks.html

Timeline @ http://www.hfmgov.org/smartfun/timeline/timeline.html

Outline of the Civil War With Links to Reconstruction @ http://members.

tripod.com/great americanhistory/gr02006.htm

Freedmen and Southern Society Project @ http://www.inform.umd.edu/ARHU/Depts/History/Freedman/home.html

Freedom: A History of US @ http://www.pbs.org/wnet/historyofus/menu.html

Note to the Teacher: Although the students define important vocabulary from their assigned chapters, the following list includes important words and people from Chapters 1 through 7 of *Reconstructing America*.

Vocabulary

Words to Remember

***Reconstruction** — twelve years of readjustment following the Civil War when the nation faced problems of rebuilding the South, reuniting the states, and ensuring the rights and protection of the newly freed African Americans

***"Seward's Folly"** — purchase of Alaska from Russia in 1867 by Secretary of State William Seward. It was considered a foolish act at the time, but turned out to be a great real estate deal

***Presidential Reconstruction** — first two years of Reconstruction, when Lincoln and his successor Johnson controlled Reconstruction policy

***Freedmen's Bureau** — organization devoted to helping newly freed blacks. It established schools and hospitals, taught blacks to read and write, helped them find work, and intervened in crisis situations.

***Thirteenth Amendment** — abolished slavery

***Fourteenth Amendment** — guaranteed that no state can take away a citizen's rights; the "equal protection under the law" amendment

***amendment** — a change or addition to a formal document or set of rules

***ratify** — to approve and make official

***radical** — extreme

***veto** — the power of the president to prevent a bill from becoming law

***carpetbagger** — Northerner who went South after the war to teach or help with social programs; some took advantage of the disorder for personal profit

***Congressional Reconstruction** — also called Radical or Military Reconstruction, the ten years (1867-77) of Northern occupation in the South meant to guarantee the rights and freedom of former slaves

***scalawag** — Southerner who cooperated with the North

***Fifteenth Amendment** — granted the right to vote to all men, regardless of race

***abolitionist** — one who works for the end of slavery

***impeach** — to charge a public official before a governing, legislative body with misconduct while in office; presidential impeachment requires a charge of treason, bribery, or other high crimes and misdemeanors

People to Remember

***Andrew Johnson** — vice president who became president upon the assassination of Abraham Lincoln and who presided over the first few years of Reconstruction; first president to be impeached but was acquitted by one vote in the Senate

***Edmund G. Ross** — senator from the Radical Republican state of Kansas who cast the deciding not guilty vote at Andrew Johnson's impeachment trial

***Thaddeus Stevens** — radical Republican who authored the Thirteenth and Fourteenth amendments

Lesson 2   Reconstruction

The Lesson

Focus Activity – 5 minutes

1. Introduce the song "Good Ol' Rebel Soldier" by explaining that some former Confederates refused to forgive and forget. While the victor extended a welcoming hand, the defeated often harbored stubborn and acrid feelings.

2. Display the Transparency: *"Good Ol' Rebel Soldier"* and read the lyrics to the students. Play the song if a recording is available.

3. Ask the students to **Think-Team-Share**:

   - What does this song tell you about some Southern reactions to Reconstruction?

   - Why might Reconstruction be a turbulent time in the South?

   - What do you predict will be the ultimate fate of Reconstruction?

4. Explain that in this song the old rebel still clings to his Confederate ideas and won't be reconstructed. Ask the students to **Speculate**:

   - Why was the song "respectfully dedicated to the Honorable Thaddeus Stevens"? (If necessary, explain the sarcasm intended by this dedication to the one man most responsible for Radical Reconstruction.)

Teaching Activity – 10 minutes

1. Briefly introduce Reconstruction by reading and commenting on the chapter titles as the students preview Chapters 1 through 7 in *Reconstructing America*.

2. Explain the research and teaching activity for the next three lessons to the students. As you explain the assignment, summarize each of the following steps on chart paper for future student reference.

   > - Each team will be assigned a specific chapter (Chapters 1 through 7 in *Reconstructing America*) to research and then teach to the class.

Notes

> - Students will receive the Student Sheets: *Chapter Summary* to guide their research.
> - After each student reads the assigned chapter and completes the *Chapter Summary*, the teams will discuss the important vocabulary, ideas, events, and people in their chapter.
> - During that discussion team members add information and make revisions to their Student Sheets: *Chapter Summary*.
> - Each team plans and then presents a five minute lesson to teach its chapter to the class. Each member of the team must have a specific part in the presentation. Teams should create an interesting presentation that actively involves classmates.
> - Teams prepare their presentations during this lesson (Lesson 2) and teach their chapters to the class during Lessons 3 and 4.

3. Distribute and explain the Student Sheet: *Evaluation Form* that the students will use to assess team presentations. Teams should keep the criteria in mind as they plan their presentations.

4. Assign **one** of the Chapters 1 through 7 in *Reconstructing America* to each team. Distribute the Student Sheets: *Chapter Summary,* that correspond to each team's assigned chapter.

   Note to the Teacher: You may assign chapters randomly, based on student interest, or according to chapter difficulty. Chapters 3, 4, 5, and 6 are very content rich, so you may wish to assign them to more capable teams. If you have more than seven teams, divide the longer or more difficult chapters between two teams.

Student Team Learning Activity – 40 minutes

Researching a topic

1. **Reading for a Purpose:** Team members read their assigned chapters to research their topic. Introduce or help students with the vocabulary as needed.

2. Students use the Student Sheets: *Chapter Summary* to guide and focus their research. After team members complete their individual chapter summaries, the team decides what information to include and each team member's role in the team presentation.

3. **Circulate and Monitor:** Visit each team as students read, complete their chapter summaries, and discuss their chapter. If necessary, assist students with the vocabulary and check that they are recording accurate and complete information. Students should not copy information verbatim from the chapter but answer in their own words. Help teams plan their presentations. Check that all team members have a part in the presentation, and that the team plans a way to engage the class, such as taking notes or answering questions.

Reflection and Review Activity – 5 minutes

Each student reviews his or her responsibility in the team's presentation. The teams check their presentation plans for completeness of information, involvement of all team members, and the active engagement of the class.

Note to the Teacher: An additional resource for this lesson is the video series *Freedom: A History of US,* Episode Seven—Part Two: Making Changes, Kunhardt Productions and Thirteen/WNET for PBS. Also explore the accompanying PBS Website: Freedom: A History of US @ http://www.pbs.org/wnet/historyofus/menu.html, especially the section for teachers.

Homework

Each student prepares for and practices his or her part of the team presentation.

Library/Media Resources

Fiction
Freedom Road by Howard Fast, M.E. Sharpe

Out From This Place by Joyce Hansen, Camelot

Cold Sassy Tree by Olive A. Burns, Delta

Gone With the Wind by Margaret Mitchell, Warner Books

Nonfiction

Reconstruction: America After the Civil War by Zak Mettger, Lodestar Books

Reconstruction: The Great Experiment by Allen W. Trelease, Harper and Row

The Era of Reconstruction by Kenneth M. Stampp, Alfred Knopf

Up From Slavery by Booker T. Washington, Doubleday

Worth Fighting For by Agnes McCarthy and Lawrence Reddick, Zenith Books

Cobblestone Magazine

Civil War: Reconstruction

Black History Month: The Struggle for Rights

Old-Time Schools in America (the establishment of free schools for blacks)

Video

The Civil War, Episode Nine: 1865—The Better Angels of Our Nature by Ken Burns

Reconstruction (Changing a Nation: 1865—1880), Film Rental Center at Syracuse University

Civil War: Postwar Period, Film Rental Center at Syracuse University

Freedom: A History of US, Episode Seven—Part Two, Kunhardt Productions and Thirteen/WNET for PBS

CD Rom

Story of America 2: The Civil War, National Geographic Society

Reconstruction, Clearvue and ZCI Publishing, Inc.

Connections

Science — During the Civil War, many men lost arms or legs. As Joy Hakim points out in Chapter 1, Mississippi spent a fifth of its state income on artificial arms and legs for veterans. Students research modern advances in bio-mechanics and how artificial limbs are made and attached.

Library — Students read biographies or research the lives of prominent persons during the Reconstruction era. To share this information with others, the students perform short first-person vignettes.

Music — Besides "Good Ol' Rebel Soldier," what songs came out of the Reconstruction era? Students find and sing these songs. Students can visit Poetry and Music of the War Between the States @ http://users.erols.com/kfraser to help them search.

Lesson 3
Reconstruction
Chapters 1 through 4

Theme

During the first two years of Reconstruction, the work of the Freedmen's Bureau and the passage of the Thirteenth and Fourteenth Amendments led many to hope that rebuilding the South would assure African Americans their full and equal rights.

Overview

Upon Lincoln's assassination by John Wilkes Booth, Andrew Johnson became president. Johnson—a Southern Democrat and former slaveholder—had demonstrated his loyalty by staying with the Union. His life had often been threatened because of this choice, but Johnson showed exceptional bravery and stubbornly held to what he thought right. Throughout the war, he held the post of military governor in his home state of Tennessee, and so impressed Lincoln that he was asked to serve as vice president. In many ways Johnson seemed an ideal post-war president. He stood for the preservation of the country but was sensitive to Southerners and understood their post-war problems and need for rebuilding.

America struggled with a long series of growing pains as newly-freed slaves endured the poverty of life without land or a paying job, the lack of guaranteed rights, and life in a society with little law and order. During the first two years of Johnson's administration, there was some measure of success as schools for former slaves were established with the aid of Northern missionaries and teachers. The Freedmen's Bureau (established by Lincoln before the end of the war) prevented people from starving and distributed clothing to those in need, regardless of color. Northern soldiers kept order in the South, trying to maintain the hard-won equality of the freedmen and women.

But before long, some Southerners fought back. The newly formed Ku Klux Klan—an organization of white supremacists cloaked as ghosts of dead Confederates—terrorized both black and white people who supported black rights. The Klan actively prevented black men from voting through threats and violence—including lynching—and put the civil rights of freed blacks in jeopardy. Democrat President Andrew Johnson supported the return of white rule to the South and saw no need to protect or expand the rights of freed slaves. Johnson, who pardoned former Confederate officials and military officers, made life difficult for Southerners who had supported the Union, seemingly forgetting that he had held that very same position during the war.

Congress and President Johnson fought bitterly over civil rights laws. In the latter half of his presidency, Johnson vetoed several civil rights bills. Congress eventually overrode Johnson's vetoes and passed the measures. The Civil Rights Act of 1866 declared that all persons born in the United States were citizens; the Fourteenth Amendment made all former slaves United States citizens, and granted them due process and the equal protection of the laws. Johnson clearly sided with white supremacists that might have accepted the end of slavery but would never embrace the idea of black equality. He actually favored the policy of states' rights and believed that each state—not the federal government—should protect the rights of its citizens, including African Americans. Johnson seemed blind to the reality that the former Confederate states had no intention of protecting their freed slave populations, and in fact were moving in the opposite direction by institutionalizing segregation and discrimination.

Congressional opposition to Johnson was led by his arch rival Thaddeus Stevens, who fought the president on all political and social matters and spearheaded the process of Johnson's impeachment. Stevens, sympathetic to the plight of black Americans, defended them and their rights at high personal cost. He labored tirelessly for justice and equality for former slaves. Johnson's retrogressive ideas, coupled with his questionable character traits, led him to be impeached by the House of Representatives but acquitted by the Senate by only a one-vote margin.

Meanwhile the South nursed its ongoing resentment of the Northern presence in its affairs. The label carpetbaggers—the name Southerners applied to Northerners who moved south during Reconstruction with only one suitcase, a carpetbag—reflected the stereotype of Northerners who intended to stay in the region just long enough to profit from the South's misfortune and stir up trouble between whites and blacks. For many white Southerners, the term also applied to those who went South to aid with education and other social programs for former slaves. Conservative Southerners sought ways to limit the social and political rights of African Americans and reestablish white control of Southern society.

References

The Annals of America, 1858-1865: The Crisis of the Union. 1976. Chicago: Encyclopedia Britannica, Inc.

Bailey, Thomas A. and David M. Kennedy. 1998. *The American Spirit.* "The Ordeal of Reconstruction, 1865-1877." Boston: Houghton Mifflin Company.

"The Civil Rights Act of 1866." *Historical Documents. Americans.net.* http://www.africanamericans.com/CivilRightsActof1866.htm. Access date October 1988.

Dick, Everett. 1993. 1948 Reprint. *The Dixie Frontier: A Social History.* Norman: University of Oklahoma Press.

Douglass, Frederick. "Reconstruction." *Atlantic Monthly.* http://www.theatlantic.com/unbound/flashbks/black/douglas.htm. Access date October 1998.

Du Bois, W. E. Burghardt. "The Freedmen's Bureau." *Atlantic Monthly* 87. University of Virginia Library. http://wyllie.lib.virginia.edu:8086/ perl/toccer-new?id=DubFree.sgm&images=images/modeng&data= /texts/english/modeng/parsed&tag=public&part=1&division=div. Access date October 1998.

"Finding Precedent: The Impeachment of Andrew Johnson." *HarpWeek, LLC.* http://www.impeach-andrewjohnson.com/. Access date October 1998

Foner, Eric. "June 13, 1866 Equality Before the Law." McPherson, James M. ed. 2001. *Days of Destiny: Crossroads in American History.* Society of American Historians. New York: A Dorling Kindersley Book.

Foner, Eric. 1999. *The Story of American Freedom.* New York: W.W. Norton & Company.

Foner, Eric. 1988. *Reconstruction: America's Unfinished Revolution, 1863-1877.* New York: Perennial.

Frankel, Noralee. 1996. *Break Those Chains at Last: African Americans, 1860-1880.* New York: Oxford University Press.

Grob, Gerald N. and George Athan Billias, ed. 1992. *Interpretations of American History: Patterns and Perspectives.* "The Reconstruction Era: Constructive or Destructive?" New York: The Free Press.

Marcus, Robert D. and David Burner. 2001. *America Firsthand.* Caleb G. Forshey and Reverend James Sinclair. "White Southerners' Reactions to Reconstruction." Boston: Bedford/St. Martin's.

Meyer, Howard. 2000. *The Amendment that Refused to Die: Equality and Justice Deferred. The History of the 14th Amendment.* New York: Madison Books.

Murphy, Richard W. 1987. *The Nation Reunited: War's Aftermath.* Alexandria, Virginia: Time-Life Books.

"Reconstruction and Its Aftermath." *American Memory.* Library of Congress. http://memory.loc.gov/ammem/aaohtml/exhibit/ aopart5b.html; http://memory.loc.gov/ammem/aaohtml/exhibit/aopart5.html#05a. Access date October 1998.

Stevens, Thaddeus. "Speech of December 18, 1865." *From Revolution to Reconstruction.* http://odur.let.rug.nl/~usa/D/1851-1875/reconstruction/steven.htm. Access date October 1998.

Trefousse, Hans L. "Andrew Johnson: 17th President: 1865-1869." McPherson, James M. ed. 2000. *"To the Best of My Ability": The American Presidents.* Society of American Historians. New York: A Dorling Kindersley Book.

Standards

Historical Thinking

The student will

Chronological Thinking

- identify in historical narratives the temporal structure of a historical narrative or story

Historical Comprehension

- reconstruct the literal meaning of a historical passage
- identify the central question(s) the historical narrative addresses
- read historical narratives imaginatively
- draw upon visual, literary, and musical sources

Historical Analysis and Interpretation

- compare or contrast differing sets of ideas, values, personalities, behaviors, and institutions
- consider multiple perspectives
- analyze cause and effect relationships and multiple causation, including the importance of the individual, the influence of ideas, and the role of chance
- hypothesize the influence of the past

Historical Research Capabilities

- formulate historical questions
- obtain historical data
- support interpretation with historical events

Analysis and Decision-Making

- identify issues and problems in the past
- marshal evidence of antecedent circumstances and contemporary factors contributing to problems and alternative courses of action

Content

The student will demonstrate understanding of

How various reconstruction plans succeeded or failed

- The political controversy over Reconstruction
    - contrast the Reconstruction policies advocated by Lincoln, Andrew Johnson, and sharply divided Congressional leaders, while assessing these policies as responses to changing events
    - analyze the escalating conflict between President Johnson and Republican legislators, and explain

Lesson 3   Reconstruction

the reasons for and consequences of Johnson's impeachment and trial

- explain the provisions of the Fourteenth and Fifteenth Amendments and the political forces supporting and opposing each

• The Reconstruction programs to transform social relations in the South

- explain the economic and social problems facing the South and appraise their impact on different groups of people

- evaluate the goals and accomplishments of the Freedman's Bureau

- analyze how African Americans attempted to improve their economic position during Reconstruction and explain factors involved in their quest for land ownership

Resources

For each student

Reconstructing America by Joy Hakim: Chapters 1 through 4

Four *Evaluation Forms*, one for each team presentation

For each team

Materials needed for its presentation

For the teacher

Chart paper

Markers

Four *Evaluation Forms*, one for each team presentation

Timer

Web sites

Civil War and Reconstruction Hot Links @ http://www.sinc.sunysb.edu/Class/is265/hotlinks.html

Timeline @ http://hfmgv.org/smartfun/timeline/timeline.html

Outline of the Civil War with Links to Reconstruction @ http://members.tripod.com/greatamericanhistory/gr02006.htm

Freedmen and Southern Society Project @ http://www.inform.umd.edu/ARHU/Depts/History/Freedman/home.html

Freedom: A History of US @ http://www.pbs.org/wnet/historyofus/menu.html

Note to the Teacher: This vocabulary list includes *Words* and *People to Remember* from Chapters 1 through 4 of *Reconstructing America*.

Vocabulary

Words to Remember

*Reconstruction — twelve years of readjustment following the Civil War; the movement to reunite the states and usher newly freed blacks into full citizenship and participation in government

guerrilla — one who participates in war for an independent cause or fights independent of a centralized military force

loot — to rob, steal, or plunder, especially during a war or crisis

*"Seward's Folly" — purchase of Alaska from Russia in 1867 by Secretary of State William Seward; considered a foolish act at the time but it turned out to be a great real estate deal.

*Presidential Reconstruction — first two years of Reconstruction when Lincoln and his successor Johnson controlled Reconstruction policy

*Freedmen's Bureau — organization that established schools and hospitals, taught blacks to read and write, helped them find work, and intervened in crisis situations

martial law — rule by military forces in an occupied territory

temperance — moderation in using alcohol

missionary — person who goes to a foreign country or unfamiliar place to carry out humanitarian or religious services

Ku Klux Klan — white supremacy hate group

*****Thirteenth Amendment** — abolished slavery

*****Fourteenth Amendment** — guaranteed that no state can take away a person's rights; the "equal protection under the law" amendment

*****amendment** — change or addition to a rule or set of rules

*****ratify** — to approve and make official

tyrannical — oppressive ruling or governing of a nation or people

*****radical** — extreme

nullify — to make valueless and without legal or binding force

*****veto** — power of the president to prevent a bill from becoming law

People to Remember

*****Andrew Johnson** — vice president who became president upon the assassination of Abraham Lincoln and who presided over the first two years of Reconstruction. Johnson was the first president to be impeached but was acquitted by one vote in the Senate.

The Lesson

Focus Activity – 5 minutes

Allow a few minutes for the teams to organize their presentations.

Student Team Learning Activity – 30 minutes

Teaching about a chapter

1. Briefly review the presentation guidelines (use the chart from Lesson 2), the time limitations for each team presentation, and the *Evaluation Form*.

2. Four teams teach their assigned chapters to the class, beginning with Chapter 1 and continuing though Chapter 4.

    Use a timer to limit each presentation to five minutes and permit one or two minutes for questions.

3. Be sure each team member participates in the presentation and that the team involves the class during its presentation.

4. The students and the teacher assess each team's presentation using the *Evaluation Forms*.

Teaching Activity – 5 minutes following each team presentation (20 minutes total)

Following each presentation, briefly review the vocabulary and the major concepts of the chapter. If necessary, add any essential information about the chapter that the team failed to include in its presentation and correct any misconceptions or inaccurate information.

Notes

Reflection and Review Activity – 5 minutes

1. Teams write a summary statement for each chapter, 1 through 4.

2. If time permits, teams use **Numbered Heads** to share their summary statements with the class as the teacher writes the statements on chart paper.

   Note to the Teacher: An additional resource for this lesson is the video series *Freedom: A History of US,* Episode Seven—Part Two: Making Changes, Kunhardt Productions and Thirteen/WNET for PBS. Also explore the accompanying PBS Website: Freedom: A History of US @ http://www.pbs.org/wnet/historyofus/menu.html, especially the section for teachers.

Homework

Choose one of your summary statements, and draw an illustration for it.

Library/Media Resources

Fiction

Freedom Road by Howard Fast, M. E. Sharpe

Out From This Place by Joyce Hansen, Camelot

Cold Sassy Tree by Olive A. Burns, Delta

Gone With the Wind by Margaret Mitchell, Warner Books

Nonfiction

Reconstruction: America After the Civil War by Zak Mettger, Lodestar Books

Reconstruction: The Great Experiment by Allen W. Trelease, Harper and Row

The Era of Reconstruction by Kenneth M. Stampp, Alfred Knopf

Up From Slavery by Booker T. Washington, Doubleday

Worth Fighting For by Agnes McCarthy and Lawrence Reddick, Zenith Books

Cobblestone Magazine

Civil War: Reconstruction

Lesson 3 Reconstruction

Old-Time Schools in America (the establishment of free schools for blacks)

Video

The Civil War, Episode Nine: 1865–The Better Angels of Our Nature by Ken Burns

Reconstruction (Changing a Nation: 1865–1880), Film Rental Center at Syracuse University

Civil War: Postwar Period, Film Rental Center at Syracuse University

Freedom: A History of US, Episode Seven—Part Two, Kunhardt Productions and Thirteen/WNET for PBS

CD Rom

Story of America 2: The Civil War, National Geographic Society

Reconstruction, Clearvue and ZCI Publishing, Inc.

Connections

Science — The purchase of Alaska was initially viewed as a mammoth blunder. People were unfamiliar with the natural resources, ecology, and beauty of this area. Students study the ecosystem of Alaska and the arctic region.

Science — The author mentions that some carpetbaggers bought huge tracts of land cheaply in the South during Reconstruction. Students research how land is measured with the metric system and how surveying is done.

Answers for Chapter 1
"Reconstruction Means Rebuilding"

Explain the vocabulary using the information in the chapter.

Reconstruction — the twelve years of readjustment following the Civil War to reunite the states and usher newly freed blacks into full citizenship and participation in government

guerrilla — one who participates in war for an independent cause or fights independent of a centralized military force

loot — to rob, steal, or plunder especially during a war or crisis

Answer the Big Four!

1. **How did Abraham Lincoln's plan for Reconstruction differ from that of most people?** Lincoln wanted to accept the Southern states back into the Union with kindness and forgiveness. He wanted to make the process as painless as possible, believing that separation from the Union, the destruction of the Southern economy, and the heavy loss of life had been punishment enough for the South.

2. **How did Northerners and Southerners feel about Reconstruction?** Northerners were incredibly angry at the South for seceding from the Union and for their continuing desires for a decentralized government and an aristocracy based on slavery. Many Northerners wanted the South to be punished. The South was angry and bitter toward the North for telling them their way of life was wrong. The South also struggled with its significant loss of brothers, sons, and fathers and its war-torn condition, which rendered plantations desolate and abandoned. The South did not eagerly embrace Reconstruction.

3. **How do each of the three photographs in Chapter 1 show the nation's need for healing and rebuilding after the Civil War?** The photographs of a man without legs, a destroyed railway depot, and a dispossessed family illustrate the brokenness, destruction, and loss of the period. They also show how much work was needed to restore the country and solve its problems. The photographs demonstrate that individual people, families, buildings, and land all suffered the effects of the war; nothing escaped the damage it caused.

4. **Explain Mark Twain's quotation from *Life on the Mississippi*. What effect did immigration have on America during the 1860s?** Mark Twain's quotation points out that the war had a greater impact on Southerners than on Northerners. Southerners defined themselves as a defeated people; the war had been a shattering experience, leaving their land, people, and economy ravaged. The North, on the other hand, had won and achieved its war aims—to secure the Union and free the slaves—and was ready to move forward. The South, in its loss and visible damage, could neither forget nor forgive. It was the defining event in the South's regional history.

Immigration in the 1860s affected all regions of the country as people came to America in droves in search of better lives. Even with the death toll of the war, the population was greater than when the war began. Many immigrants settled in the North and West. In some areas, there were so many German settlers that Native Americans began speaking German!

Answers for Chapter 2
"Who Was Andrew Johnson?"

Explain the vocabulary using the information in the chapter.

Andrew Johnson — vice president who became president upon the assassination of Abraham Lincoln; presided over the first two years of Reconstruction; first president to be impeached but was acquitted by one vote in the Senate

"Seward's Folly" — purchase of Alaska from Russia in 1867 by Secretary of State William Seward; considered a foolish act at the time but turned out to be a great real estate deal

Answer the Big Four!

1. **What do the cartoons of Andrew Johnson reveal about how some people viewed him?** At first many people, including many members of the press, considered Johnson to be the perfect man to reunite the North and South. The cartoon on page 16, which shows Johnson using his skills as a tailor to make a unified suit of the states, demonstrates the role Johnson was expected to take as he assumed the presidency. In the other drawing he is depicted as a parrot, constantly squawking about the Constitution.

2. **Why did Andrew Johnson seem like the best person to bring peace between the North and South after the war?** Johnson was Lincoln's vice president and a Southern Democrat who had remained loyal to the Union during the Civil War. It was assumed he would maintain his loyalty to the Union, but would also usher the South back into the "family" of states with fairness because of his own Southern roots and interests.

3. **Which character traits of Andrew Johnson made him a promising leader and politician? Which ones made him a poor leader?** Andrew Johnson demonstrated courage as a Southern Democrat who remained loyal to the Union, but he was also "mulishly" stubborn and refused to compromise or listen to advice. Through his own determination, and the help of his wife, he overcame his lack of education and rose to great political power. But being unyielding and unwilling to compromise led to great difficulty with the majority Radical Republican Congress.

4. **How did Andrew Johnson demonstrate his loyalty to the United States and its citizens during the Civil War?** Andrew Johnson did not agree with the secession of the Southern states and did not join the Confederacy as did many of his fellow Southern politicians. He demonstrated loyalty and courage by holding onto his political beliefs and supporting unity above all else.

Answers for Chapter 3
"Presidential Reconstruction"

Explain the vocabulary using the information in the chapter.

Presidential Reconstruction — first two years of Reconstruction when Lincoln and his successor Johnson controlled Reconstruction policy

Freedmen's Bureau — organization devoted to establishing schools and hospitals for newly freed blacks, teaching blacks to read and write, helping them find work, and intervening in crisis situations

martial law — law enforced by the military, as in an occupied territory

temperance — moderation in using alcohol

missionary — person who goes to a foreign country or unfamiliar place to carry out humanitarian or religious services

Ku Klux Klan — white supremacy hate group

Answer the Big Four!

1. **Describe the first two years of Reconstruction.** The first two years of Reconstruction were guided by President Lincoln and his successor, President Johnson. During Lincoln's tenure, Congress established the Freedmen's Bureau, which helped newly freed blacks by setting up schools and hospitals and providing food and clothing. However, Johnson supported the return to white rule in the South and saw no need to protect or extend the rights of the freed slaves. Many Southern blacks saw little difference between freedom and their former way of life as few of the economic, social, and political benefits of Reconstruction were extensive or long-lasting.

2. **What role did the Freedmen's Bureau play during Reconstruction? How did Northerners help during these first crucial years?** In March 1865, President Abraham Lincoln signed into law a congressional bill that created the Freedmen's Bureau. Its purpose was to feed needy blacks and whites in the South, set up schools and hospitals, help former slaves find jobs, and protect them from discrimination and violence. Many Northerners, called "carpetbaggers" by Southerners, moved to the South as teachers and missionaries to help the former slaves, or to take advantage of the disorder for their own profit.

3. **What were black codes? How did they hurt efforts to rebuild Southern society and bring the newly freed blacks into that society?** Black codes were laws that conservative white Southerners passed limiting the freedom and rights of blacks, practically making them slaves again. The codes keep former slaves from voting, serving on juries, and joining the state militia. Conversely, the codes gave whites almost unlimited power.

4. **Use the photographs and sidebar information to summarize Chapter 3.** Teachers from the North came to the South to educate blacks, while Northern soldiers occupied the South to ensure law and order. In the political realm, Uncle Sam is pictured as a stern schoolmaster punishing the South for her rebelliousness. The press portrayed Johnson as a Roman emperor, who watches the violence and uncivilized behavior of the South from afar with mild amusement. The Ku Klux Klan has its grand debut of terrorism and revenge for the lost Southern way of life.

Answers for Chapter 4
"Presidential Reconstruction"

Explain the vocabulary using the information in the chapter.

Thirteenth Amendment — abolished slavery

Fourteenth Amendment — guaranteed that no state can take away a person's rights; the "equal protection under the law" amendment

Amendment — change or addition to a formal document or set of rules

ratify — to approve and make official

tyrannical — oppressive ruling or governing of a nation or people

radical — extreme

nullify — having no legal or binding force

veto — power of the president to prevent a bill from becoming law

Answer the Big Four!

1. **Explain the Thirteenth Amendment, the key part of the Fourteenth Amendment, and the section of the Declaration of Independence in Chapter 4. How do these documents define freedom for a United States citizen? Did the newly freed blacks in the South think they were truly free?** The 13th Amendment states that slavery and involuntary servitude in United States can exist only as a punishment for a crime, of which a person must be convicted before service can begin. The Declaration of Independence, in its opening paragraph, states that it is perfectly obvious that human beings are created equal and free by their Creator. Therefore, no other person can take their basic rights and freedoms from them. The partial quotation from the 14th Amendment states that no one can be deprived of equal protection under the law, or the right to own property. Freedom, based upon the summations of these government documents, is the right to pursue your interests (as long as they are not in conflict with the law, or another person's rights), your work, all civil liberties, and happiness in accordance with the law of the land. Newly freed blacks did not think they were truly free because while they were no longer officially slaves, they did not receive equal treatment under the law and could not vote.

2. **Describe President Johnson's war with the Radical Republicans. On what issues did they have differing opinions?** President Johnson and the Radical Republicans differed on every issue. Johnson consistently vetoed or opposed civil rights laws in accordance with Reconstruction efforts. The Radical Republicans persisted with bills that supported the rights of blacks to the same liberties under the law as whites. Johnson was a strong proponent of states' rights—the right of states to decide individually about the rights it would grant to blacks—instead of allowing a central government to determine a state's responsibility. Republicans supported the Constitution and believed in its superiority over state constitutions.

3. **What steps did the Radical Republicans take to ensure civil rights for blacks?** They wrote laws to protect the civil rights of blacks, passed the Civil Rights Act in 1866 (which was designed to end the black codes), and wrote the Fourteenth Amendment entitling all citizens to the safeguards of the Constitution. This amendment protects citizens from abuses by states and establishes the superiority of the United States government over state governments.

4. **What is states' rights? Why did the South argue for it so strongly?** States' rights is the idea that each state decides for itself what its laws and policies will be. It is the absence of accountability to a central government. The South argued for states' rights so strongly because Southerners wanted to continue their way of doing things as much as possible. They didn't want to afford blacks equal rights, or treat them as equal to white citizens.

Lesson 4
Reconstruction
Chapters 5 through 7

Theme

After the first two years of Reconstruction, Congress took matters into its own hands to ensure the liberty of former slaves by enacting civil rights legislation, sending the military to enforce the principles of equality in the South, and impeaching President Andrew Johnson.

Overview

After two years of Johnson's duplicitous efforts at Reconstruction, the Radical Republican Congress began to exercise its own power by overriding presidential vetoes and initiating reform legislation such as the Reconstruction Act. Congress divided the South into five military districts, and sent Northern soldiers south to maintain order. By demonstrating a formidable presence at polling places, the troops ensured that black men could exercise their new right to vote. With the opportunity to vote came the chance to elect local officials who realized the need to protect African Americans from racism, violence, and discrimination.

In addition to the military rule, the North maintained an irritating presence in the South in other ways. Northern abolitionists, teachers, and agents with the Freedmen's Bureau traveled south to establish schools and relief programs and to help the dispossessed secure jobs and wages. White Southerners resented this influx, calling them "carpetbaggers" and accusing them of exploiting the troubles of that once glorious and aristocratic region. And in some cases that was true, for there was profit to be made amid the chaos and destruction.

Congressional Reconstruction was an unprecedented time in the nation's history: its initial venture into a biracial democracy. For the first time, illiterate white men who did not own land and former male slaves could vote in favor of their own interests. Between 1869 and 1876, Southern states elected fourteen black men to the House of Representatives. Mississippi boasted two black senators, Blanche Bruce and Hiram Revels—the latter of whom occupied Jefferson Davis' old seat in the Senate. More than six hundred African Americans served in state legislatures. Some were former slaves, others had been born free, and several were college educated. They served with honor and distinction and brought about reform in civil rights for all Americans.

The Radical Republican Congress, led by Thaddeus Stevens, made much of this reform possible. A white abolitionist representative from Pennsylvania, Stevens sympathized with the plight of black Americans and relentlessly defended them and their rights. Without ceasing, he labored for justice for former slaves. As early as 1838, he refused to sign the Pennsylvania constitution because it denied black men the right to vote.

Stevens was a man of exceptional character—he could not be bribed, duped, or moved from his convictions. He was often stern and without humor, but he was a fair man. And his compassion for the poor led him to act on their behalf. For instance, Stevens once purchased a widow's farm that was being auctioned for payment of her debts, and then gave it back to her.

This fierce politician would not compromise because he sincerely believed in the moral validity of every single ideal he held. As a radical, Stevens did not just support the ideas of the Constitution, he carried out its ideals in practical, helpful ways. Among his most pivotal contributions to American government was his authorship of the Thirteenth and Fourteenth Amendments. Their passage guaranteed the right to vote to black men and protected the rights of all citizens by asserting that no state government is superior to the central government of the United States and that all Americans have the right to due process of law.

In a less dignified fight—and one that later clouded his legacy—Stevens opposed President Johnson on political and social matters and spearheaded the process of his impeachment. Johnson's presidency was imperiled by his own conflicting statements of ideology, his inability to compromise, and by the public disdain Johnson and Thaddeus Stevens had for each other, stemming from their differing political agendas. Both men were uncompromising and implacable in their respective widely divergent beliefs.

By 1868, the tension in Washington and throughout the United States was palpable: politicians and citizens alike anxiously waited to hear Johnson's fate. Following Johnson's impeachment by the House of Representatives, many people believed the Senate should vote to rid the White House of a man who had burdened his office with fits of anger, counterproductive programs, and subversive anti-reconstruction ideals and practices. Johnson's veto of several civil rights bills—although eventually overridden by Congress—clearly indicated his sympathy with white supremacists who would never embrace the idea of black equality. The nation as a whole was thoroughly engaged with this drama and invested in its outcome. Admission tickets to the Senate vote were printed and sold to the public at high cost, which many were willing to pay.

In the context of the times, the popular desire to impeach President Johnson was understandable, but the impeachment charges were not necessarily legally valid. An elected official cannot be removed from office simply because the opposing political party disagrees with his politics, or even because he demonstrates poor leadership skills. A president must stand trial for and be convicted of "bribery, treason, or high crimes and misdemeanors."

Eventually, Johnson's fate came down to one man who did not support Johnson personally or politically, but who was determined to uphold the principles of the Constitution even at his own political expense. Senator Edmund G. Ross bore the tremendous burden of deciding in favor of his conscience when his constituency from the Radical Republican state of Kansas and most of his fellow legislators clamored for the impeachment of the president. But Ross would not be influenced, and with great courage he cast his vote for acquittal. Ross knew that as obstructive as Johnson was, he was not guilty of "bribery, treason, or high crimes and misdemeanors." And so the Senate acquitted Johnson because of that one-vote margin, and he finished out his term as president.

Even though the country had made significant strides toward rebuilding and reforming itself, the progress would soon be eradicated with the end of Reconstruction and the re-establishment of white supremacy in each of the Southern states. In the days to come, political power shifted away from Radical Republicanism and reform, due in some degree to the influence of the three pillars of the Democratic Party—the Irish immigrant, the Wall Street financier, and the Confederate veteran.

References

The Annals of America, 1858-1865: The Crisis of the Union. 1976. Chicago: Encyclopedia Britannica, Inc.

Bailey, Thomas A. and David M. Kennedy. 1998. *The American Spirit.* "The Ordeal of Reconstruction, 1865-1877." Boston: Houghton Mifflin Company.

"The Civil Rights Act of 1866." Historical Documents. *Americans.net.* http://www.africanamericans.com/CivilRightsActof1866.htm. Access date October 1988.

Douglass, Frederick. "Reconstruction." *Atlantic Monthly.* http://www.theatlantic.com/unbound/flashbks/black/douglas.htm. Access date October 1998.

"Finding Precedent: The Impeachment of Andrew Johnson." *HarpWeek, LLC.* http://www.impeach-andrewjohnson.com/. Access date October 1998

Foner, Eric. "June 13, 1866 Equality Before the Law." McPherson, James M. ed. 2001. *Days of Destiny: Crossroads in American History.* Society of American Historians. New York: A Dorling Kindersley Book.

Foner, Eric. 1999. *The Story of American Freedom.* New York: W.W. Norton & Company.

Foner, Eric. 1988. *Reconstruction: America's Unfinished Revolution, 1863-1877.* New York: Perennial.

Linder, Douglas O. "Famous American Trials. The Andrew Johnson Impeachment Trial. 1868." *Famous Trials Homepage.* http://www.law.umkc.edu/faculty/projects/ftrials/impeach/impeachmt.htm. Access date January 1999.

Grob, Gerald N. and George Athan Billias, ed. 1992. *Interpretations of American History: Patterns and Perspectives.* "The Reconstruction Era: Constructive or Destructive?" New York: The Free Press.

Marcus, Robert D. and David Burner. 2001. *America Firsthand.* Caleb G. Forshey and Reverend James Sinclair. "White Southerners' Reactions to Reconstruction." Boston: Bedford/St. Martin's.

Meyer, Howard. 2000.*The Amendment that Refused to Die: Equality and Justice Deferred. The History of the 14th Amendment.* New York: Madison Books.

"Military Reconstruction: The Impeachment of Andrew Johnson." *HarpWeek, LLC.* http://www.impeach-andrewjohnson.com/06FirstImpeachmentDiscussions/MilitaryReconstruction.htm. Access date October 1998.

Murphy, Richard W. 1987. *The Nation Reunited: War's Aftermath.* Alexandria, Virginia: Time-Life Books.

"Reconstruction and Its Aftermath." *American Memory.* Library of Congress. http://memory.loc.gov/ammem/aaohtml/exhibit/aopart5b.html; http://memory.loc.gov/ammem/aaohtml/exhibit/aopart5.html#05a. Access date October 1998.

Stevens, Thaddeus. "From the Closing Arguments of Hon. Thaddeus Stevens." *Impeachment Trial Homepage.* http://www.law.umkc.edu/faculty/projects/ftrials/impeach/StevensClosing.html. Access date October 1998.

Trefousse, Hans L. "Andrew Johnson: 17th President: 1865-1869." McPherson, James M. ed. 2000. *"To the Best of My Ability": The American Presidents.* Society of American Historians. New York: A Dorling Kindersley Book.

Standards

Historical Thinking

The student will

Chronological Thinking

- identify in historical narratives the temporal structure of a historical narrative or story

Historical Comprehension

- reconstruct the literal meaning of a historical passage

- identify the central question(s) the historical narrative addresses
- read historical narratives imaginatively
- draw upon visual, literary, and musical sources

Historical Analysis and Interpretation

- compare or contrast differing sets of ideas, values, personalities, behaviors, and institutions
- consider multiple perspectives
- analyze cause and effect relationships and multiple causation, including the importance of the individual, the influence of ideas, and the role of chance
- hypothesize the influence of the past

Historical Research Capabilities

- formulate historical questions
- obtain historical data
- question historical data
- support interpretation with historical evidence

Analysis and Decision-Making

- identify issues and problems in the past
- marshal evidence of antecedent circumstances and contemporary factors contributing to problems and alternative courses of action

Content

The student will demonstrate understanding of

How various reconstruction plans succeeded or failed

- The political controversy over Reconstruction
    - contrast the Reconstruction policies advocated by Lincoln, Andrew Johnson, and sharply divided Congressional leaders, while assessing these policies as responses to changing events
    - analyze the escalating conflict between President Johnson and Republican legislators, and explain the reasons for and consequences of Johnson's impeachment and trial
    - explain the provisions of the Fourteenth and Fifteenth Amendments and the political forces supporting and opposing each
- The Reconstruction programs to transform social relations in the South
    - explain the economic and social problems facing the South and appraise their impact on different groups of people
    - evaluate the goals and accomplishments of the Freedman's Bureau
    - analyze how African Americans attempted to improve their economic position during Reconstruction and explain factors involved in their quest for land ownership

Resources

For each student

Reconstructing America by Joy Hakim: Chapters 5 through 7

Three Evaluation forms, one for each team presentation

For each team

Materials needed for its presentation

For the teacher

Chart paper

Markers

Lesson 4 Reconstruction

Three Evaluation forms, one for each team presentation
Timer

Web sites

Civil War and Reconstruction Hot Links @ http://www.sinc.sunysb.edu/Class/is265/hotlinks.html

Timeline @ http://hfmgv.org/smartfun/timeline/timeline.html

Outline of the Civil War with Links to Reconstruction @ http://members.tripod.com`greatamericanhistory/gr02006.htm#[VIIK]

Freedmen and Southern Society Project @ http://www.inform.umd.edu/ARHU/Depts/History/Freedman/home.html

Freedom: A History of US @ http://www.pbs.org/wnet/historyofus/menu.html

Note to the Teacher: This vocabulary list includes *Words and People to Remember* from Chapters 5 through 7 of *Reconstructing America*.

Vocabulary

Words to Remember

*carpetbagger — Northerner who went South after the war to teach or help with social programs; some took advantage of the disorder for personal profit

*Congressional Reconstruction — also called Radical or Military Reconstruction, the ten years (1867-77) of Northern occupation in the South meant to guarantee the rights and freedom of former slaves

*radical — extreme

*scalawag — Southerner who cooperated with the North

integrity — keeping to a code of ethics, morals, and values

democracy — government by the people; rule by the majority

illiterate — unable to read or write

*Fourteenth Amendment — protects the rights of all citizens regardless of race or color

*Fifteenth Amendment — granted the right to vote to African American men

sovereign — supreme power and authority

*abolitionist — one who labors for the end of slavery

*impeach — to charge a public official before a governing, legislative body with misconduct while in office; presidential impeachment requires the charge of treason, bribery, or other high crimes and misdemeanors.

People to Remember

*Edmund G. Ross — radical Republican senator who cast the deciding vote of not guilty at Johnson's impeachment trial

*Thaddeus Stevens — radical Republican who fought for reform and the rights of blacks, and who authored the Thirteenth and Fourteenth Amendments

Ben Butler — radical Republican congressman who read impeachment evidence against President Andrew Johnson

D. R. Anthony — principal signer of the telegram to Edmund Ross demanding the conviction of President Johnson

The Lesson

Focus Activity – 5 minutes

Notes

Allow a few minutes for the teams that will present Chapters 5 through 7 to organize their presentations.

Student Team Learning Activity – 25 minutes

Teaching about a chapter

1. Briefly review the presentation guidelines using the chart from Lesson 2, the time limitations for each team presentation, and the *Evaluation Form*.
2. Each team presents its assigned chapter to the class, beginning with Chapter 5 and continuing though Chapter 7. Use a timer to limit each presentation to five minutes and permit one or two minutes for questions.
3. Be sure each team member participates in the presentation and that the team involves the class during its presentation.
4. The students and the teacher assess each team's presentation using the *Evaluation Forms*.

Teaching Activity – 5 minutes following each team presentation (15 minutes total)

Following each presentation, briefly review the vocabulary and the major concepts of the chapter. If necessary, add any essential information about the chapter that the team failed to include in its presentation and correct any misconceptions or inaccurate information.

Reflection and Review Activity – 5 minutes

1. Teams write a summary statement for each chapter, 5 through 7.

2. If time permits, teams use **Numbered Heads** to share their summary statements with the class as the teacher writes the statements on chart paper.

Note to the Teacher: An additional resource for this lesson is the video series *Freedom: A History of US,* Episode Seven—Part Three: Reconstruction and Rebuilding, Kunhardt Productions and Thirteen/WNET for PBS. Also explore the accompanying PBS Website: Freedom: A History of US @ http://www.pbs.org/wnet/historyofus/menu.html, especially the section for teachers.

Homework

Choose one of your summary statements and draw an illustration for it.

Library/Media Resources

Fiction

Freedom Road by Howard Fast, M. E. Sharpe

Out From This Place by Joyce Hansen, Camelot

Cold Sassy Tree by Olive A. Burns, Delta

Gone With the Wind by Margaret Mitchell, Warner Books

Nonfiction

Reconstruction: America After the Civil War by Zak Mettger, Lodestar Books

Reconstruction: The Great Experiment by Allen W. Trelease, Harper and Row

The Era of Reconstruction by Kenneth M. Stampp, Alfred Knopf

Up From Slavery by Booker T. Washington, Doubleday

Worth Fighting For by Agnes McCarthy and Lawrence Reddick, Zenith Books

Remembering Slavery (book and tape) edited by Ira Berlin, The New Press

Cobblestone Magazine

Civil War: Reconstruction

Black History Month: The Struggle for Rights

Old-Time Schools in America (the establishment of free schools for blacks)

Video

The Civil War, Episode Nine: 1865–The Better Angels of Our Nature by Ken Burns

Reconstruction (Changing a Nation: 1865–1880), Film Rental Center at Syracuse University

Civil War: Postwar Period, Film Rental Center at Syracuse University

Freedom: A History of US, Episode Seven—Part Three, Kunhardt Productions and Thirteen/WNET for PBS

CD Rom

Story of America 2: The Civil War, National Geographic Society

Reconstruction, Clearvue and ZCI Publishing, Inc.

Connections

Writing — Students write a letter nominating Thaddeus Stevens to the History Hall of Fame. In their letters, students explain why he is important and should be honored.

Answers for Chapter 5
"Congressional Reconstruction"

Explain the vocabulary using the information in the chapter.

carpetbagger — Northerner who went South after the war to teach or help with social programs or to take advantage of the disorder for personal profit

Congressional Reconstruction — (sometimes called Military or Radical Reconstruction), ten years (1867-77) of radical reform measures and federal military occupation in the South to safeguard the rights and freedom of former slaves

radical — extreme

scalawag — Southerner who cooperated with the North

integrity — keeping to a code of ethics, morals, and values

democracy — government by the people, rule by the majority

illiterate — unable to read or write

Fourteenth Amendment — protects the rights of all citizens regardless of race or color

Fifteenth Amendment — granted the right to vote to African American men

Answer the Big Four!

1. **What was Congressional Reconstruction? What happened during this period?** Congressional Reconstruction is the ten year period (1867-77) when Congress passed the Civil Rights Act and took control of Reconstruction by writing bills and passing laws that afforded greater civil and legal rights for blacks. Congress overrode many of Johnson's vetoes of civil rights legislation. Northern military forces occupied the South to guarantee the freedom and rights of former slaves.

2. **How did Reconstruction efforts change federal and state legislatures?** Blacks began to serve in both houses of Congress and in the Southern state legislatures as elected officials.

3. **According to James Madison, what is a democratic society? How did the freed blacks and poor whites use their rights as citizens of a democracy during congressional Reconstruction?** A democratic society is one in which people vote in favor of their interests, and where every voice is heard. Madison believed that if everyone was heard, all the needs and interests would balance each other. Before Congressional Reconstruction, Southern blacks and illiterate whites were denied the right to vote. Both groups exercised their rights as citizens by voting during Congressional Reconstruction.

4. **Based on the map on page 26, would you say that Congressional Reconstruction was ultimately successful? Hint: Look at the legend. What does the re-establishment of white supremacy mean?** The map illustrates that Congressional Reconstruction ultimately failed. The re-establishment of white supremacy means that although slavery ended, the Southern states reverted back to their former way of treating blacks, namely by suppressing their rights and freedom.

Answers for Chapter 6
"Thaddeus Stevens: Radical"

Explain the vocabulary using the information in the chapter.

Thaddeus Stevens — Congressional leader of the Radical Republicans who fought for reform and the rights of blacks, and who authored the 13th and 14th amendments

sovereign — supreme power and authority

abolitionist — one who labors for the end of slavery

impeach — to charge a public official before a governing, legislative body with misconduct while in office; presidential impeachment requires the charge of treason, bribery, or other high crimes and misdemeanors.

Answer the Big Four!

1. **Describe Thaddeus Stevens. Use the sidebar information, the political cartoons, and the text to describe his relationship with Andrew Johnson.** Thaddeus Stevens was a very honest man whose political opinions and feelings did not change depending on whom he was talking to about important issues. Stevens could not be bribed or bought. He fought hard for his principles, stood up for what he thought was right, and could not be manipulated. Stevens and Johnson hated each other; their political opinions were completely opposite, and they were both incapable of compromise.

2. **How did Thaddeus Stevens impact the Constitution?** Thaddeus Stevens wrote the Thirteenth Amendment (making slavery illegal) and the Fourteenth Amendment (protecting the rights of all American citizens, regardless of race or color), and laid the foundation for the Fifteenth Amendment (guaranteeing all male citizens the right to vote). These amendments paved the way for greater freedom for blacks and all Americans.

3. **Why did Thaddeus Stevens want to impeach President Johnson? What did Stevens mean when he said the country had a moral necessity to impeach Johnson?** Stevens wanted to impeach President Johnson because he believed that Johnson was illegally obstructing the freedom and equality of blacks. By moral necessity, Stevens believed that for the good of the country and to uphold the character and dignity of America, Johnson should be removed from office because he did not lend character or dignity to the presidency. Stevens felt that Johnson's actions were morally wrong.

4. **Explain the impeachment process. See the boxed section titled "How to Impeach" on page 30.** The House of Representatives has sole power to impeach. If the majority of the House votes to impeach a president, he will be brought to trial in the Senate. The Senate tries the case and votes. To convict, at least two-thirds of Senate members must vote in agreement with the impeachment charges or the president is acquitted. The chief justice of the United States Supreme Court presides over the trial.

Answers for Chapter 7
"Impeaching a President"

Explain the vocabulary using the information in the chapter.

Edmund G. Ross — radical Republican senator who voted not guilty and saved Andrew Johnson from being convicted of impeachment

impartial — not biased or prejudiced in judgment

high crimes — serious criminal acts

misdemeanor — a crime that is less serious than a felony; a wrongful act

treason — acts or plans to betray or overthrow one's country

bribery — to influence or be influenced with money or favors

Answer the Big Four!

1. **Why did Edmund G. Ross bear a large burden during Johnson's impeachment trial?** Edmund G. Ross was from the Radical Republican state of Kansas, and was himself a Radical Republican. But unlike the other Senator from Kansas and most of the residents of his state, he was not convinced that the acts for which Johnson was on trial deserved impeachment. Ross was the only senator who had not announced how he would vote, and the Senate was one vote short of the necessary two-thirds to convict Johnson. Ross knew that if he voted his conscience, which told him to vote *not guilty*, he would be a hated man and be voted out of his position as senator from his home state.

2. **What was the country's response to Johnson's trial? Compare it to the public's response to other recent trials of famous men.** The country was consumed with Johnson's impeachment by the House and the ensuing trial in the Senate. People clamored for tickets as they would for a boxing match or rock concert today. One woman camped outside her congressman's house until he promised her a ticket of admission. The public obsession with Johnson's trial is comparable to that during the O.J. Simpson trial, and to the attention paid to President Clinton's impeachment trial.

3. **Even though Edmund Ross disliked President Johnson, he voted not guilty. Explain why he voted this way.** As a Radical Republican, Ross was a staunch believer in the Constitution. He took the idea of impeachment very seriously and did not believe Johnson had committed "treason, bribery, or high crimes and misdemeanors," which are the grounds for presidential impeachment.

4. **What lasting impression did Thaddeus Stevens make on the politics of the Unites States? How did he demonstrate in his death what he valued throughout his life?** Thaddeus Stevens wrote two of the most powerful amendments to the Constitution (the Thirteenth and Fourteenth), and he paved the way for the Fifteenth Amendment, which gave black men the right to vote. Stevens, who died a few days after Johnson's trial, was buried in a cemetery where blacks and whites lay side by side—an unusual arrangement in that day—as an illustration of his belief in the principle of equality.

Lesson 5
Collapse of Reconstruction
Chapters 8 and 9

Theme

In order to secure the promises of freedom hard won by the Civil War, Southern freed blacks needed to gain political and economic power, goals that vanished with the rise of Southern Conservative Democrats and the growing disinterest of Northern Radical Republicans.

Overview

Following the Civil War, Southern freed blacks knew that the keys to their social and political equality lay in securing the right to vote, the ability to read and write, and the opportunity to own land. Through voting rights, African American men elected state and national legislators who enacted policies to advance their cause and local officials who protected them and their rights. Free public schools, open to all, appeared in the South for the first time. Former slaves well knew the value of reading and writing: an educated, knowledgeable person cannot be taken advantage of as easily as someone kept in ignorance. To achieve economic independence and to feed, clothe, and shelter themselves, blacks needed to earn their own livings. For both blacks and whites in the post-war, agrarian South, this meant owning farmland. To achieve these economic and political goals, blacks exercised their franchise and headed to the ballot box.

"America's Second Revolution"—the attempt at a genuine interracial democracy—began with the meeting of the South Carolina legislature on January 14, 1868, to write a new state constitution. Composed of seventy-six black men—a direct result of the Fifteenth Amendment, which granted black men the right to vote—and forty-eight white men, the legislature asserted equal rights and equal public privileges for all classes of American citizens and composed a state constitution that reflected those beliefs.

All across the South, similar state legislatures worked to achieve the goals of Reconstruction: freedom and voting rights for former slaves, reunification of the nation, and rebuilding the South. Striving to represent all Southerners, including freed slaves and poor whites, the Reconstruction legislatures voted for free public schools, road construction to rebuild transportation systems, and the protection of equal rights for blacks. What they did not do was demand revenge on former Confederates.

Reluctantly, a number of white Southerners came to recognize the intelligence and political savvy of the black legislators. An emerging class of black leaders and eloquent spokesmen—all duly elected as a result of the black male franchise—took political office and began to affect change, reform society, and champion civil rights. Little did these optimistic leaders realize that any power they had to change government and society would be limited by the fear, hatred, and ignorance of many of their white counterparts and the citizens of the states they served.

Almost immediately, reform measures met a backlash of intimidation, violence, and voting restrictions, unleashed by the resurgence of a white Southern Democrat party. Controlled by former Confederates, these Redeemer governments, one by one, reclaimed the Southern state legislatures and instituted policies of discrimination and segregation. The political hope of the freed slaves for equal and exact justice ended.

Likewise, on the economic front, freed men and women saw their desire to own farmland dashed. At the end of the war, planters, small farmers, businesses, banks, and charitable organizations—individuals and institutions at every level of Southern society—were broke. War debt and worthless Confederate paper money, war bonds, and treasury notes crippled the Southern economy. In addition, the federal government taxed Southern agricultural products and other goods to help pay the Northern war debt. Southern landowners were destitute: they had no financial resources to buy seed, livestock, and machinery to make a new start, and no slave workforce to sow and harvest fields. Neither planters nor freedmen were prepared for how the end of slavery changed their relationship; neither knew how to develop a new form of labor relations based not on owner and slave but on employer and employee.

Most Northerners felt that the best way for former slaves to get used to the free labor system—as well as to restart large-scale Southern agriculture—was for them to return to work on the plantations under contract. The Freedmen's Bureau was given the task of approving the contracts to ensure fairness to both parties. But neither freedmen nor planters adapted quickly or easily to this new way of working. Former slaves had trouble adjusting to using wages to pay for all their needs, and their working and living conditions did not differ much from slavery. Planters felt stymied by their inability to rely on punishment to get the best from their workers, did not like to pay wages for what they formerly got for free, and resented having to clear labor relations through Northern officials. Even so, most contracts benefited the planters: wages were low and paid in a lump sum at the end of the year with extra costs deducted, and workers often had to ask permission to leave the plantation or carry passes and could be punished for disobedience or disrespect.

In cotton and tobacco growing regions, a form of wage labor called sharecropping became common. Under this arrangement, planters provided freedmen with a piece of land, a place to live, livestock, seed, and farm machinery. In exchange, croppers planted and raised cotton or tobacco, corn, and other grains, and turned the harvest over to the planter. Generally, planters sold the crop and gave croppers a quarter to a half of the profit after deducting expenses.

Other freedmen became share renters who supplied their own seed and machinery and owned the crop they planted and sowed. In return for the use of the land they paid one-quarter to one-third of their crop to the landowner. Both sides preferred sharecropping or renting to wage labor (contract work). Landowners did not have to pay cash wages in a time of scarce money, and the workers produced more than contract workers because they shared the harvest. Freedmen liked the independence and lack of white supervision, and they hoped to earn enough money to eventually buy land.

But getting ahead financially and buying land of their own escaped contract workers, croppers, and renters. Money intended to purchase land went instead to pay for food, clothes, farming supplies, and other necessities—usually bought on credit and too often on terms that cheated the ex-slaves. Years of bad weather following the war led to poor harvests and low crop prices. Rather than saving money, workers went further into debt.

After a decade of struggle, the hope of financial independence vanished for most freedmen and their families. The support and protection of the Freedmen's Bureau, the Northern carpetbaggers, and the federal army terminated with the Compromise of 1877, which ended Congressional Reconstruction and military occupation. Southern Democrats gradually reclaimed the southern political system, and the Radical Republicans had their own troubles with political corruption and shifting public opinion. The South, with its newly freed slaves, would have to solve its own problems.

References

The Annals of America, 1858-1865: The Crisis of the Union. 1976. Chicago: Encyclopedia Britannica, Inc.

Bailey, Thomas A. and David M. Kennedy. 1998. *The American Spirit.* "The Ordeal of Reconstruction, 1865-1877." Boston: Houghton Mifflin Company.

Benedict, Michael Les. "Ulysses S. Grant: 18th President: 1869-1877." McPherson, James M. ed. 2000. *"To the Best of My Ability": The American Presidents*. Society of American Historians. New York: A Dorling Kindersley Book.

Douglass, Frederick. "Reconstruction." *Atlantic Monthly.* http://www.theatlantic.com/unbound/flashbks/black/douglas.htm. Access date October 1998.

Foner, Eric. "June 13, 1866 Equality Before the Law." McPherson, James M. ed. 2001. *Days of Destiny: Crossroads in American History.* Society of American Historians. New York: A Dorling Kindersley Book.

Foner, Eric. 1999. *The Story of American Freedom*. New York: W.W. Norton & Company.

Foner, Eric. 1988. *Reconstruction: America's Unfinished Revolution, 1863-1877.* New York: Perennial.

Frankel, Noralee. 1996. *Break Those Chains at Last: African Americans, 1860-1880.* New York: Oxford University Press.

Grob, Gerald N. and George Athan Billias, ed. 1992. *Interpretations of American History: Patterns and Perspectives.* "The Reconstruction Era: Constructive or Destructive?" New York: The Free Press.

Kolchin, Peter. "Reconstruction." *Microsoft Encarta 97.* http://www.stanford.edu/~paherman/reconstruction.htm. Access date October 1998.

Marcus, Robert D. and David Burner. 2001. *America Firsthand.* Caleb G. Forshey and Reverend James Sinclair, "White Southerners' Reactions to Reconstruction." Boston: Bedford/St. Martin's.

Meyer, Howard. 2000.*The Amendment that Refused to Die: Equality and Justice Deferred. The History of the 14th Amendment.* New York: Madison Books.

"Military Reconstruction." *HarpWeek, LLC.* http://www.impeach-andrewjohnson.com/06FirstImpeachmentDiscussions/MilitaryReconstruction.htm. Access date October 1998.

Murphy, Richard W. 1987. *The Nation Reunited: War's Aftermath.* Alexandria, Virginia: Time-Life Books.

"Reconstruction and Its Aftermath." *American Memory. Library of Congress.* http://memory.loc.gov/ammem/aaohtml/exhibit/aopart5b.html, http://memory.loc.gov/ammem/aaohtml/exhibit/aopart5.html#05a. Access date October 1998.

"Reconstruction and its Failure." *Rochester Institute of Technology.* http://www.rit.edu/~nrcgsh/bx/bx06b.html. Access date December 1998

Sutherland, Daniel E. 1989. *The Expansion of Everyday Life 1860-1876.* New York: Harper & Row.

Standards

Historical Thinking

The student will

Chronological Thinking

- establish temporal order in constructing historical narratives of his or her own

Lesson 5   Collapse of Reconstruction   49

Historical Comprehension

- reconstruct the literal meaning of a historical passage
- identify the central question(s) the historical narrative addresses
- read historical narratives imaginatively
- draw upon visual, literary, and musical sources

Historical Analysis and Interpretation

- compare or contrast differing sets of ideas, values, personalities, behaviors, and institutions
- consider multiple perspectives
- analyze cause and effect relationships and multiple causation, including the importance of the individual, the influence of ideas, and the role of chance
- hypothesize the influence of the past

Historical Research Capabilities

- formulate historical questions
- obtain historical data
- support interpretation with historical evidence

Analysis and Decision-Making

- identify issues and problems in the past
- marshal evidence of antecedent circumstances and contemporary factors contributing to problems and alternative courses of action

Content

The student will demonstrate understanding of

How various reconstruction plans succeeded or failed

- The political controversy over Reconstruction

  - contrast the Reconstruction policies advocated by Lincoln, Andrew Johnson, and sharply divided Congressional leaders, while assessing these policies as responses to changing events
  - explain the provisions of the Fourteenth and Fifteenth Amendments and the political forces supporting and opposing each
  - evaluate why the Republican party abandoned African Americans in the South and analyze the causes and consequences of the Compromise of 1877

- The Reconstruction programs to transform social relations in the South

  - explain the economic and social problems facing the South and appraise their impact on different groups of people
  - analyze how African Americans attempted to improve their economic position during Reconstruction and explain factors involved in their quest for land ownership

- The successes and failures of Reconstruction in the South, North, and West

  - examine the progress of "Black Reconstruction" and legislative reform programs promoted by reconstructed state governments
  - evaluate Reconstruction as a revolution
  - assess how the political and economic position of African Americans in the northern and western states changed during Reconstruction
  - evaluate why corruption increased in the postwar period

Resources

For each student

Reconstructing America by Joy Hakim: Chapter 8, "Welcome to Meeting Street" and Chapter 9, "A Southern Girl's Diary"

For each team

Team Sheets:
> *Ordering Reconstruction Events*
> *Reconstruction Amendments* (two per team)

Scissors

For the teacher

Chart paper
Markers
Timer

Web sites

Civil War and Reconstruction Hot Links @ http://www.sinc.sunysb.edu/Class/is265/hotlinks.html

Timeline @ http://www.hfmgov.org/smartfun/timeline/timeline.html

Outline of the Civil War With Links to Reconstruction @ http://members.tripod.com/greatamericanhistory/gr02006.htm

Freedmen and Southern Society Project @ http://www.inform.umd.edu/ARHU/Depts/History/Freedman/home.html

Freedom: A History of US @ http://www.pbs.org/wnet/historyofus/menu.html

Vocabulary

Words to Remember

- ***America's Second Revolution** — Reconstruction state legislatures gave voice to poor whites and freed slaves in the South
- ***Reconstruction legislatures** — state governing bodies with black and white representatives that passed laws asserting equal rights and privileges for all Americans
- ***Thirteenth Amendment** — outlaws slavery
- ***Fourteenth Amendment** — forbids states to deprive citizens of life, liberty, or property without due process of law
- ***Fifteenth Amendment** — guarantees all men the right to vote, regardless of race
- **legislator** — person who serves in a state or federal lawmaking body
- **polling place** or **polls** — place where people vote during elections
- **contract farming** — agreement that planters would pay former slaves for their labor
- ***sharecropping** — agreement between a landowner and a worker who pays a portion of the harvest for use of the land

People to Remember

- ***Robert Brown Elliott** — black congressman from South Carolina who worked for the passage of civil rights laws
- ***Robert Smalls** — delivered a Confederate steamer to Union lines during the Civil War and became a successful businessman and black legislator after the war
- ***Benjamin T. Montgomery** — former slave who organized the profitable black farming community called Davis Bend
- ***Mary Virginia Montgomery** — college educated freed woman who taught school and was a bookkeeper at Davis Bend
- ***Davis Bend** — successful, profitable plantation community owned and operated by freed blacks

Lesson 5   Collapse of Reconstruction

The Lesson

Focus Activity – 10 minutes

Notes

1. Distribute one copy of the Team Sheet: *Ordering Reconstruction Events* to each team.

2. Each team reviews the major events of Reconstruction by putting the events in chronological order and explaining their impact on the South.

	Ordering Reconstruction Events
1865	Freedmen's Bureau is established to aid African Americans.
1865	The Civil War ends and Lincoln is assassinated.
1865	The states ratify the Thirteenth Amendment abolishing slavery.
1866	Johnson outlines Reconstruction policies and pardons former Confederates.
1867	President Johnson is impeached but not convicted. Congress now controls Reconstruction policies.
1868	The states ratify the Fourteenth Amendment granting rights and privileges of American citizenship and giving federal protection of individual rights to African Americans.
1870	The Fifteenth Amendment guarantees the right to vote to black men.
1871	For the first time, blacks serve in Southern state legislatures.
1877	President Rutherford B. Hayes withdraws the last federal soldiers from the South, leaving the rights of African Americans unprotected.

If time permits, students comment on the effect of each event from the viewpoint of

- Northern carpetbaggers

- Southern former Confederates
- Southern freed blacks

Teaching Activity – 20 minutes

1. Review the goals of Reconstruction (rebuild the South, reunite the states, and ensure the rights and protection of the freed slaves) and the efforts of freed men and women to gain equality, justice, and economic independence using information from the Overview.

    Explain that these goals and efforts stemmed from the passage of three civil rights amendments to the Constitution during Reconstruction.

2. Distribute two copies of the Team Sheet: *Reconstruction Amendments* to each team.

    Read the amendments and help students identify the rights granted by each amendment and who benefited.

3. Ask the students to consider this situation: You are a freed black in the South during Reconstruction. Discuss the situation in the South (refer to the Focus Activity) and your rights as assured by the three Reconstruction amendments to the Constitution.

    Students use **Think-Pair-Share**:

    - What are your two most important goals?

    Help students conclude that the two greatest needs of freed blacks during Reconstruction were for economic and political power.

    - **Economic power** — Explain the need for former slaves to become financially independent and self-sufficient in order to feed, clothe, and house themselves. Blacks could not depend on former owners now that they were free, and the Freedmen's Bureau was limited in the help it could give. Because the key to economic independence in the South was to own farmland, blacks struggled to achieve such ownership, but instead were forced to sharecrop or become contract farmers. Use the information from the Overview to briefly describe sharecropping and contract farming.

    - **Political power** — Explain that blacks needed the right to vote to elect local and state officials sympathetic to

Lesson 5 Collapse of Reconstruction

their cause. Through equal representation, blacks could pass laws and elect local officials to protect them from discrimination and violence.

4. Help the students interpret this quotation from Frederick Douglass.

   The arm of the Federal government is long but it is far too short to protect the rights of individuals in the interior of distant States. They must have the power to protect themselves, or they will go unprotected, in spite of all the laws the Federal government can put on the national statue-book.

5. Briefly introduce Chapter 8, "Welcome to Meeting Street" and Chapter 9 "A Southern Girl's Diary" of *Reconstructing America*. Explain that Chapter 8 recounts the freed slaves' struggle to attain and use political power and that Chapter 9 concerns their struggle to gain economic power through land acquisition.

6. Explain the Student Team Learning Activity and introduce the Vocabulary *Words and People to Remember*

Student Team Learning Activity – 25 minutes

Conducting a television news interview

1. **Reading for a Purpose:** Each student works with a team partner. One partnership reads Chapter 8, and the other reads Chapter 9.

   Each partnership tells the story of its chapter through a mock television news interview. One partner role plays a television reporter interviewing the other partner who role plays a major figure in the chapter. Be sure that students understand that an interview makes use of a question and answer format.

2. Partners plan their interview questions and answers using information in their chapter.

3. Each partnership presents a three minute interview to the other students in their team.

   Circulate and Monitor: As team partners plan and present their television interview to their teammates, help them develop good interview questions and accurate, complete answers to convey the story of their chapter. Use a timer to limit the interview presentations to three minutes.

4. Following the interviews, the teams briefly discuss:

   - How does each chapter illustrate a way in which black Southerners attempted to secure equality and freedom? (Chapter 8 describes the use of political power—voting and electing representatives to promote equality and freedom. Chapter 9 addresses economic power—the financial success of a black farming community that actually purchased and owned land.)

   - Why were political and economic power both necessary for black Southerners to enjoy equal justice? (Civil rights needed to be protected through state and federal government, and ex-slaves needed to be paid a fair wage for their work or own farmland to make an independent living in order to become economically free.)

   - What happened to change the promise of political equality? Of economic equality? (The rise of white supremacy, the conservative Southern Democratic Party, and the growth of "Redeemer" legislatures—all of which had the goal of segregation and were racist)

5. Discuss the collapse of Reconstruction with the class. Use questions such as the following to guide the discussion and review Chapters 8 and 9:

   - What were some of the difficult questions faced by Reconstruction legislatures? (How to redistribute land, treat former Confederates, extend justice and equality to all, create an interracial society)

   - What did these legislatures achieve? (Established free public schools for all, built roads, treated former Confederates fairly)

   - Why was education especially important to Southern blacks? (It enabled them to better protect their rights, obtain fair contracts.)

   - What were the "Redeemer" governments? (Southern conservative Democrats and former Confederates who seized power in the Southern state legislatures)

   - How did the Redeemer governments seize power? (By using fear tactics, terrorism, and voting requirements such as the poll tax to keep blacks from voting and to scare white supporters of black rights.)

Lesson 5   Collapse of Reconstruction

- How did the Montgomery family gain control of Davis Bend? (By renting and then buying land from Joseph Montgomery and creating a successful working community of freed blacks.)

- What freedoms did African Americans enjoy at Davis Bend? (The right to own property, share in the profits of free enterprise, and elect judges, sheriffs, and political leaders)

- How did the Montgomery family lose Davis Bend? (Jefferson Davis confiscated the land when political power shifted.)

Reflection and Review Activity – 5 minutes

1. Teams use a one-minute **Roundtable** to review and list the conditions endured by enslaved African Americans.

2. Teams determine
   - Which of those conditions did the Civil War end?
   - What new restrictions on liberty emerged during the collapse of Reconstruction?

3. Students turn to page 14 in *Reconstructing America*. Teams study the photograph and discuss the question posed in the caption: ". . . without land, without law and order, without civil rights backed by guarantees, what did 'freedom' mean?"

4. Ask the students: Even without full freedom, would most freed men and women return to the conditions of the past? Why or why not?

   Note to the Teacher: An additional resource for this lesson is the video series *Freedom: A History of US,* Episode Seven—Part Five: A Failed Revolution, Kunhardt Productions and Thirteen/WNET for PBS. Also explore the accompanying PBS Website: Freedom: A History of US @ http://www.pbs.org/wnet/historyofus/menu.html, especially the section for teachers.

Homework

Design a historical marker for the black community at Davis Bend or the site of one of the Reconstruction legislatures. What reasons would you give for preserving these places as national landmarks?

Library/Media Resources

Fiction
Freedom Road by Howard Fast, M.E. Sharpe

Out From This Place by Joyce Hansen, Camelot

Cold Sassy Tree by Olive A. Burns, Delta

Gone With the Wind by Margaret Mitchell, Warner Books

Nonfiction
Reconstruction: America After the Civil War by Zak Mettger, Lodestar Books

Reconstruction: The Great Experiment by Allen W. Trelease, Harper and Row

The Era of Reconstruction by Kenneth M. Stampp, Alfred Knopf

Up From Slavery by Booker T. Washington, Doubleday

Worth Fighting For by Agnes McCarthy and Lawrence Reddick, Zenith Books

Remembering Slavery (book and tape) edited by Ira Berlin, The New Press

From Slave to Civil War Hero: The Life and Times of Robert Smalls by Michael L. Cooper, Lodestar Books

Cobblestone Magazine
Civil War: Reconstruction

Black History Month: The Struggle for Rights

Old-Time Schools in America (the establishment of free schools for blacks)

Video
The Civil War, Episode Nine: 1865—The Better Angels of Our Nature by Ken Burns

Reconstruction (Changing a Nation: 1865–1880), Film Rental Center at Syracuse University

Civil War: Postwar Period, Film Rental Center at Syracuse University

Freedom: A History of US, Episode Seven—Part Five, Kunhardt Productions and Thirteen/WNET for PBS

CD Rom
Story of America 2: The Civil War, National Geographic Society

Reconstruction, Clearvue and ZCI Publishing, Inc.

Connections

Language Arts — Students write a storyboard for a play or skit that tells the story of individual black Reconstruction legislators or of the Davis Bend community.

Geography — Students draw a map of the United States that communicates the dates or the order in which the former Confederate states adopted their Reconstruction constitutions.

Lesson 6
A Failed Revolution
Chapter 10

Theme

Corruption, lack of leadership, and insufficient popular support for Reconstruction allowed the rise of the old Southern political system and the use of segregation and violence to end the attempt at racial equality and justice. With the Compromise of 1877, the revolution of Reconstruction ended.

Overview

For a brief decade after the Civil War, the United States came close to living up to the promise contained in the Declaration of Independence: an America where all men were not only created equal but also treated as such. Sadly, this attempt was not to last.

The great experiment of Reconstruction and political equality ended in 1877 as a result of a disputed presidential election that required the recounting of contested Southern ballots. The Republicans let it be known that if their candidate Rutherford B. Hayes should emerge the victor, he would withdraw all federal troops from the South. Subsequently judged the winner, Hayes kept his word to Southern whites.

During the next few years, the conservative Southern Democrats rapidly recaptured their states' governments. These Redeemer legislatures lost no time passing Jim Crow laws that segregated blacks and deprived them of their right to vote by a variety of means—often carefully created to be just within the law—that included poll taxes, residency stipulations, and literacy tests. Most of these laws, upheld by the Supreme Court in the 1890s, endured until the Civil Rights Movement of the 1960s.

Reconstruction was a period of great hope and crushing disappointment. Although the outcome of the Civil War united the nation and freed the slaves, it did not bring to African Americans the equality or justice for which they had hoped. And peace didn't return the former Confederates to their lost but cherished way of life although they did regain political and social power at a great price. The following decades of animosity, discrimination, and economic backwardness kept the entire South—white and black alike—from realizing its full potential and promise.

Southern whites were not the only ones to cause Reconstruction to fail. With the death of the great Radical Republican Thaddeus Stevens in 1868, much of the reconstructive fire went out of the United States Congress and with it the Northern commitment to the freed slaves. Nevertheless, as long as federal soldiers were present in the South, blacks could resist physical and economic intimidation. By 1870, Northern interest in reconstructing the South began to wane. Furthermore, the North had never really supported the one program that might have truly safeguarded the former slaves: land reform. To break up the plantations and redistribute the land to the people who as slaves had worked the soil for two hundred years was simply too extreme an idea for all but a few of the most radical Republicans.

With the closing of the Freedmen's Bureau in 1872 and with President Ulysses S.

Grant—although a firm ally of equal rights and justice for African Americans— made ineffective by the scandals surrounding his presidency, Southern blacks lost the last vestiges of Northern support. The Compromise of 1877 dealt the final blow when federal troops left the South and Reconstruction officially ended.

By 1900, most of the former slaves and their descendents belonged to an impoverished caste system of sharecroppers, racially isolated from the white world all around them, and intimidated by lynchings and violence. Blacks, forbidden by law to use the same public buildings and services as whites, seldom dared to speak out against the pervasive, legalized racism that dominated their lives. Thus both the Civil War and Reconstruction had failed to secure the promise of freedom and equality for the victims of slavery.

In spite of its failures, important progress during Reconstruction helped lay the groundwork for momentous changes in American life. A thread of continuity links the Emancipation Proclamation and the Fourteenth and Fifteenth Amendments to the civil rights movement of modern times. In ways neither black nor white citizens of that time would see, Reconstruction brought America closer to realizing the promise of equality for all.

References

The Annals of America, 1858-1865: The Crisis of the Union. 1976. Chicago: Encyclopedia Britannica, Inc.

Bailey, Thomas A. and David M. Kennedy. 1998. *The American Spirit.* "The Ordeal of Reconstruction, 1865-1877." Boston: Houghton Mifflin Company.

Benedict, Michael Les. "Ulysses S. Grant: 18th President: 1869-1877." McPherson, James M. ed. 2000. *"To the Best of My Ability": The American Presidents.* Society of American Historians. New York: A Dorling Kindersley Book.

Douglass, Frederick. "Reconstruction." *Atlantic Monthly.* http://www.theatlantic.com/unbound/flashbks/black/douglas.htm. Access date October 1998.

Foner, Eric. "June 13, 1866 Equality Before the Law." McPherson, James M. ed. 2001. *Days of Destiny: Crossroads in American History.* Society of American Historians. New York: A Dorling Kindersley Book.

Foner, Eric. 1999. *The Story of American Freedom.* New York: W.W. Norton & Company.

Foner, Eric. 1988. *Reconstruction: America's Unfinished Revolution, 1863-1877.* New York: Perennial.

Frankel, Noralee. 1996. *Break Those Chains at Last: African Americans, 1860-1880.* New York: Oxford University Press.

Grob, Gerald N. and George Athan Billias, ed. 1992. *Interpretations of American History: Patterns and Perspectives.* "The Reconstruction Era: Constructive or Destructive?" New York: The Free Press.

Kolchin, Peter. "Reconstruction." *Microsoft Encarta 97.* http://www.stanford.edu/~paherman/reconstruction.htm. Access date October 1998.

Meyer, Howard. 2000.*The Amendment that Refused to Die: Equality and Justice Deferred. The History of the 14th Amendment.* New York: Madison Books.

"Military Reconstruction." *HarpWeek, LLC.* http://www.impeach-andrewjohnson.com/06FirstImpeachmentDiscussions/MilitaryReconstruction.htm. Access date October 1998.

Murphy, Richard W. 1987. *The Nation Reunited: War's Aftermath.* Alexandria, Virginia: Time-Life Books.

Rawley, James A. "Rutherford B. Hayes: 19th President: 1877-1881." McPherson, James M. ed. 2000. *"To the Best of My Ability": The American Presidents.* Society of American Historians. New York: A Dorling Kindersley Book.

"Reconstruction and Its Aftermath." *American Memory.* Library of Congress. http://memory.loc.gov/ammem/aaohtml/exhibit/aopart5b.

html, http://memory.loc.gov/ammem/aaohtml/exhibit/ aopart5.html#05a. Access date October 1998.

"Reconstruction and its Failure." Rochester Institute of Technology. http://www.rit.edu/~nrcgsh/bx/bx06b.html. Access date December 1998

Sutherland, Daniel E. 1989. *The Expansion of Everyday Life 1860-1876.* New York: Harper & Row.

Standards

Historical Thinking

The student will

Chronological Thinking

- identify in historical narratives the temporal structure of a historical narrative or story

Historical Comprehension

- reconstruct the literal meaning of a historical passage
- identify the central question(s) the historical narrative addresses
- read historical narratives imaginatively
- draw upon visual, literary, and musical sources

Historical Analysis and Interpretation

- compare or contrast differing sets of ideas, values, personalities, behaviors, and institutions
- consider multiple perspectives
- analyze cause and effect relationships and multiple causation, including the importance of the individual, the influence of ideas, and the role of chance
- hypothesize the influence of the past

Historical Research Capabilities

- formulate historical questions
- obtain historical data
- support interpretation with historical evidence

Analysis and Decision-Making

- identify issues and problems in the past
- marshal evidence of antecedent circumstances and contemporary factors contributing to problems and alternative courses of action

Content

The student will demonstrate understanding of

How various reconstruction plans succeeded or failed

- The political controversy over Reconstruction
    - contrast the Reconstruction policies advocated by Lincoln, Andrew Johnson, and sharply divided Congressional leaders, while assessing these policies as responses to changing events
- The Reconstruction programs to transform social relations in the South
    - explain the economic and social problems facing the South and appraise their impact on different groups of people
    - analyze how African Americans attempted to improve their economic position during Reconstruction and explain factors involved in their quest for land ownership
- The successes and failures of Reconstruction in the South, North, and West
    - examine the progress of "Black Reconstruction" and legislative reform programs promoted by reconstructed state governments

Lesson 6 A Failed Revolution

- evaluate Reconstruction as a revolution
- assess how the political and economic position of African Americans in the northern and western states changed during Reconstruction
- evaluate why corruption increased in the postwar period

Resources

For each student
Reconstructing America by Joy Hakim: Chapter 10, "A Failed Revolution"

For each team
Team Cards: *The End of Reconstruction*

A copy of the *Cartoon Analyzer* for each partnership

For the teacher
Chart paper

Markers

Timer

Web sites
Civil War and Reconstruction Hot Links @ http://www.sinc.sunysb.edu/Class/his265/hotlinks.html

Outline of the Civil War With Links to Reconstruction @ http://members.tripod.com/~greatamericanhistory/gr02006.htm#[VIIIK]

Freedmen and Southern Society Project @ http://www.inform.umd.edu/ARHU/Depts/History/Freedman/home.html

Freedom: A History of US @ http://www.pbs.org/wnet/historyofus/menu.html

Vocabulary

Words to Remember
*****Radical Republicans** — political party that opposed slavery and supported Reconstruction policies to grant voting and civil rights to blacks

*****segregation** — separation of the races

*****lynching** — execution without due process of law, especially by hanging

*****white supremacy** — belief that the white race is superior

Ku Klux Klan — white supremacy group that intimidated freed slaves and their white supporters through violence

*****Conservative Democrats** — political party that supported slavery and obstructed Reconstruction efforts to expand the civil and voting rights of blacks

redeem — to recover or set free

*****"Redeemers"** — Conservative Democrats who regained control of the Southern state legislatures, drove the Republicans from power, and instituted segregation and voting requirements for freed slaves

*****polling place or polls** — place where people vote during elections

*****poll tax** — tax that voters must pay

*****sharecropping** — agreement in which a landowner supplied land, tools, and seed to a landless farmer, who then gave the owner a portion of all he grew

*****Compromise of 1877** — Rutherford B. Hayes was judged president in a contested race in return for the withdrawal of federal troops from the South

People to Remember
*****Ulysses S. Grant** — general in charge of the Union armies who became president; although Grant supported equal rights, scandals surrounding his presidency made him ineffective

*****Rutherford B. Hayes** — elected president in the contested 1877 election in return for withdrawing federal troops from the South

Wade Hampton — former Confederate general who later supported voting rights for blacks and became governor of South Carolina and a United States senator

The Lesson

Focus Activity – 5 minutes

1. Write "Retreat from the South" and "A Failed Revolution" on the chalkboard.

2. Ask the students to **Think-Team-Share**:

   - What does retreat mean? Who do you think is retreating?

   - How will this retreat impact the struggle for equal justice for blacks? Why?

   - What is a revolution? What do you think is the "failed revolution"?

   - What changes will the "failed revolution" bring about for blacks and whites?

   - What is the relationship between the "retreat from the South" and "a failed revolution"?

3. Teams use **Numbered Heads** to share their explanations with the class.

Teaching Activity – 25 minutes

1. Introduce Chapter 10, "A Failed Revolution" in *Reconstructing America*. Ask the students to summarize the situation in the South in the late 1870s:

   - What events are taking place in the South?

   - How do those events affect Northern carpetbaggers? Former Confederates? Southern freed blacks?

   If necessary, explain that most Radical Republicans and Northern carpetbaggers have left the South or have lost interest in Reconstruction. Other problems consume their energy: the scandals of Grant's presidency, Indian problems in the West, massive numbers of immigrants in the Northeast, and a weariness with the problems of the South and the newly freed slaves. Southern Democrats have begun to gain political and social power that prevents freed slaves from voting, buying land, getting an education, or gaining equal rights. Southern free blacks are losing their right to vote through intimidation and violence.

Notes

Lesson 6 A Failed Revolution

2. Introduce the Vocabulary *Words and People to Remember*.

3. Distribute a set of eight Team Cards: *The End of Reconstruction* to each team. The team divides the cards among its members.

   Reading for a Purpose: Each student reads Chapter 10 of *Reconstructing America* to research how the event or circumstance on his or her cards influenced the end of Reconstruction.

   - Increased taxes
   - Sharecropping
   - Poor leadership
   - Problems in the North
   - Rise of Southern white hate groups
   - Compromise of 1877
   - Poll tax
   - "Redeemer" state legislatures

   Each student writes the explanations on the back of his or her cards.

4. **Circulate and Monitor**: Visit each team to guide the students in reading the chapter and finding the information to write on their cards.

5. Use **Numbered Heads** for students to discuss the significance of the eight events or circumstances to the failure of Reconstruction.

6. Ask the students to discuss:
   - What changes did Radical Republicans try to bring to the South?
   - What advances did the freed slaves make during Reconstruction?
   - What techniques did white Southerners use to take government away from blacks?

Student Team Learning Activity – 25 minutes

Analyzing political cartoons

1. Explain the Student Team Learning Activity. Each student works with a team partner. One partnership analyzes the political cartoon on page 45 and the other analyzes the one on page 48 of *Reconstructing America*.

2. Explain the purpose of political cartoons.

   Political cartoons express a specific viewpoint. By making fun of political figures and issues, the cartoonist expresses his or her political opinion about an issue or idea. Political cartoons use *caricature* and *satire* to create humor. *Caricature* is the exaggeration of personal characteristics. *Satire* is the use of irony or sarcasm to make fun of a person or event. To understand a political cartoon the reader must first understand what the cartoon *symbols* represent and then determine the overall *meaning* of the cartoon.

3. Distribute a copy of the Team Sheet: *Cartoon Analyzer* to each team partnership and briefly explain each section of the analyzer.

4. Working in pairs, team members use the *Cartoon Analyzer* to identify the symbols used and the meaning of their cartoon. Then each pair shares the cartoon and its analysis with the other team partnership.

   Note to the Teacher: If the students have little experience analyzing cartoons, guide them through the process and discuss each completed section of the worksheet before beginning the next section.

5. **Circulate and Monitor**: Visit each team as students use the *Cartoon Analyzer* and help them identify the symbols and meaning of their cartoons.

6. Use **Numbered Heads** for students to share and compare their understanding of the cartoons' symbols and overall meaning. Ask the students:

   - What does the cartoon tell us about the failure of Reconstruction?

7. Each student on the team chooses one of the events or circumstances that influenced the end of Reconstruction (See Teaching Activity #3) and creates a political cartoon based on that event. Remind the students to first identify a caption or the overall meaning of their cartoon (the point they want to make) and then choose symbols that express that meaning.

   Note to the Teacher: Students begin this activity in class and finish their cartoons for homework.

Lesson 6   A Failed Revolution

8. **Circulate and Monitor**: Visit each team to help the students plan their political cartoons, especially to determine the overall point the student wishes to make and the symbols that express that point.

Reflection and Review Activity – 5 minutes

Students read the quotation by Eric Foner on page 45 of *Reconstructing America* and discuss the questions beneath that quotation.

Note to the Teacher: An additional resource for this lesson is the video series *Freedom: A History of US,* Episode Seven—Part Five: A Failed Revolution, Kunhardt Productions and Thirteen/WNET for PBS. Also explore the accompanying PBS Website: Freedom: A History of US @ http://www.pbs.org/wnet/historyofus/menu.html, especially the section for teachers.

Homework

Complete your political cartoon.

Library/Media Resources

Fiction

Freedom Road by Howard Fast, M. E. Sharpe

Out From This Place by Joyce Hansen, Camelot

Cold Sassy Tree by Olive A. Burns, Delta

Gone With the Wind by Margaret Mitchell, Warner Books

Nonfiction

Reconstruction: America After the Civil War by Zak Mettger, Lodestar Books

Reconstruction: The Great Experiment by Allen W. Trelease, Harper and Row

The Era of Reconstruction by Kenneth M. Stampp, Alfred Knopf

Up From Slavery by Booker T. Washington, Doubleday

Worth Fighting For by Agnes McCarthy and Lawrence Reddick, Zenith Books

Remembering Slavery (book and tape) edited by Ira Berlin, The New Press

From Slave to Civil War Hero: The Life and Times of Robert Smalls by Michael L. Cooper, Lodestar Books

Cobblestone Magazine

Civil War: Reconstruction

Black History Month: The Struggle for Rights

Old-Time Schools in America (the establishment of free schools for blacks)

Video

The Civil War, Episode Nine: 1865—The Better Angels of Our Nature by Ken Burns

Reconstruction (Changing a Nation: 1865–1880), Film Rental Center at Syracuse University

Civil War: Postwar Period, Film Rental Center at Syracuse University

Freedom: A History of US, Episode Seven—Part Five, Kunhardt Productions and Thirteen/WNET for PBS

CD Rom

Story of America 2: The Civil War, National Geographic Society

Reconstruction, Clearvue and ZCI Publishing, Inc.

Connections

Math — Students compose "Sharecropper Math Problems" using the sharecropper's payment of one-half or one-third of his harvest to the landowner. For example: How many bales of cotton would a sharecropper pay if he raised two hundred bales and paid the landowner one-third of his harvest?

Music — Laborers have always sung work songs to make their toil seem easier. Many freed slaves farmed or did other manual labor. Students research and perform the work songs that farmers and laborers sang during the late 1800s.

Library — Students research first person accounts about slavery and the Reconstruction period by consulting the book and tape *Remembering Slavery* (edited by Ira Berlin). Some accounts depict freedom as harder than slavery. How would students explain this opinion?

Technology/Library — Students use the web sites listed in the lesson to research first person accounts of slavery and the change to freedom.

Review Lesson I
Lessons 1 through 6
Preface through Chapter 10

In the Review Lesson, students revisit essential ideas and vocabulary from the first six lessons to prepare for the Assessment Lesson. The Review Lesson is in the form of a card game.

If time allows, the teams may play more than one round of *Reconstructing America Review*. Even though one team member will win each round, all students win by reviewing ideas, facts, and vocabulary from the previous lessons. The goal of the game is to successfully prepare *each* member of the team for the assessment.

Reconstructing America Review I: Rise and Fall of Reconstruction

1. To ensure that each student has a chance to play, students remain in their cooperative learning teams of four or five.

2. Each team receives a set of game cards and the answer sheet.

3. Cards are shuffled, separated into their respective piles (Who Did What?, The Name Game, Legal Eagle, etc.), and placed face down in the center of the table.

4. One team member is designated as the first player (i.e. the student whose name is last in the alphabet). The student to his or her right has the answer sheet, keeping it face down on the desk. This person is the fact checker.

5. The first player chooses a card, reads the number and the question aloud, and attempts to answer it. The fact checker turns the answer sheet over, finds the correct question number, and checks the first player's response. If the student answers correctly, he or she keeps the card. If the answer is wrong, the card is placed at the bottom of the pile. The fact checker quickly turns the answer sheet face down again.

6. Play passes to the left, and the student who was the first player is now the fact checker.

7. The game ends when all the cards are gone. The student with the most cards wins.

Reconstructing America Review I: Rise and Fall of Reconstruction Questions and Answers

Who Did What?

1. Who was Edmund G. Ross, and what did he do? United States Senator from Kansas who cast the deciding not guilty vote at President Andrew Johnson's impeachment trial

2. Who was Thaddeus Stevens, and what did he do? Radical Republican United States congressman who wrote and supported civil rights legislation for freed blacks and led the movement to impeach President Andrew Johnson

3. Who was Andrew Johnson, and what did he do? Vice president who became president on the death of Lincoln; he supported the South and was impeached but not convicted.

4. Who was Rutherford B. Hayes, and what did he do? President after Grant who in a contested presidential election promised if elected to withdraw federal troops from the South

5. Who was Robert Brown Elliott, and what did he do? A black representative to the South Carolina Reconstruction legislature and a congressman who worked to get civil rights legislation passed

6. Who was Benjamin T. Montgomery, and what did he do? A former slave who created a profitable black farming community on plantations bought from Joseph Davis

The Name Game

7. What were carpetbaggers? Northerners who went South to teach, help with aid programs, organize state governments, and sometimes make money for themselves

8. What were scalawags? Southerners who cooperated with the North

9. What were black codes? Laws passed by white legislatures in the South that limited the freedom of former slaves

10. What were sharecroppers? Workers who agreed to pay a portion of their harvest for use of the land

11. What were poll taxes? A tax that voters must pay. Poll taxes were used in the South to keep blacks from voting.

12. What were Redeemers? Conservative Southern Democrats who gained control of the state legislatures and instituted segregation and voting requirements for blacks

Legal Eagle

13. Which Constitutional amendment granted the right to vote to black men? Fifteenth

14. Which Constitutional amendment provided equal protection under the law to all citizens? Fourteenth

15. Which Constitutional amendment made slavery illegal in the United States? Thirteenth

16. What process brings the United States president to trial for treason, bribery, or high crimes and misdemeanors? Impeachment

17. What can a president do to stop a bill from becoming law? Veto (refuse to sign) the bill

18. How much of the total Senate vote is needed to convict an impeached president? Two-thirds

The Rise of Reconstruction

19. What were the three major goals of Reconstruction? Rebuild the South, reunite the states, and ensure the rights and protection of the newly freed slaves

20. What were the first two years of Reconstruction called and why? Presidential Reconstruction because President Lincoln and then President Johnson controlled the practices and policies of Reconstruction

21. What was Congressional Reconstruction? Last ten years of Reconstruction when Congress passed legislation to secure and protect the rights of freed slaves and required Southern states to grant certain rights to former slaves before the state could rejoin the Union

22. What did the Freedmen's Bureau do? Helped newly freed men, women, and children to integrate into free society by setting up schools, distributing food and other supplies, settling disputes, and aiding with other problems

23. What was Abraham Lincoln's plan for Reconstruction? He wanted to bring the South back into the Union without harsh treatment, believing everyone had suffered enough already.

24. What did the Southern Reconstruction legislatures achieve? Free public schools for all, road construction, treated former Confederates fairly, and supported voting and equal civil rights for all

The Fall of Reconstruction

25. What effect did the Compromise of 1877 have on ending Reconstruction? Reconstruction ended when Rutherford B. Hayes, a Republican, kept his promise to Southern Democrats that he would withdraw federal forces from the South if they would support him in the disputed presidential election.

26. What effect did the "Redeemer" legislatures have on ending Reconstruction? Conservative Southern Democrats and former Confederates used fear tactics and voting requirements to keep former slaves and their white supporters from voting, took control of the state legislatures, and enacted segregation policies.

27. What effect did sharecropping have on ending Reconstruction? Because most freedmen and women could not afford to buy land and farming equipment, they agreed to pay a portion of their crop in exchange for the use of the land. Sharecroppers were economically dependent on the landowners, who often cheated them or made them pay additional costs.

28. What effect did the Ku Klux Klan have on ending Reconstruction? This Southern white hate group used terrorist tactics including lynching to frighten blacks and their white supporters from voting.

29. What effect did problems in the North have on ending Reconstruction? The scandals of Grant's presidency, the "Indian problems" in the West, the "immigrant problems" in the Northeast, and a weariness with the problems of the freed blacks and the Southern people drew Northerners' attention from Southern reform and rebuilding.

30. What effect did the poll tax have on ending Reconstruction? Many freedmen did not have the money to pay the poll tax and so could not vote for representatives who supported their civil rights.

Lesson 7
Out West
Chapter 11

Theme

After the Civil War, settlers rushed into the western territories and transformed the Great Plains from open prairie to the nation's breadbasket. In the process, they robbed the Native Americans of their ancestral lands and changed the nation forever.

Overview

From the time the nation was founded, Americans viewed the West as a never-ending source of new living space. Just beyond the edge of civilization, that vast open land provided room and opportunity for a better life with plentiful, rich earth free to anyone who was daring and hard working enough to claim it and use it.

After the Civil War, veterans of both armies looked to the western lands for a new start in life. They came as farmers under the Homestead Act or acquired inexpensive farmland through railroad land subsidies. Those who desired more adventure—and were not afraid of back-breaking hard work—joined the fraternity of the cowboys and drove cattle over the great trails to rail centers. Others became part of the most ambitious enterprise of the century: building a railroad across an entire rugged continent. Some remained soldiers and joined the United States cavalry, fighting Indians instead of each other.

For many freed blacks, the West offered opportunities to own land rather than sharecrop, or to join the ranks of the cowboys, who offered African Americans more equality than was available elsewhere in the nation at that time. Some blacks stayed in the federal army and earned the sobriquet "buffalo soldiers," a name given to them by Native Americans because of their physical characteristics.

Women—some widowed by the Civil War—also found a more open society in the West. The need to populate the land and establish communities created an unusual acceptance of women as homesteaders and entrepreneurs. Some territories granted full rights of citizenship to women, including suffrage. Women were frequently welcomed as a civilizing influence in rough frontier towns that desired to become respectable communities. And so, women in the West enjoyed greater autonomy, status, and respect long before they did in the more established and conservative east.

The promise of the great American West reached beyond the nation itself, drawing immigrants from Europe, Russia, and China. Some settled in ethnic enclaves so that entire Western communities spoke German, or grew Russian wheat, or ate Swedish meatballs. Immigrant Irish railroad gangs building from eastern terminals met their exotic Chinese counterparts laying track from the west coast.

In the early 1800s, national leaders predicted that it would take half a millennium to settle and populate the West's vast terrain. But by the 1890s, America's most dramatic era of expansion was over. Railway tracks crisscrossed the prairies, and farms and towns prospered where Native

Americans had hunted buffalo only a few decades earlier. Inherent in the great western movement was the sacrifice of an entire ancient culture. The solutions to the "Indian problem" were tragic for this once-proud people. Forced from their ancestral lands, robbed of their traditional way of life, denied justice and equality, and often massacred, the western Indian tribes were eventually subdued and contained on reservations.

The passing of the Old West was mostly brought about by the arrival of modern technology. Inventions of mechanical farm machinery and advances in farming techniques turned agriculture into an industry and the small, self-sufficient sodbuster into a businessman. The flat, grassy plains that had defied profitable cultivation became the bread-basket of the world. With advances in communication and transportation, rural life became less isolated, and suddenly the great distances shrank. As the West embraced countless new varieties of technological advancement, even the cowboy on horseback—the very symbol of the American West—finally grew obsolete as the guardian of the range.

References

Brash, Sarah, ed. 1997. *Defiant Chiefs: The American Story.* Alexandria, Virginia: Time-Life Books.

Brash, Sarah, ed. 1996. *Settling the West: The American Story.* Alexandria, Virginia: Time-Life Books.

Brown, Dee. 1994. *The American West.* New York: Simon & Schuster.

Colbert, David. ed. 1998. *Eyewitness to the American West.* New York: Penguin Books.

Dick, Everett. 1993 (1948 Reprint). *The Dixie Frontier: A Social History*. Norman: University of Oklahoma Press.

Fleet, Cameron, ed. 1997. *First Nations—Firsthand.* Edison, New Jersey: Chartwell Books, Inc.

Horn, Huston and the Editors of Time-Life. 1974. *The Pioneers: The Old West.* New York: Time Life Books.

Hoxie, Frederick E., ed. 1996. *Encyclopedia of North American Indians: Native American History, Culture, and Life from Paleo-Indians to the Present.* New York: Houghton Mifflin.

Lamar, Howard R. 1998. *The New Encyclopedia of the American West.* New York: Harper Collins.

Milner, Clyde A., II, Carol A. O'Connor, and Martha A. Sandweiss, ed. 1994. *The American West.* New York: Oxford University Press.

Murphy, Richard W. 1987. *The Nation Reunited: War's Aftermath.* Alexandria, Virginia: Time-Life Books.

Sutherland, Daniel E. 1989. *The Expansion of Everyday Life 1860-1876.* New York: Harper & Row.

Trails West. 1979. Special Publications Division. Washington, D.C.: National Geographic Society.

Ward, Geoffrey C. 1996. *The West: An Illustrated History*. Boston: Little, Brown and Company.

Wheeler, Keith and the Editors of Time-Life. 1976. *The Chroniclers: The Old West.* New York: Time Life Books.

Standards

Historical Thinking

The student will

Historical Comprehension

- identify the central question(s) the historical narrative addresses
- evidence historical perspectives
- draw upon visual, literary, and musical sources

Historical Analysis and Interpretation

- identify the author or source of the historical document or narrative
- compare or contrast differing sets of ideas, values, personalities, behaviors, and institutions

Lesson 7 Out West

- differentiate between historical facts and historical interpretation
- consider multiple perspectives

Historical Research Capabilities

- obtain historical data

Analysis and Decision-Making

- identify issues and problems in the past

Content

The student will demonstrate understanding of

Federal Indian policy and United States foreign policy after the Civil War

- Various perspectives on federal Indian policy, westward expansion, and the resulting struggles
    - identify and compare the attitudes and policies toward Native Americans by government officials, the U.S. Army, missionaries, and settlers

Resources

For each student
Reconstructing America by Joy Hakim: Chapter 11, "Meanwhile, Out West"
Notebook

For each team
Sheet of chart paper
Markers or crayons
Team Sheets:
  Aboriginal Susceptibility
  Avarice of Indian Agents
  Two copies of the Cartoon Analyzer

For the teacher
Transparencies:
  Symbols
  Suitors
  Indian Bureau
Chart Paper
Markers

Web sites

America's West — Development and History @ http://www.americanwest.com/index.htm#post

Famous People in American History @ http://www.studyweb.com/lit/bio/famous.htm

Images of the American West @ http://www.treasurenet.com/images/americanwest.html

Events in THE WEST—1860-1870 @ http://www3.pbs.org/weta/thewest/wpages/wpgs200/w21860.htm

Events in THE WEST—1870-1880 @ http://www3.pbs.org/weta/thewest/wpages/wpgs200/w21870.htm

Events in THE WEST—1880-1890 @ http://www3.pbs.org/weta/thewest/wpages/wpgs200/w21880.htm

People of Color on the Western Frontier @ http://www.coax.net/people/lwf/western.html

Places in THE WEST — Texas Cattle Trails @ http://www3.pbs.org/weta/thewest/wpages/wpgs300/3cattle.htm

HarpWeek @ http://thewest.harpweek.com/

Freedom: A History of US @ http://www.pbs.org/wnet/historyofus/menu.html

Vocabulary

Words to Remember

*homesteader — person who lives on and cultivates a tract of United States public land under the homestead law

Homestead Act — legislative act authorizing the sale of public lands to settlers

nation's bread basket — midsection of the United States that produces most of the country's wheat for bread

- ***prairie** — large area of level land that has deep fertile soil, tall coarse grasses, and few trees
- **buffalo chips** — dried buffalo dung used for fuel
- **capital** — large amounts of money needed to start a business or farm
- **land rush** — race to claim a tract of land in the West
- ***political cartoon** — humorous way to present news or a viewpoint about a political figure or event
- ***caricature** — exaggeration of personal characteristics
- ***symbol** — something that stands for or suggests something else
- ***stereotype** — hurtful symbols used to describe or attack a group of people

People to Remember

- ***Walt Whitman** — late nineteenth century writer and poet who captured the mission, destiny, and spirit of the American people

Lesson 7 Out West

The Lesson

Focus Activity – 10 minutes

1. Introduce the western movement of the late 1800s. Explain that as soon as the Civil War ended, settlers rushed to the Great Plains in the midsection of the United States to make new lives.

   Help the students locate the Great Plains and the area of western settlement on the map on page 75 of *Reconstructing America*.

   Explain that for many of these people, the move was a new start. For example, settlers included Confederate veterans whose homes and way of life were destroyed by war, northern immigrants who wanted their own land, African Americans who left the segregated South, Civil War soldiers who remained in the military; and adventurers who sought excitement.

2. Distribute a sheet of chart paper and markers to each team. Teams have two minutes to list on the chart paper as many words as possible that they think describe the "Old West."

3. Teams share their lists by displaying them in the classroom.

Teaching Activity – 20 minutes

1. Introduce Chapter 11 of *Reconstructing America* by asking the teams to consider their lists of words about the "Old West":

   - What words appear on all or most of the lists? Teams place a checkmark next to each of those words.

   - Based on the lists, what impressions do we share about the "Old West"?

   Students **Speculate:**

   - Why would people head west after the Civil War?

   - What difficulties would settlers encounter?

   - Why would people take such risks?

Notes

2. **Reading for a Purpose**: After introducing the Vocabulary *Words and People to Remember,* direct the students to read Chapter 11, "Meanwhile, Out West" in *Reconstructing America* in order to discuss the following questions with their teammates.

   - What difficulties did settlers encounter in the West? (Indians, buffalo, the terrain itself, new kind of farming)
   - Why did the settlers take such risks? (To own land, to farm, to make a better life, for adventure, to escape the South during Reconstruction, to escape the industrialized life of the North)

3. **Circulate and Monitor**: Visit each team as the students read the chapter and discuss the questions.

4. Discuss the problems and promises of the West with the class. (Refer to the chapter and add information from the Overview.)

5. Direct the students to listen as you read the poem by Walt Whitman on page 51 in *Reconstructing America*.

   Help the students interpret the poem by asking

   - What types of growth does Whitman mention in his poem? (Growth of cities, communication, transportation, farming, and industry)
   - What does Whitman's poem tell you about the West? (The West is growing, changing, and progressing; it is becoming industrialized and less wild.)

Student Team Learning Activity – 25 minutes

Recognizing symbols and stereotypes

1. Using the Transparency: *Symbols*, ask the students to identify each object and what it represents. Guide the students in defining the term *symbol,* and write the word and its definition on the vocabulary chart.

2. Ask the students:
   - Which of the words on their team lists are *symbols* of the Old West? (Focus Activity #2)

   Students circle the words that are symbols on their team lists.

Connect the term *symbol* to political cartoons: Explain that objects and political caricatures are often used in political cartoons as *symbols*. Define the term *caricature*, and write the word and its definition on the vocabulary chart. Explain that cartoonists often seize on obvious differences in clothing, facial characteristics, and hairstyles to *symbolize* or *caricature* particular groups of people.

3. Using the Transparency: *Suitors*, help the students identify the *symbols* and *caricatures* in the cartoon by asking

   - What groups of people are depicted in this political cartoon?
   - What clothing, facial characteristics, and hairstyles did the cartoonist use to symbolize them?
   - What other symbols did the cartoonist use?

4. Then ask the students to **Speculate:**

   - How does a cartoonist turn a *caricature* into a sympathetic or cruel portrait?
   - How does the use of caricature express the cartoonist's point of view, bias, or attitude toward the character?

   Use the Transparency: *Indian Bureau*. Ask the students to describe the cartoonist's attitude or point of view and explain how he uses *symbols* and *caricature* to make his point.

5. Explain that hurtful symbols that are used to attack groups of people are called *stereotypes*. Add the term and its definition to the vocabulary list.

   Then ask the students to again consider their lists of words about the Old West:

   - Are any of the words or symbols *stereotypes* of the Old West?
   - What groups of people or ideas about the Old West might be victims of stereotyping?

6. Use the example of stereotyping Indians to introduce the next activity.

   Distribute one copy of *Aboriginal Susceptibility* and one of *Avarice of Indian Agents* and two copies of the *Cartoon Analyzer* to each team.

   Explain the Student Team Learning Activity. If necessary, help students define the terms *aboriginal, susceptibility* and *avarice*.

7. During this Student Team Learning Activity, each student works with a team partner. One partnership uses the *Cartoon Analyzer* to analyze the cartoon *Aboriginal Susceptibility* while the other partnership analyses *Avarice of Indian Agents*. Then the team discusses the two cartoons:

   - How does the cartoonist use symbols, caricatures, and stereotypes to express his point of view about Native Americans? United States officials?

   - How does the cartoonist use these symbols, caricatures, and stereotypes to persuade the reader to his point of view?

   - What is your reaction to these cartoons?

   Circulate and Monitor: Visit each team as students analyze the two cartoons, discuss each cartoonist's use of symbols, caricatures, and stereotypes to express his point of view, and students' reactions to the cartoons.

8. Remind students that the stereotypes in these cartoons reveal fears and dislikes of people who lived over one hundred years ago, and it is natural for us to react strongly to those stereotypes today.

   Explain that not just cartoonists, but many people use stereotypes when they think about or describe groups of people. Often people use hurtful symbols and words to attack those who are unlike themselves or have a different viewpoint. Even historians sometimes allow bias or their own viewpoint to influence the way they report the stories of the past.

9. Lead the class in a discussion of how stereotypes can lead to dehumanizing people. Ask students to consider how stereotypes hinder cooperation, equality, and justice. Remind them that negative feelings behind stereotypes can incite violent behavior. Ask them for examples of this behavior in our history, such as battles between the Indians and the cavalry in the West.

Reflection and Review Activity – 5 minutes

1. Teams **Think-Team-Share** to consider

   - As you study the West, what stereotypes do you think will emerge?

- After scanning Chapters 12 through 18 in *Reconstructing America*, **Predict**:

- What people or events might be stereotyped? (Americans, farmers, homesteaders, cowboys, ranchers, gunfighters and outlaws, marshals and sheriffs, railroaders)

2. Use **Numbered Heads** for the teams to share their responses.

   Note to the Teacher: An additional resource for this lesson is the video series *Freedom: A History of US,* Episode Eight—Part One, Meanwhile, Out West, Kunhardt Productions and Thirteen/WNET for PBS. Also explore the accompanying PBS Website: Freedom: A History of US @ http://www.pbs.org/wnet/historyofus/menu.html, especially the section for teachers.

Homework

Suppose you were a political cartoonist in the West in the late 1800s. What symbols would you use to represent the following groups of people?

   Native Americans

   Cowboys

   United States cavalrymen

   Homesteaders

Draw at least two symbols for each of the groups.

Library/Media Resources

Fiction
Little House on the Prairie by Laura Ingalls Wilder, Harper Trophy
Little Town on the Prairie by Laura Ingalls Wilder, Harper Trophy
The Long Winter by Laura Ingalls Wilder, Harper Trophy

Nonfiction
Songs of the Wild West by Dan Fox, Simon & Schuster
Time-Life Series: Books of the Old West, Time-Life Books
Prairie Visions: The Life and Times of Solomon Butcher by Pam Conrad, Harper Trophy

The Prairie Traveler: The Bestselling Classic Handbook for America's Pioneers by Randolph B. Marcy, Perigee Books

Cobblestone Magazine

Americans Who Were the First

Willa Cather

Annie Oakley

Outlaws of the West

Plains Indians

Walt Whitman

CD Rom

Story of America 1: The Western Movement, National Geographic Society

Video

The West: Video Set, Book, and Music CD by Ken Burns

Freedom: A History of US, Episode Eight—Part One, Kunhardt Productions and Thirteen/WNET for PBS

Connections

Language Arts/Library — Students read *Caddie Woodlawn* by Carol Ryrie Brink. Partner Discussion Guide available from Talent Development Middle Schools, Johns Hopkins University.

Language Arts/Library — Students read excerpts from *The Prairie Traveler*, a reprint of the 1859 best selling guide written by army captain Randolph B. Marcy for settlers traveling across the American frontier. This guide became the essential handbook for westward-bound pioneers, outlining exactly how to prepare for the trip and what to expect. Students will enjoy such fascinating frontier lore as why mules can cross rivers only if they don't get their ears wet, how to interpret smoke signals, and treatments for rattlesnake bite.

Science/Library — Students study the ecology of the prairie and how the grasslands are different from other ecosystems. The science of life on the prairie includes such topics as prairie plants and why they grow there; interesting prairie animals and their life cycles; the composition of the soil; and weather on the prairie.

Music — Students sing or listen to the songs of the Old West.

Physical Education — Barn dances were popular social events for prairie communities. Students learn to square dance and explore dances of ethnic groups that settled in particular western regions.

Technology/Library — The Teaching With Historic Places program has a lesson about Adeline Hornbek, a single mother of four who homesteaded in Colorado in the 1870s. Students visit the site @ www.cr.nps.gov/nr/twhp/wwwlps/lessons/67hornbek/67hornbek.htm

Lesson 8
The Cowboy
Chapter 12

Theme

For the brief span of a generation, the rugged American cowboy endured physically punishing, arduous work as he drove the Texas longhorns along the cattle trails of the Great Plains to markets and railway terminals.

Overview

The rugged era of the American cowboy lasted a mere generation, from the end of the Civil War until the mid-1880s, when bad weather, poor range management, and calamitous cattle market prices forced an end to his free-ranging life. In that brief span, about 40,000 cowboys rode the cattle trails of the Great Plains. Most were young (their average age was twenty-four), adventurous, and unsophisticated. Theirs was a stoic, arduous life, far different from the mythic legends that grew around them. They were men of a particular time and place, who lived by a code that combined hard-fisted frontier toughness with Victorian era social values. They performed body-punishing and hazardous jobs, and pitted themselves against a vast, magnificent land of austere beauty that offered monumental doses of tribulation.

In the 1800s, the American West seemed like an entirely separate country to the civilized Easterners: a wasteland of desolate plains, harsh mountain ranges, and sparse frontier settlements. For half a century, Americans had probed for a way to exploit the West. But not until after the Civil War and the slaughter of over seventy-five million buffalo was the opportunity made clear: vast expanses of unused grass awaited a grazing creature that could withstand the climate, and that creature was the hardy Texas longhorn, a descendent of the cattle brought by the early Spanish conquistadors. From 1867 to 1887, cowboys moved a total of 5.5 million head of cattle north on cattle trails to be shipped from Kansas railheads to the beef-hungry East. This mountain of animals, men, and money drew settlers and merchants to a region that had long been considered worthless. And the chief agents of colonization were the mounted cattle tenders of the West, the cowboys.

A wide spectrum of humanity made up the fraternity of the cowboy. About one cowhand in six was Mexican, one in four was black, and a smaller percentage was Indian; there were even a few women. After the Civil War, many of the cowboys were mustered-out Union soldiers who, for a variety of reasons, could not bear to return home to the rocky farms, the boring small towns, or the large cities overrun with recent immigrants. A greater number were former Confederate soldiers who were looking for a new life or fast action to ease the frustration of the Lost Cause. Others were former slaves—many of whom had been freed from Texas cattle ranches and possessed the skills of roping and riding necessary for a life on the cattle trails. Black cowboys frequently enjoyed greater opportunities for a dignified life in the territories and new states of the American West than did blacks in other regions of the nation. African American cowboys worked, ate, slept, played, and on occasion, fought side by side with their white comrades, and their ability and courage won respect, even admiration. Rounding out the society of the cowhand were a few immigrant peasants, remittance men (paid to stay away from their upright families), drifters, adventurers, and those on the dodge from the law.

The cowboy got his name from working the West's sprawling herds of cattle. In his job, he employed a multitude of activities, styles, and techniques that extended from rounding up, branding, and driving half-wild longhorns across a thousand miles of untamed range to a more settled life of ranch chores and breeding shorthorns. Most cowboys found city jobs in the winter when the ranches and cattle barons laid off their help. Others went bounty hunting for wolves or "batched it" with friends until the spring roundup. Most cowboys spent an average of seven years caring for the unpredictable, panic-prone, thick-headed, long-horned cattle before settling permanently in towns or on ranches of their own.

Besides his unique work-dress of broad-brimmed hat, bandanna, leather vest, leg-protective chaps, and spurred, high-heeled boots, the cowboy used three basic tools—the horse, the rope, and the pistol. His horse was essential to the cowboy's work: a serviceable tool that greatly expanded the muscle power and mobility of the rider. The range was no place for a man on foot—the distances were too great and without horses it was impossible to round up, brand, and drive thousands of cattle to market. So the horse was a practical arrangement as well as the major element in the cowboy's self-image. As cowpuncher Jo Mora put it, dismounted the cowboy was: ". . . just a plain bowlegged human who smelled very horsey at times, slept in his underwear, and was subject to boils and dyspepsia." On a horse, he was a cavalier.

The cowboy's rope or lariat was also indispensable to his image and function. Expertly thrown, the rope enabled a man to capture and subdue a thousand-pound animal. Multi-functional, the lariat became an instant corral, a horse hobble, a way to drag firewood or a mired cow from a bog, or in extreme cases, a hangman's noose for frontier justice.

Although the use of the famous Colt revolver figures prominently in frontier myth, cowboys used their guns most often for target practice, hunting game, killing rattlesnakes, or turning aside stampeding cattle. Hot-headed shoot-outs rarely occurred, with a few exceptions—mostly caused by skittish greenhorns, the trail-end's spree in town, the Southern tradition (brought west) of defending honor, and the lawlessness of a small number of thugs and bullies. Contrary to legendary tales of gunfights and gangs of hard-riding, pistol-packing desperadoes, the most common cause of death among cowboys was to be dragged by a horse while tending cattle.

The most important job of the cowboy was the cattle drive, delivering steaks on the hoof to the railway terminals of Abilene, Wichita, or Dodge City. Smooth-faced youngsters turned into fully mature and tested cowboys on what might be a 1,200 mile journey. For two-thirds of that distance the herds would follow the main northern route of most cattle drives, the Chisholm Trail. Named for Scotch-Cherokee trader Jesse Chisholm, who had mapped out a straight, level wagon road with easy river fords between southern Kansas and his trading post, the trail opened as a cattle drive in 1867. Within five years, over a million cattle had tramped and bawled up that road, which was littered with the bones of cattle, horses, and the shallow graves of men who did not make it—victims of swollen streams, rattlesnakes, or stampeding cattle. Every man who set out understood the risks and knew that on the trail he was considered less valuable than the cattle he drove. Nevertheless, the challenges and excitement, and sometimes the sheer necessity of having a job, drew men to the trail.

Through it all, the cowboy carried himself with vinegary pride, fully convinced that he was the aristocrat among workmen. The cattle drive proved a hard way to earn a hundred dollars—three or four months of dust, thirst, blisters, cold, and danger for the price of a new hat and fancy boots. But there were compensations: the comradeship of the trail, the epic sight of cattle on the move, the satisfaction of passing the tough tests of the trade, and a proud awareness of being part of something fundamental and grand.

References

Adams, Andy. 1903. *The Log of a Cowboy: A Narrative of the Old Trail Days*. Lincoln: University of Nebraska.

Brash, Sarah. ed. 1996. *Settling the West: The American Story*. Alexandria, Virginia: Time-Life Books.

Brown, Dee. 1994. *The American West*. New York: Simon & Schuster.

Clay, John. 1962. *My Life on the Range*. Norman: University of Oklahoma Press.

Colbert, David. ed. 1998. *Eyewitness to the American West*. New York: Penguin Books.

Colloson, Frank. 1963. *Life in the Saddle*. Edited by Mary Whatley. Norman: University of Oklahoma Press.

Forbis, William H. and the Editors of Time-Life. 1973. *The Cowboys: The Old West*. New York: Time Life Books.

Hoig, Stan. 1970. *The Humor of the American Cowboy*. University of Nebraska Press: A Bison Book.

Horn, Huston and the Editors of Time-Life. 1974. *The Pioneers: The Old West*. New York: Time Life Books.

Lamar, Howard R. 1998. *The New Encyclopedia of the American West*. New York: HarperCollins.

Milner, Clyde A. II. Carol A. O'Connor, and Martha A. Sandweiss, ed. 1994. *The American West*. New York: Oxford University Press.

Porter, Kenneth Wiggins. 1970. *The Negro on the American Frontier: The American Negro, His History and Literature*. New York: Ayers Company Publishers.

Ward, Geoffrey C. 1996. *The West: An Illustrated History*. Boston: Little, Brown and Company.

Wheeler, Keith and the Editors of Time-Life. 1976. *The Chroniclers: The Old West*. New York: Time Life Books.

Standards

Historical Thinking

The student will

Historical Comprehension

- read historical narratives imaginatively
- evidence historical perspectives
- draw upon visual, literary, and musical sources

Historical Analysis and Interpretation

- identify the author or source of the historical document or narrative
- differentiate between historical facts and historical interpretation

Historical Research Capabilities

- obtain historical data

Content

The student will demonstrate understanding of

How the rise of big business, heavy industry, and mechanized farming transformed the American peoples

- How agriculture, mining, and ranching were transformed

Lesson 8 The Cowboy

- explain the major geographical and technological influences affecting farming, mining, and ranching
- explain the conflicts that arose during the settlement of the "last frontier" among farmers, ranchers, and miners
- evaluate the gender and ethnic diversity of farmers, miners, and ranchers in the West

Resources

For each student

Reconstructing America by Joy Hakim: Chapter 12, "Riding the Trail"

Notebook

Homework Sheet: *Help Wanted: Cowboy*

For each team

A copy of the Team Sheet: Don't Fence Me In **or** Home on the Range

A copy of **one** of the following Team Sheets:

Indian Cowboy

Cowboys Driving Longhorns

Roundup with Chuckwagons

Dan Lohr Ranch

Roundup on the Sherman Ranch

Black Cowboy

Cowgirls

Trail Boss

A copy of **one** of the Team Sheets: *Cowboy Voices*

For the teacher

Chart paper

Markers

Web sites

Freedom: A History of US @ http://www.pbs.org/wnet/historyofus/menu.html

America's West — Development and History @ http://www.americanwest.com/index.htm#post

Famous People in American History @ http://www.studyweb.com/lit/bio/famous.htm

Images of the American West @ http://www.treasurenet.com/images/americanwest.html

People of Color on the Western Frontier @ http://www.coax.net/people/lwf/western.html

Black Cowboys @ http://www.coax.net/people/lwf/bkcowboy.html

The Chisholm Trail, Kansas State Historical Society @ http://www.ukans.edu/heritage/kshs/perspect/chisholm.htm

Events in THE WEST—1860-1870 @ http://www3.pbs.org/weta/thewest/wpages/wpgs200/w21860.htm

Events in THE WEST—1870-1880 @ http://www3.pbs.org/weta/thewest/wpages/wpgs200/w21870.htm

Places in THE WEST — Texas Cattle Trails @ http://www3.pbs.org/weta/thewest/wpages/wpgs300/3cattle.htm

Jesse Chisholm's Grave @ http://www.findagrave.com/pictures/chisholmjesse.html

Jane Canary "Calamity Jane's" Grave @ http://www.findagrave.com/pictures/janecalamity.html

Wild Bill Hickok — Article from WILDWEST @ http://www.thehistorynet.com/WildWest/articles/0896_text.htm

Along the Chisholm Trail @ http://ww.texhoma.net/~glencbr/p40la.html

InterAct — Chuck Wagon Cooking @ http://www.netarrant.net/interact/events/cookbook/cwintro.html

Vocabulary

Words to Remember

*cowboy — person who tended cattle in the West

longhorn — hardy Texas cattle with long horns, descended from cattle brought by the Spaniards

"dogies" — stray or motherless calves

- ***range** — open land for grazing cattle
- ***stampede** — wild, uncontrollable running by a herd of cattle
- **chuck wagon** — wagon that carried food, cooking equipment, and supplies to feed the cowboys on the trail
- **chaps** — leather leggings that protected the cowboy's legs
- **lariat** — rope
- ***ranch** — large farm where cattle are bred and raised
- ***legend** or ***myth** — story from the past that is sometimes regarded as factual but is not proven true

People to Remember

- ***Jesse Chisholm** — Scotch-Cherokee trader who mapped out a straight, level trail with easy river fords between southern Kansas and his trading post; the trail opened as a cattle drive in 1867
- **Elizabeth Johnson** — cowgirl who made a fortune in the cattle business
- **Nat Love** — black cowboy known as "Deadwood Dick"
- **Wild Bill Hickok** — scout, stagecoach driver, and marshal of various western towns who was killed while playing poker
- **Bat Masterson** — frontier marshal
- **Wyatt Earp** — Western lawman known for his part in the gunfight at the OK Corral
- **Calamity Jane (Martha Jane Canary)** — horse-woman and sharpshooter who wore men's clothing and did men's work

Places to Remember

- ***Chisholm Trail** — main cattle drive trail from Texas to Abilene, Kansas
- ***Abilene, Kansas** — cattle town and railway station at the end of the Chisholm Trail
- ***Chicago, Illinois** — center of the western cattle butchering and shipping industry
- **Wichita, Kansas** — cattle town and railway center
- **Dodge City, Kansas** — cattle town and railway center

The Lesson

Focus Activity – 10 minutes

1. Distribute a copy of the Team Sheet: *Home on the Range* to half of the teams and a copy of the Team Sheet: *Don't Fence Me In* to the remainder of the teams.

2. Direct the teams to read the song lyrics and discuss these questions written on chart paper:

   - What do these songs tell us about the life of the Western cowboy?
   - What do these songs tell us about the characteristics of the Western cowboy?
   - What elements of the songs appear to be realistic or factual?
   - What elements of the songs appear to be unrealistic or not factual?

3. Students use **Numbered Heads** to share their generalizations about the life of the cowboy and the American West as depicted in the lyrics of the two songs. **Note to the Teacher**: If available, play recordings of the songs.

Teaching Activity – 25 minutes

Differentiating between fact and myth

1. Introduce Chapter 12, "Riding the Trail" in *Reconstructing America* by asking the students to share what they consider to be the popular view of cowboys, cattle drives, and life in the Old West. (For example, students might mention ways in which movies or television portrays cowboys.)

   Briefly record their responses, without comment, on chart paper under the heading: *Popular Viewpoint of Cowboy Life*.

2. Then ask the students to **Speculate**:

   - What do you think it was *really* like to be a cowboy?
   - What did cowboys *really* do?

Notes

Again record their responses, without comment, on the chart paper under a second heading: *Our Viewpoint of Cowboy Life.*

3. **Reading for a Purpose:** Explain the purpose for reading Chapter 12, "Riding the Trail" in *Reconstructing America*. Students read Chapter 12 in order to answer the following questions and record information from the chapter on a web or other graphic organizer that they design.

   Suppose you wanted to be a Western cowboy or cowgirl in the late 1860s.

   - What skills would you need?
   - What jobs would you do?
   - What conditions would you have to endure?
   - What would your everyday life be like?

   Note to the Teacher: If your students need guidance designing a graphic organizer, draw a web organizer with the four categories (skills, jobs, conditions, everyday life) on the chalkboard.

4. Before the students read the chapter, briefly introduce the Vocabulary *Words, People, and Places to Remember.*

   Circulate and Monitor: Visit each team to help students read the chapter and record information about the life and work of cowboys on their webs.

5. Use **Numbered Heads** for students to share their findings about the work of the cowboy. Summarize that information on the chalkboard web.

   Share additional information about the cowboys' life and work, the cattle drives, and the Chisholm Trail from the Overview with the students. Review the sidebar information in Chapter 12 and discuss the map on page 55 with the students.

6. Direct the students to compare their lists of the *Popular Viewpoint of Cowboy Life* and *Our Viewpoint of Cowboy Life* with the information recorded on their webs from Chapter 12. Encourage the students to explain the popular concepts of the cowboy (theirs and that of others) and how that viewpoint is the same as or different from the reality of cowboy life.

7. Introduce and define the concepts of *legend* and *myth* in history. Use the following questions to guide the discussion:

- How do legends and myths based on historical information develop?

- What legends and myths grew out of the American West and cowboy life?

- Why do myths and legends occur in history?

- Why is it important to distinguish fact from myth in history?

Help the students realize that myths grew up around cowboy life and the West even as the great cattle drives were ending. In part, the cowboys themselves created their own legends as did popular books and magazines and "Wild West" shows. These legends and myths expanded as movies, novels, tall tales, and other forms of popular entertainment further romanticized the cowboy as a symbol of American individualism.

Student Team Learning Activity – 25 minutes

Distinguishing fact from myth

1. Distribute the eight photographs, one to each team. Ask each team to create a list of details about cowboy life from analyzing its photograph. Team members take turns recording that information.

   Circulate and Monitor: Visit each team as the students examine their photographs and record information. If necessary, guide the students in completing the task.

2. Use **Numbered Heads** for each team to display its photograph and briefly share its findings with the class. After each presentation, help the students determine if the primary source photograph supports or contradicts the mythic view of cowboys.

3. Distribute copies of one of the three Team Sheets: *Cowboy Voices* to each team. After the team members read their particular first person account, the students briefly share their accounts and note the similarities of three cowboy experiences with stampedes on cattle drives. Ask the students to **Speculate**:

   - What would it be like to be a cowboy during a stampede?

Reflection and Review Activity – 5 minutes

1. Students scan Chapters 13 through 18 in *Reconstructing America*. Teams **Think-Team-Share**:
   - As you continue to study the West, what other myths do you think will emerge?
   - In what ways do the myths and legends of the cowboy and the West continue today?
2. Use **Numbered Heads** for the teams to share their responses.

   Note to the Teacher: An additional resource for this lesson is the video series *Freedom: A History of US,* Episode Eight—Part One, Meanwhile, Out West, Kunhardt Productions and Thirteen/WNET for PBS. Also explore the accompanying PBS Website: Freedom: A History of US @ http://www.pbs.org/wnet/historyofus/menu.html, especially the section for teachers.

Homework

Create a "Help Wanted" ad for a cowboy that includes a description of the job and the skills needed to fill it.

Library/Media Resources

Fiction
Riders of the Purple Sage by Zane Gray, Dover

The Zebra Riding Cowboy: A Folk Song from the Old West by Angela Shelf Medearis, Owlet

Roughing It by Mark Twain, Signet Books, Signet

Nonfiction
The Cowboys by William H. Forbis and the Editors of Time-Life Books of the Old West

Cowboys of the Wild West by Russell Freedman, Clarion Books

Wild Bill Hickok by Carl R. Green, Enslow Publishers, Inc.

Cowboys by Elaine Landau, Franklin Watts

Cobblestone Magazine

Cowboys

CD Rom

The Story of America 1: The Western Movement, National Geographic Society

Video

Freedom: A History of US, Episode Eight—Part One, Kunhardt Productions and Thirteen/WNET for PBS

The West by Ken Burns, PBS (Video Series, Book, and Music CD)

Heritage of the Black West, National Geographic Society

The West That Was, National Geographic Society

Connections

Music — Students sing or listen to the songs of the cowboys. Students determine which are traditional work songs.

Library — Students research the western cattle industry, its trails, and the rough-and-tumble cattle barons.

Geography/Art — Students research, draw, and illustrate a map of the most famous cattle trails.

Math — Students locate and interpret statistics and trends in the cattle industry from the 1860s through the 1890s.

Language Arts/Library — Students research western writers and poets such as Zane Gray and Bret Harte and read one of their works. Students explain how these writers portrayed the cowboy and western frontier life and determine if the authors perpetuated the legends and myths of the Old West.

Language Arts/Library — Students read books of cowboy humor such as *The Humor of the American Cowboy* by Stan Huig, University of Nebraska Press.

Language Arts/Library — Students read an example of Mark Twain's literature about the West, such as *Roughing It* and "The Celebrated Frog of Calaveras County."

Art/Library — Students examine the works of Frederick Remington, who is best known for his paintings of the West.

Lesson 9
The Railroads
Chapters 13 and 14

Theme

By connecting the east with the west, the transcontinental railroad brought about the settlement and ultimate taming of the American West.

Overview

To most Americans in the late 1850s, the idea of a railroad across the American continent seemed as remote as traveling to the moon. In the first place, many doubted whether railroad technology could overcome the sheer physical challenge posed by the Western landscape. In addition to the mind-numbing distance across that wilderness were the blistering desolate deserts, the towering snow-topped mountain ranges, and the steep canyons with their rushing rivers. And because problems with Native Americans remained unresolved, trains crossing sacred lands and hunting grounds would surely cause violent reactions.

In the East, railroads primarily connected large cities, transporting passengers and freight at many points along the route. However, the West contained thousands of miles of sparsely populated wilderness. What the skeptics overlooked—but the visionaries and entrepreneurs did not—was that with federal loans and land grants the impossible could be accomplished. Then the settlement and taming of the American West would surely follow.

In the spring of 1864, two railway building tycoons, Collis P. Huntington (of the Central Pacific Railroad bound east from Sacramento) and Thomas C. Durant (of the Union Pacific heading westward from Omaha) went to Washington to influence political friends to pass legislation to build the railroad. Engineers Theodore Judah and Grenville Dodge had already surveyed and mapped the route of a transcontinental line across two thousand miles of wilderness. Congress itself had chartered the road in the Railroad Act of 1862, which offered free land and government loans once construction began. Nevertheless, the railway planners needed up-front money to start the actual task. Although the two companies were empowered to raise money through stock options, few investors during the turbulent Civil War years wanted to risk their money on such a wild scheme. Besides, over a hundred million dollars was needed to build the line—more money than had ever been spent before on any single enterprise. And both railroad companies were broke.

By buying the needed votes, Huntington and Durant assured that a new Pacific Railroad Act of 1864 sailed through Congress. The act granted twenty square miles of land for every mile of track laid (eventually totaling twenty-one million acres), and released two-thirds of the federal building loans (as much as $48,000 per track mile) as soon as each twenty miles of roadbed had been prepared. It seemed of little consequence that in the process, these daring and triumphant entrepreneurs bent laws, broke rivals, bribed government officials, trampled ordinary ethics, and amassed their own personal empires and fortunes. Although greedy and unscrupulous, such men turned the dream of connecting the east and west into a reality. Most Americans gave the railroad barons begrudging respect: one newsman described Huntington as "ruthless as a crocodile" and meant it as a sincere compliment.

With government funds and land grants secure, Durant organized the Credit Mobilier (the French word for movable loan), a corporation set up by the directors of the Union Pacific to perform the physical task of building the railroad. By giving its own company a contract to grade roadbed, dig tunnels, and lay track, the directors of the Union Pacific would, in effect, be doing business with themselves. Soon the Union Pacific paid grossly inflated construction bills, and an inner ring of stockholders and Union Pacific officials were pocketed the difference between the actual and stated costs. A similar construction company (the Contract & Finance Company) was created to milk the Central Pacific.

The bubble of embezzlement and fraud finally burst in the summer of 1872. The scandal spilled into the courts, and the ensuing publicity forced Congress to investigate the Credit Mobilier and its shady dealings. The scandal implicated numerous congressmen as well as Vice President Schuyler Colfax, and it tarnished President Grant. Although public wrath was aroused against corrupt railroad and government officials, shameless profiteering, shoddy ethics, and unscrupulous behavior, almost everyone in both the Union Pacific and the Central Pacific safely escaped: no crime was proven and no indictments brought.

In spite of the fact that the financing of the transcontinental railroad is a study in greed, graft, and unethical government practices, the actual building of the railroad is a tribute to the heart, soul, and tenacity of the American laborer. Its construction was a task of monumental proportions—a dangerous, sweaty, backbreaking, brawling business. And it was accomplished by the most cosmopolitan work crew in American history—Civil War veterans, freed slaves, Irish, German, and Chinese immigrants, Mormons, and Native Americans. The work crews laid two to five miles of track a day. They filled in sheer ravines, ran spidery trestles across rivers and valleys, and hand dug their way through mountains. And they did most of it with their own muscle power.

Flatcars, traveling on tracks just laid, carried the rails to within half a mile of the railhead. There rails were loaded onto carts. An eyewitness described the procedure:

> *A light car, drawn by a single horse, gallops up to the front with its load of rails. Two men seize the end of the rail and start forward, the rest of the gang taking hold by twos until it is clear of the car. They come forward at a run. At the word of command, the rail is dropped in its place, right side up. Less than thirty seconds to a rail for each gang, and so four rails go down to the minute.*

In this way, tens of thousands of dogged workers completed the most ambitious enterprise of the nineteenth century. By laying track across the entire continent, railroad tycoons and laborers created a new social order and turned the western wilderness into a home for any farmer, doctor, lawyer, tradesman, schoolmarm, bank clerk, or seamstress who could scrape up the price of a ticket.

References

"The American West: Railroads." *HarpWeek*. http://thewest.harpweek.com/. Access date October 1998.

Bain, David Haward. 1999, *Empire Express: Building the First Transcontinental Railroad*. New York: Penguin Books.

Brash, Sarah. ed. 1996. *Settling the West: The American Story.* Alexandria, Virginia: Time-Life Books.

Brown, Dee. 1994. *The American West.* New York: Simon & Schuster.

Combs, Barry B. 1969. *Westward to Promontory: Building the Union Pacific Across the Plains and Mountains.* Palo Alto, California: American West Publishing.

Galloway, John Debo. 1983. *The First Transcontinental Railroad: Central Pacific, Union Pacific.* Westport, Connecticut: Greenwood Press.

Horn, Huston and the Editors of Time-Life. 1974. *The Pioneers: The Old West.* New York: Time Life Books.

Huntington, Collis P. "Race to the Last Spike." Colbert, David. ed. 1998. *Eyewitness to the American West.* New York: Penguin Books.

Jensen, Oliver. 1975. *The American Heritage History of Railroads in America.* New York: Bonanza Books.

Lamar, Howard R. 1998. *The New Encyclopedia of the American West.* New York: Harper Collins.

Milner, Clyde A., II., Carol A. O'Connor, and Martha A. Sandweiss. eds. 1994. *The American West.* New York: Oxford University Press.

Wheeler, Keith and the Editors of Time-Life. 1773. *The Railroaders: The Old West.* New York: Time Life Books.

Wheeler, Keith and the Editors of Time-Life. 1976. *The Chroniclers: The Old West.* New York: Time Life Books.

Ward, Geoffrey C. 1996. *The West: An Illustrated History.* Boston: Little, Brown and Company.

Standards

Historical Thinking

The student will

Historical Comprehension

- read historical narratives imaginatively
- evidence historical perspectives
- draw upon data in historical maps
- draw upon visual, literary, and musical sources

Historical Analysis and Interpretation

- consider multiple perspectives
- analyze cause and effect relationships and multiple causation, including the importance of the individual, the influence of ideas, and the role of chance

Historical Research Capabilities

- obtain historical data

Analysis and Decision-Making

- identify issues and problems in the past

Content

The student will demonstrate understanding of

The building of the transcontinental railroad

- The impact of the transcontinental railroad on settlement of the West, the physical environment, the Native Americans, and the nation.
- The role of big business and the railroad workers in the construction of the transcontinental railroad.
- A railway journey west
  - identify information about the transcontinental railroads, the early journeys west, and the impact of the railroad

Resources

For each student

Reconstructing America by Joy Hakim: Chapter 13, "Rails Across the Country" and Chapter 14, "Taking the Train"

Notebook

Lesson 9 The Railroads

Crayons or markers

Optional web or other graphic organizer

For the teacher

Transparencies:
- *The Old Way Across the Plains*
- *Reporting the News*
- *Train on Trestle*

Headlines written on chart paper

Markers

For the classroom

Overhead projector

Web sites

America's West – Development and History @ http://www.americanwest.com/index.htm#post

Railroad Museum Transcontinental Railroad @ http://www.csrmf.org/transbuild.html

Transcontinental Railroad @ http://www.sfmuseum.org/hist1/rail.html

HarpWeek @ http://thewest.harpweek.com/

Freedom: A History of US @ http://www.pbs.org/wnet/historyofus/menu.html

Vocabulary

Words to Remember

*transcontinental — across a continent

*tycoon — businessman of great wealth and power

*Pacific Railroad Act of 1864 — provided land grants and money to build the transcontinental railway

visionary — someone with insight and imagination

Central Pacific — railroad company that laid track from the west to Promontory Point, Utah

Union Pacific — railroad company that laid track from the east to Promontory Point, Utah

*subsidy — grant of money or land

ties — logs upon which iron rails were laid to construct railroad track

King Midas — mythical king who turned items to gold simply by touching them

emigrant cars — train coaches that were inexpensive to ride

Pullman cars — train coaches that were expensive to ride

Golden Spike — last spike driven to celebrate the completion of the transcontinental railroad

People to Remember

*Leland Stanford — railway builder and tycoon who used unethical business practices to become wealthy

*Thomas Durant — railway owner of the Central Pacific who used unethical business practices

*George Pullman — entrepreneur who built comfortable train coaches for passengers and tried to set up a model company for his workers

Places to Remember

*Promontory Point, Utah — point at which the Union Pacific and the Central Pacific railroads met to create the first transcontinental railway

The Lesson

Focus Activity – 5 minutes

1. Show the Transparency: *The Old Way Across the Plains*.
2. Ask the students to **Think-Team-Share**:
   - After the Civil War, what new way do you think replaced this old way across the plains?

Teaching Activity – 20 minutes

1. Introduce Chapter 13, "Rails Across the Country" in *Reconstructing America* by asking the students to **Predict**:
   - What changes occurred in the West as a result of railroads? (more settlers moved west, it was easier and faster for Easterners to visit the West, changed the environment including the wild animal population, angered the Native Americans, etc.)

2. **Reading for a Purpose:** Explain the purpose for reading Chapter 13, "Rails Across the Country."

   The joining of the two railroads at Promontory, Utah was a great event. Newspaper reporters and telegraph operations spread the news to the folks back east. Working with your teammates, discover the stories behind the following newspaper headlines by reading Chapter 13.

   Display the chart with the following headlines:

A Miss and a Hit
Two Pacifics Meet
East Races West
Go Over or Go Under
A Dollar a Day
Tycoon or Crook?
Indians See Red
A Ten-Day Trip

Notes

Lesson 9　The Railroads

2. Use the Transparency: *Reporting the News* to briefly review the "who, what, where, when, why, and how" format. Team members use this format to record facts for each of the headlines. Teams should assign specific headlines to their members.

3. Briefly introduce the Vocabulary *Words, People, and Places to Remember*.

4. **Circulate and Monitor:** Visit each team while the students read the chapter. Help them locate information and record "who, what, where, when, why, and how" on their graphic organizers.

5. Teams use **Numbered Heads** to share the story behind each headline. As time permits, share additional information about the early railroads, their construction, and their impact on the West with the students using information in the Overview.

6. **Reading for a Purpose:** Read the poem on page 63 of *Reconstructing America* to the students. Help them understand the event depicted in the first stanza, the message of the eastern engine in the second stanza, and the message of the western engine in the third stanza.

Student Team Learning Activity – 25 minutes

Describing a train ride through the Old West

1. Explain the Student Team Learning Activity.

   Reading for a Purpose: Read Chapter 14, "Taking the Train" to the class, while the students visualize the early trains and the journey west. Students imagine they are taking the train out west and sending a postcard to their folks or friends back home. They must listen carefully and take notes in order to draw a postcard picture and write a message accurately describing the trip.

2. As you read the chapter to the students, pause periodically to emphasize information, ask questions, and guide students in recording details. (For example, page 65 of *Reconstructing America* gives information about the emigrant cars and page 66 relates information about the Pullman cars. The student's description of the trip greatly depends upon the car in which he or she is traveling.)

Encourage the students to examine the sidebar photographs and illustrations as you read.

3. **Circulate and Monitor:** Visit each team as students collect information from Chapters 13 and 14 to incorporate in their postcard pictures and messages. Check that students have sufficient details to create accurate postcards and messages.

4. Students begin designing their postcards and composing their messages. **Note to the Teacher:** Students work on this assignment until ten minutes before the end of the class and then finish it for homework.

Reflection and Review Activity – 10 minutes

1. Briefly review the following questions with the students.
   - What expenses and problems did the railroad companies face in building railroads?
   - What benefits could a railroad company expect to receive in exchange for building a railroad?
   - What benefits did the public and the nation receive from the construction of railroads?
   - What were some of the environmental consequences of constructing railroads?
   - What might have happened in the West if the railroad had not been built?

2. Show the Transparency: *Train on Trestle*. Ask the students:
   - What does this photograph reveal about the engineering skill necessary to build railroads across the continent?

Note to the Teacher: An additional resource for this lesson is the video series *Freedom: A History of US,* Episode Eight—Part One, Meanwhile, Out West, Kunhardt Productions and Thirteen/WNET for PBS. Also explore the accompanying PBS Website: Freedom: A History of US @ http://www.pbs.org/wnet/historyofus/menu.html, especially the section for teachers.

Homework

Complete your postcard and message home about your train trip through the wild West.

Library/Media Resources

Fiction

Death of the Iron Horse by Paul Goble, Aladdin Library

Nonfiction

The Railroaders by Keith Wheeler, Time-Life Books

Transcontinental Railroad by Jean Blashfield, Compass Point Books

The Transcontinental Railroad: America at Its Best? by Robert Young, Dillon Press

Songs of the Wild West by Dan Fox, Simon & Schuster

Trail of the Wild West by Paul Robert Walker, National Geographic Society

Full Steam Ahead: The Race to Build a Transcontinental Railroad by Rhoda Blumberg, National Geographic

Nothing Like It in the World: The Men Who Built the Transcontinental Railroad 1863-1969 by Stephen E. Ambrose, Simon & Schuster

Cobblestone Magazine

The Transcontinental Railroad

CD Rom

The Story of America 1: The Western Movement, National Geographic Society

Video

The West, video series, book, and music CD by Ken Burns

Heritage of the Black West, National Geographic Society

The West That Was, National Geographic Society

Freedom: A History of US, Episode Eight—Part One, Kunhardt Productions and Thirteen/WNET for PBS

Connections

Geography/Library — Students research the topography and physical geography of the region over which the transcontinental railroad was built.

Music — Students sing or listen to the songs of the railroad labor crews. How did the rhythms of the songs help the men work as a team?

Library — Students research the ethnic groups that built the transcontinental railroad. In particular, students research the story of the Chinese immigrant workers.

Geography/Art — Students research, draw, and illustrate a map of the transcontinental railroad.

Math — Students create or solve math problems about the transcontinental railroad such as measurement and distance, task-time for laying rails, and cost analysis.

Language Arts/Library — Students research the tall tales and stories of the railroaders, such as "John Henry." How do these perpetuate the legends and myths of the Old West?

Science/Library — Students study the role of technology in supporting the settlement of the West. For example, students consider the ways in which the railroad made one-crop agriculture possible, the use of refrigerator cars to send meat east, the impact of the railroad on western ecology, and the adverse effect of the railroad on the western ecosystem.

Science/Library — Students research the inventions and engineering advancements that made the building of the transcontinental railway possible.

Lesson 10
The Homesteaders
Chapters 15 and 16

Theme

With the advent of the transcontinental railroad, the Homestead Act, and a handful of inventions, settlers populated the Great Plains, and within a generation, the self-sufficient "sodbuster" became the industrialized farmer of the nation's bread-basket.

Overview

For decades, pioneers and settlers had crossed the vast, desolate grasslands of the Great Plains. But few of them thought of settling in that treeless ocean of grass with its matted sod and brutal climate: temperatures rose to over a hundred degrees in summer and burned crops to a crisp, then plunged to forty degrees below zero in winter, bringing sudden horrendous snowstorms that caused men to lose their way and freeze to death between barn and house. With so little rainfall and so much barren landscape, early travelers called it the "Great American Desert" and hurried on to the fertile valleys of the far West. But after the Civil War, tens of thousands of pioneers swarmed onto this inhospitable great prairie—and stayed. In two decades, they brought more new land under cultivation in the United States than in the previous two and a half centuries. These hardy pioneers not only survived; they converted the bleak prairie expanse into some of the most productive farmland in the world.

Many factors combined to spur that conquest. Foremost were the growing shortages of arable lands in the Old South and the overcrowded cities in the Northeast. The prairie settlers came with a hunger for land, an urge to escape poverty or persecution, a thirst for adventure, or simply a desire for a fresh start in life. Civil War veterans and freed slaves alike looked to the West for a new beginning, a freedom and equality not possible back home, and an opportunity to own their own land. Likewise, for wave after wave of European immigrants, the plains offered the chance to rise from peasant to proprietor. Millions of pamphlets and posters, printed in a variety of languages, drew overwhelming numbers of Swedes, Dutch, Norwegians, Danes, Germans, English, and Welsh with promises of "Land for the Landless! Homes for the Homeless!"

With the completion of the transcontinental railway and its subsequent trunk lines, most prairie settlers, whether European immigrants or American born, could travel to their destinations with relative comfort. Getting there was considerably easier—and less costly—than in the days of the Conestoga wagons. Furthermore, the newly built railroads, eager for business, wooed settlers with promotional campaigns and sold affordable farmland for $2.50 an acre from their enormous land grant subsidies. In a like manner, the federal government encouraged settlers with the Homestead Act of 1862. Under its terms, a person could stake a claim to a piece of unoccupied public land by living on it and cultivating it for five years—after which he or she could file for ownership. Among the homesteading men and families, thousands of single women (many alone or widowed after the Civil War) carved out new lives and embraced a more liberated lifestyle than was then usual for women.

But the railroads, land grants, and mass immigration could not have populated the plains without the advent of a number of inventions that moved the Industrial Revolution from urban to rural settings. The prairie settler had to surmount formidable obstacles. The first was a dependable water supply in a land that was often bone-dry even with torrential spring downpours. Windmills—harnessing the grasslands' most reliable and handiest energy source—pumped hand-dug wells, many over 280 feet deep. Perfected by David Halladay in 1854, the prairie windmill pivoted to face the wind and adjusted to withstand high wind pressure. During a normal prairie day, the mill could lift hundreds of gallons from the deep wells to water livestock and irrigate fields. Its stilt-legged tower, stark against the wide sky, became the lofty symbol of a homesteader's victory over the trials of prairie living.

The modification of the plow claimed a like victory over the sod. The buffalo grass of the prairies sprouted from densely tangled roots that filled the top three inches of soil and made plowing with the conventional cast-iron plow impossible. With the advent of the steel plow, invented by John Deere, the prairie farmers could at last "bust the sod" and turn the prairie soil efficiently. This advance in metallurgy was then applied to making a special plow that could cut sod for building purposes, thus providing the universal building material for prairie homes, schools, and other structures in a landscape without timber, rocks, or clay. A well-constructed "soddie" was a great improvement over the underground dugout—drier, sturdier, generally more comfortable, and not likely to collapse during a rainy spell. It offered so many advantages that settlers continued to build sod houses long after imported lumber became readily available for conventional frame buildings.

Now that the plow had broken the plains, the farmers needed a fast harvesting method to cut grain before it spoiled. The answer appeared when a hard-working, serious Scotch-Irishman from Virginia, Cyrus McCormick, invented a reaping machine that symbolized the mechanical revolution in agriculture. Coming at a time when the rich prairie wheat lands necessitated a practical way to harvest huge crops, the mechanical reaper provided a substitute for hand labor and an efficient way to cut grain on the flat, stoneless prairie. Pulled by as many as thirty-two horses or mules, the reaper heralded the beginning of farming as both scientific enterprise and big business. By the 1870s, mobile steam engines, with an auxiliary wagon to carry the water supply, replaced the horses and powered improved threshers.

For decades the homesteaders—and the western ranchers—sought a way to fence in their crops and stock. The prairie lacked rocks and wood for traditional farm fences. Plain wire fences were ineffective, and thorn hedges required years to grow. In 1874 a canny Illinois farmer, Joseph Glidden, combined the concepts of smooth wire and prickly hedges and devised the first practical barbed wire. He concocted a barbing machine from an old-fashioned coffee mill with its casing cut away and its grinder altered to cut and coil small lengths of wire. The barbs were strung by hand between lengths of twisted wire. Within a decade, 120 million pounds of barbed wire were sold each year, changing the open range of the cowboy to enclosed pasture and farmland.

But even with these new inventions, homesteaders struggled to survive on the prairie. To many it was a dismal existence. Distances were great and neighbors nonexistent. The flat, seemingly endless prairie stretched as far as the eye could see, with no trees, human inhabitants, or geographic ripple to break the monotony. The wind blew constantly with a low ceaseless moan that literally drove some homesteaders mad. Natural disasters—drought, hailstorms, prairie fires, plagues of locusts and grasshoppers, and sudden winter blizzards with arctic temperatures—were unpredictable but common occurrences that could leave homesteaders destitute in minutes.

Ordinary sicknesses and accidents took a high toll in areas where the nearest doctor lived a day's ride away in good weather. In addition to back-breaking farm labor, the everyday chores of housekeeping—meal preparation using cow chips for fuel, keeping a sodhouse "clean", and washday blues—dismayed and disillusioned many wives and mothers. Furthermore, the threat of Indians—often more imagined than real, although not entirely groundless—terrified the sodbusters. Even though most Indians had been resettled to reservations and what few encounters that occurred were amicable, some tribes, beginning to feel the shock of injustice and betrayal, settled their many grievances with violence against the homesteaders.

But before long even the occasional Indian threat subsided, and masses of homesteaders moved onto the plains. By the 1870s, windmills sprouted across the grasslands and irrigation ditches crisscrossed the arid plains, watering a new kind of wheat. Introduced from Russia by Mennonite immigrants, this wheat proved hardy enough to withstand severe extremes of climate and gradually replaced the prairie grass. Giant new machines—plows and reapers and combines pulled by lumbering steam tractors—allowed a sodbuster to cultivate in one afternoon the same acreage that would have taken weeks to work by hand. With their land embraced by barbed-wire fences, the prairie settlers were there to stay, and they held as stubbornly as the matted sod beneath their feet.

References

Brash, Sarah. ed. 1996. *Settling the West: The American Story*. Alexandria, Virginia: Time-Life Books.

Brown, Dee. 1994. *The American West*. New York: Simon & Schuster.

Dick, Everett. 1993 (1948 Reprint). *The Dixie Frontier: A Social History*. Norman, Oklahoma: University of Oklahoma Press.

Dick, Everett. 1954. *The Sod-House Frontier 1854-1890*. Lincoln, Nebraska: Johnsen Publishing.

"Glidden's Patent Application for Barbed Wire." U.S. National Archives and Record Administration. http://www.archives.gov/digital_classroom/lessons/barbed_wire_patent/barbed_wire_patent.html. Access date June 1999.

"The Homestead Act of 1862." U.S. National Archives and Record Administration. http://www.archives.gov/digital_classroom/lessons/homestead_act_1862/homestead_act.html. Access date December 2003.

Horn, Huston and the Editors of Time-Life. 1974. *The Pioneers: The Old West*. New York: Time Life Books.

Lamar, Howard R. 1998. *The New Encyclopedia of the American West*. New York: Harper Collins.

Milner, Clyde A., II, Carol A. O'Connor, and Martha A. Sandweiss. eds. 1994. *The American West*. New York: Oxford University Press.

Schlissel, Lillian. 1992. *Woman's Diaries of the Westward Journey*. New York: Schocken Books.

Sutherland, Daniel E. 1989. *The Expansion of Everyday Life 1860-1876*. New York: Harper & Row.

Trails West. 1979. Special Publications Division. Washington, D.C.: National Geographic Society.

Ward, Geoffrey C. 1996. *The West: An Illustrated History*. Boston: Little, Brown and Company.

Wheeler, Keith and the Editors of Time-Life. 1976. *The Chroniclers: The Old West*. New York: Time Life Books.

Standards

Historical Thinking

The student will

Historical Comprehension

- read historical narratives imaginatively
- evidence historical perspectives
- draw upon data in historical maps
- draw upon visual, literary, and musical sources

Historical Analysis and Interpretation

- consider multiple perspectives
- analyze cause and effect relationships and multiple causation, including the importance of the individual, the influence of ideas, and the role of chance

Historical Research Capabilities

- obtain historical data

Analysis and Decision-Making

- identify issues and problems in the past

Content

The student will demonstrate understanding of

How the rise of big business, heavy industry, and mechanized farming transformed the American peoples

- How agriculture, mining, and ranching were transformed
  - explain the major geographical and technological influences affecting farming, mining, and ranching
  - explain the conflicts that arose during the settlement of the "last frontier" among farmers, ranchers, and miners
  - explain how commercial farming differed in the Northeast, South, Great Plains, and West in terms of crop production, farm labor, financing, and transportation
  - evaluate the gender and ethnic diversity of farmers, miners, and ranchers in the West
  - explain the significance of farm organizations

Resources

For each student

Reconstructing America by Joy Hakim: Chapter 15, "Fencing the Homestead" and Chapter 16, "Reaping a Harvest"

Student Sheet: *Innovations that Changed Farming*

Notebook

For each team

Document Packet: Homesteading on the Plains

For the teacher

Excerpt: *Sod House Frontier*

Web sites

HarpWeek @ http://thewest.harpweek.com/

Freedom: A History of US @ http://www.pbs.org/wnet/historyofus/menu.html

America's West – Development and History @ http://www.americanwest.com/index.htm#post

Famous People in American History @ http://www.studyweb.com/lit/bio/famous.htm

Images of the American West @ http://www.treasurenet.com/images/americanwest.html

Lesson 10 The Homesteaders

People of Color on the Western Frontier @ http://www.coax.net/people/lwf/western.html

Events in THE WEST—1860-1870 @ http://www3.pbs.org/weta/thewest/wpages/wpgs200/w21860.htm

Events in THE WEST—1870-1880 @ http://www3.pbs.org/weta/thewest/wpages/wpgs200/w21870.htm

Western Migration and Homesteading @ http://lcweb.loc.gov/exhibits/african/afam009.html

Vocabulary

Words to Remember

***Great Plains** — flat grassland stretching from Texas to Canada and from Kansas to the Rocky Mountains

***prairie** — flat, treeless grasslands

***Homestead Act of 1862** — act that provided for settlement; ownership required settlers to live on land and cultivate it for five years

"Great American Desert" — scornful term for the Great Plains based on its appearance as a dry, flat wasteland

***McCormick Reaper** — horse-drawn machine, invented by Cyrus McCormick, that cut and harvested grain and revolutionized farming in the Great Plains

***barbed wire** — twisted wire with small sharp spikes that allowed farmers in the midwest to fence their lands

Grange — social and political organization for farmers that is similar to a workers' union

Morrill Act — provided states with large land grants to establish agricultural colleges

Hatch Act — established agricultural experiment stations

***sod** — turf or grass with attached soil

***homesteader** — person who occupied and cultivated public land

self-sufficient — able to provide for oneself

industry — manufacturing that uses machines

***Industrial Revolution** — rapid, major change in producing goods brought about by power-driven machinery

People to Remember

***Cyrus Hall McCormick** — invented a mechanical reaper that harvested grain and modernized farming

***John Deere** — invented a steel plow that could "bust the sod" of the prairie

***Booker T. Washington** — developed and headed Tuskegee Institute; great orator

***Joseph Glidden** — invented barbed wire

The Lesson

Focus Activity – 10 minutes

1. Read the excerpt from *The Sod-House Frontier* to the students. Then read "Plains Writing" on page 73 of *Reconstructing America*.

2. Ask the students to **Think-Team-Share**:

   - How do the two descriptions of life on the Great Plains differ?

   - What factors do you think influenced the different points of view?

   - Which description do you think is a more true or accurate one of life on the prairie? Why?

   - How might each description simply reflect a different viewpoint?

3. During the discussion of the readings, help the students understand that the two accounts represent different views of the prairie at different times in its history, and that great changes occurred in prairie life during that time.

   The Sod-House Frontier excerpt describes the back-breaking, bone-weary work of the earlier homesteaders and their isolation from others by miles of desolate flatland.

   The Willa Cather description reflects life in the early 1900s. By then many of the obstacles to and deprivations of prairie life had been surmounted by the invention of mechanized and steam-powered farm machinery, more modern methods of communication and transportation, and the growth of cities and small towns.

Teaching Activity – 25 minutes

1. Introduce homesteading in the Plains States after the Civil War. Use the map on page 75 of *Reconstructing America* to identify the area of the Great Plains.

   Using the photographs and sidebar information in Chapters 15 and 16, the students preview the life and

Notes

hardships of the early homesteaders and describe the landscape of the prairie. Share additional information from the Overview about those topics with the students.

2. Explain that within a generation, prairie life changed dramatically and that a number of things contributed to that change. Remind the students of the two prairie descriptions that you read earlier.

3. Distribute and explain Student Sheet: *Innovations that Changed Farming*. Briefly introduce the Vocabulary *Words and People to Remember*.

4. **Reading for a Purpose:** Students **Partner Read** Chapters 15 and 16 in *Reconstructing America*. Working with their partners, the students

   - Identify and list the problems of the first prairie homesteaders.

   - Identify how the eight innovations changed farming the plains.

   Team members may assist each other to locate and discuss the information.

5. **Circulate and Monitor:** Visit each team while the students read the chapters, discuss the information, and record it on their Student Sheets. In particular, help students locate pertinent information and record it accurately. Check that all students are reading and completing their own Student Sheets.

6. Use **Numbered Heads** for teams to share the information on their Student Sheets and check for accuracy. Correct any misinformation and share additional information about each of the items and their impact on prairie farming with the students by using information in the Overview.

   Be sure students understand how agriculture changed and what brought about those changes.

Student Team Learning Activity – 25 minutes

Writing captions for photographs

1. Distribute a Document Packet: *Homesteading on the Plains* to each team and explain the Student Team Learning Activity.

2. Teams examine and discuss the photographs to determine what each of the pictures tells about the life of the prairie homesteader. Then teams compose captions for the photographs.

   Circulate and Monitor: Visit each team as students analyze and discuss the photographs and compose the captions. Check that the captions are accurate and that all students are equally involved in the activity. Students should take turns recording their team's captions.

3. Display the photographs, perhaps by attaching a copy of each to the chalkboard. Cluster all the teams' captions around each of the photographs. If time permits, teams can read a few of the captions to the class. Allow an opportunity for students to view the photographs and read the captions.

Reflection and Review Activity – 10 minutes

1. Refer students to the eight innovations that transformed farming and life on the Great Plains. For as many of the innovations as time permits, team members use **Think-Team-Share** to ponder

   - What if _____ had not been invented or happened? How do you think prairie life or farming would have been affected?

2. Use **Numbered Heads** for the teams to share their insights.

   Note to the Teacher: An additional resource for this lesson is the video series *Freedom: A History of US,* Episode Eight—Part One, Meanwhile, Out West, Kunhardt Productions and Thirteen/WNET for PBS. Also explore the accompanying PBS Website: Freedom: A History of US @ http://www.pbs.org/wnet/historyofus/menu.html, especially the section for teachers.

Homework

Design an advertisement that encourages homesteading on the Great Plains. Include information about the land and the benefits of owning a farm as well as the requirements for land ownership.

Library/Media Resources

Fiction

Cassie's Journey: Going West in the 1860s by Brett Harvey, Holiday House

Dakota Dugout by Ann Turner, Aladdin Library

Prairie Songs by Pam Conrad, Harper Trophy

Grasshopper Summer by Ann Turner, Aladdin Library

Steal Away by Jennifer Armstrong, Scholastic

Trouble River by Betsy Byers, Puffin

My Prairie Christmas by Brett Harvey, Holiday House

Little House on the Prairie by Laura Ingalls Wilder, Harper Trophy

Little Town on the Prairie by Laura Ingalls Wilder, Harper Trophy

The Long Winter by Laura Ingalls Wilder, Harper Trophy

Nonfiction

Letters of a Woman Homesteader by Elinore Pruitt Stewart, University of Nebraska Press

Songs of the Wild West by Dan Fox, Simon & Schuster

The Pioneers by Huston Horn, Time-Life Books

Prairie Visions: The Life and Times of Solomon Butcher by Pam Conrad, Harper Trophy

The Sod-House Frontier by Everett Dick, Johnsen Publishing

Cobblestone Magazine

Laura Ingalls Wilder

Wheat

Willa Cather

CD Rom

The Oregon Trail I and II, MECC

The Story of America 1: The Western Movement, National Geographic Society

Video

The West, Video series, book, and music CD by Ken Burns

Heritage of the Black West, National Geographic Society

The West That Was, National Geographic Society

Freedom: A History of US, Episode Eight—Part One, Kunhardt Productions and Thirteen/WNET for PBS

Connections

Language Arts/Library — Students read *Caddie Woodlawn* by Carol Ryrie Brink. Partner Discussion Guide is available from Talent Development Middle Schools, Johns Hopkins University.

Writing/Library — Students research and write a short biography of an author—such as Laura Ingalls Wilder or Willa Cather—who described life on the Great Plains in the late 1800s.

Geography — Students locate and label the states of the Great Plains on a United States map.

Geography — Students draw and label a products map for the Great Plains.

Research/Library — Students research the different ethnic groups that settled on the Great Plains. How do place names, local history, customs, and culture in these areas reflect that ethnic heritage?

Science — Students contrast the agricultural revolution of the late 1800s (machinery, crop selection, new uses for crops), the post Second World War agricultural revolution (mechanization, fertilizers, pesticides), and today's agricultural revolution using biotechnology.

Technology/Library — Students use the internet to investigate topics of interest about homesteading or pioneer life on the Great Plains. For example, students can explore the Library of Congress site about western migration and homesteading of African Americans (http://lcweb.loc.gov/exhibits/african/afam009.htlm) or the National Archives site about Glidden's patent for barbed wire (http://www.nara.gov/education/teaching/glidden/wire.html)

Music — Students listen to "The Plow that Broke the Plains" by Aaron Copeland.

Language Arts/Library — Students read works by Willa Cather and *Prairie Boy* by Carl Sandburg.

Art/Library — Students view works of artists such as Frederick Remington, Winslow Homer, and Thomas Moran, who captured the spirit and landscape of the West and the late 1800s.

The Sod-House Frontier

These solitary women, longing to catch a glimpse of one of their own sex, swept their eyes over the boundless prairie and thought of the old home in the East. They stared and stared across space with nothing to halt their gaze over the monotonous expanse. Sometimes the burning prairie got to staring back and they lost their courage. They saw their complexions fade as the skin became dry and leathery in the continual wind. Their hair grew lifeless and dry, their shoulders early bent, and they became stooped as they tramped round and round the hot cook-stove preparing the three regular though skimpy meals each day. There was little incentive to primp and care for one's person. Few bothered much about brushes and combs. Hollow-eyed, tired, and discouraged in the face of summer heat, drought, and poverty, they came to care little about how they looked. Some begged their husbands to hitch up the team, turn the wagon tongue eastward, and leave the accursed plains which were never meant for human habitation. They were willing to sell out for a song—anything to get out of the country. Letters from home during droughts and grasshopper years, telling of the good crops in the old home, accentuated this feeling.

How much of the retreat from the frontier from time to time was due to the women, is not known, but it is certain that many stayed until the prairie broke them in spirit or body while others fled from the monotonous terror of it.

There was nothing to do or see and nowhere to go. The conversation each day was a repetition of that of the day before and was primarily concerning the terrible place where they had to live. Even the children felt the monotony of the life. One day in the eighties in southwestern Kansas a little boy came into the house to his mother and, throwing himself on the floor in hopeless grief, exclaimed, "Mamma, will we always have to live here?" When she hopelessly replied in the affirmative, he cried out in desperation, "And will we have to die here, too?"

By no means were all the women crushed and defeated by the rude frontier. Many a member of the fairer sex bore her loneliness, disappointment, and heart aches without complaint. Brushing away the unbidden tears, she pushed ahead, maintaining her position by the side of her hardy husband, a fit companion of the resolute conqueror of the plains. Together the two unflinchingly waged a winning struggle against the odds of poverty and loneliness.

The Sod-House Frontier: 1854-1890 by Everette Dick, Johnsen Publishing

Lesson 11
The Indians
Chapters 17

Theme

When white settlers surged onto the ancestral lands and hunting grounds of the Plains Indians, two very different cultures came into conflict. Official actions to solve the "Indian problem" took such diverse strategies as confining, Americanizing, and annihilating the Indians.

Overview

In the aftermath of the Civil War, Indian policy was in utter disarray. On the frontier, federal troops clashed with Plains tribes who fought an intermittent but ferocious guerrilla war against white encroachment. Atrocities and massacres by both sides ignited passions and troubled consciences, splitting whites and Indians alike into war and peace factions.

The dichotomy of perception and duplicity of action was clearly evident in the early winter of 1864 when Colonel J. M. Chivington, a former Methodist minister and now commander of the Military District of Colorado, reported his attack of a Cheyenne village at daybreak. According to Chivington, his troopers battled a thousand warriors, killing about four hundred braves and three chiefs. For his own troops, he had praise: "All did nobly." Missing from his account was the anguish of many of the soldiers and their officers over the engagement. Eventually a different picture of the battle emerged, and Congress investigated the affair at Sand Creek. The charges were sobering: Chivington's men had murdered Indians who thought they were under Army protection; most of the Indian dead were women and children; Indian bodies had been mutilated. As it turned out, Chivington's report proved both incomplete and, according to eyewitnesses, in most cases an outright lie.

The reaction of the other Plains chiefs was quick and violent. Said one Indian leader: "What do we have to live for? The white man has taken our country, killed our game, was not satisfied with that, but killed our wives and children. Now no peace. We have now raised the battle ax until death." And so began another fierce retaliation of raiding and slaughter.

While the frontier trembled and raged, a different kind of reaction was taking shape back east. The testimony about the Sand Creek massacre created a wave of revulsion and soul searching over the issue that had plagued the West since the mid-1800s. Although some politicians continued to espouse the traditional hard-line attitude to "exterminate the whole fraternity of redskins," many, like Senator Lot M. Morrill, reflected the awakening conscience of the American people and their government. Morrill posed the central question to the Senate: "We have come to this point in the history of the country that there is no place beyond population to which you can remove the Indian, and the precise question is: Will you exterminate him or will you fix an abiding place for him?"

The basic choice was clearly between accommodation or annihilation. The "Indian problem" could no longer be postponed by pushing Native Americans further and further west. With the end of the Civil War and the settling of the frontier, there was nowhere else to move them. Another solution would have to be found. After Sand Creek, a number of religious leaders and government officials were less eager for war and advocated a fundamentally humanitarian approach, which incidentally was also a pragmatic one. It was less costly to keep an Indian alive on a reservation than to kill him in the field, and Congress, with a treasury drained by the Civil War, was looking for bargains.

Henry B. Whipple, an Episcopal bishop, had long agitated for a more enlightened approach to Indian relations, and now asked the government to fulfill its promises and administer the Indian Bureau through persons of temperance and integrity. This viewpoint espoused the assimilation of the Indian into mainstream culture—housing and feeding him through regular allotments of food, stores, and money; introducing him to modern agriculture; and teaching him a trade. Advocates hoped that through such humanitarian methods, the problems would disappear as the Indians lived a new way of life based on the values of idealized, middle-class, nineteenth-century white folks. The new Indian would be industrious, a self-supporting landowner with all the rights and duties of citizenship.

While such ideas were worth careful consideration, the government sought a practicable solution. General William T. Sherman, the greatest power in the post Civil War army, was a pragmatist who tolerated Indians as long as they behaved, but he favored the extermination of the fighting tribes. The great debate continued through the late 1860s and culminated in a peace commission set up by an act of Congress. As it turned out, the treaties utterly failed to keep the peace. The same Congress that set up the peace commission would not appropriate the provisions needed to meet its own pledges to the Native Americans. On the other side, many Indian warriors who had no intention of observing a permanent peace. Among both whites and Indians the currents of cultural conflict continued to be too strong to be reconciled. The Native Americans were a proud people whose way of life and value system was markedly different from that of the white man. What warrior would follow the plow because some white man said he should? And what white settler would let "savages" stand between himself and his farmland?

In November 1868, in a dawn raid reminiscent of the Sand Creek massacre, the United States 7th Cavalry led by George Armstrong Custer brought death and destruction to another Indian camp. Likewise Custer's report failed to mention forty murdered women and children. Yet this time no white officials questioned the raid, and Custer—already a hero—won the commendation of Generals Sheridan and Sherman, who advocated strong actions against the "fighting" Indians. For now the white man would hold no more councils, but would strike hard at any Indian band that showed the slightest armed resistance and would force any survivors onto the reservations. The following years were marked by still more treaties and broken promises, misunderstandings and betrayals, swift massacres of both whites and Indians, and basic ignorance of the realities on both sides.

And so the lines were drawn when, in June 1876, Custer and his troops set out to notify Sitting Bull's band that they must return to their reservation and remain there. In 1874, with the discovery of gold in the Black Hills, swarms of prospectors had poured over the Sioux's sacred lands and their last stronghold. In retaliation, angry warriors had raided and harassed white settlements. Thus Custer brought an ultimatum to Indians who were already in a fighting mood. What happened at the Little Bighorn—or as the Indians called it, the Greasy Grass River—echoes forever in the American consciousness and is based as much on misconception and myth as on fact. Regardless of the actual details, it was a triumph for the Sioux warrior chief—a brilliant tactician and brave fighter named Crazy Horse. Perhaps the clearest meaning of the battle was that the Plains Indian still had his dignity and would fight for his freedom. He would eventually lose the war, but he could still win a battle.

References

Ambrose, Stephen E. 1975. *Crazy Horse and Custer: The Parallel Lives of Two American Warriors.* New York: Anchor Books.

Black Elk Speaks: Being the Life Story of a Holy Man of the Ogalala Sioux. 1961 Reprint. As told to John G. Neihardt. New York: MJF Books.

Brash, Sarah. ed. 1997. *Defiant Chiefs: The American Story.* Alexandria, Virginia: Time-Life Books.

Brown, Dee. 1994. *The American West.* New York: Simon & Schuster.

Capps, Benjamin and the Editors of Time-Life. 1975. *The Great Chiefs: The Old West.* New York: Time Life Books.

Connell, Evan S. 1994. *Son of the Morning Star: Custer and the Little Big Horn.* New York: Harper Perennial.

Custer, General George Armstrong. 1990 Reprint. *A Personal Narrative: My Life on the Plains.* Secaucus, New Jersey: The Citadel Press.

Fleet, Cameron. ed. 1997. *First Nations—Firsthand.* Edison, New Jersey: Chartwell Books, Inc.

Hoxie, Frederick E. ed. 1996. *Encyclopedia of North American Indians: Native American History, Culture, and Life from Paleo-Indians to the Present.* New York: Houghton Mifflin.

Hutton, Paul Andrew, ed. 1992. *The Custer Reader.* Lincoln: University of Nebraska Press.

Mails, Thomas E. 1991. *The Mystic Warriors of the Plains.* New York: Barnes and Noble Books.

Milner, Clyde A., II, Carol A. O'Connor, and Martha A. Sandweiss. eds. 1994. *The American West.* New York: Oxford University Press.

Nevin, David and the Editors of Time-Life. 1974. *The Soldiers: The Old West.* New York: Time Life Books.

Pritzker, Barry M. 2000. *A Native American Encyclopedia: History, Culture, and Peoples.* New York: Oxford University Press.

Ward, Geoffrey C. 1996. *The West: An Illustrated History.* Boston: Little, Brown and Company.

Wheeler, Keith and the Editors of Time-Life. 1976. *The Chroniclers: The Old West.* New York: Time Life Books.

Standards

Historical Thinking

The student will

Chronological Thinking

- interpret data presented in time lines

Historical Comprehension

- read historical narratives imaginatively
- evidence historical perspectives
- draw upon data in historical maps
- draw upon visual, literary, and musical sources

Historical Analysis and Interpretation

- compare or contrast differing sets of ideas, values, personalities, behaviors, and institutions
- consider multiple perspectives
- analyze cause and effect relationships and multiple causation, including the importance of the individual, the influence of ideas, and the role of chance

Lesson 11   The Indians

Historical Research Capabilities

- obtain historical data

Analysis and Decision-Making

- identify issues and problems in the past
- identify relevant historical antecedents
- evaluate alternative courses of action

Content

The student will demonstrate understanding of

Federal Indian policy and United States foreign policy after the Civil War

- Various perspectives on federal Indian policy, westward expansion, and the resulting struggles
    - identify and compare the attitudes and policies toward Native Americans by government officials, the U.S. Army, missionaries, and settlers
    - compare survival strategies of different Native American societies in this era
    - evaluate the legacy of nineteenth century federal Indian policy

Resources

For each student

Reconstructing America by Joy Hakim: Chapter 17, "The Trail Ends on a Reservation"

Notebook

For each team

Document Packet: Visions and Voices
Team Sheet: *Cultures in Conflict*

For the teacher

Transparencies:

Cartoons from Lesson 7
General Store

For the classroom

Overhead projector

Web sites

America's West – Development and History @ http://www.americanwest.com/index.htm#post

Famous People in American History @ http://www.studyweb.com/lit/bio/famous.htm

Images of the American West @ http://www.treasurenet.com/images/americanwest.html

Events in THE WEST—1860-1870 @ http://www3.pbs.org/weta/thewest/wpages/wpgs200/w21860.htm

Events in THE WEST—1870-1880 @ http://www3.pbs.org/weta/thewest/wpages/wpgs200/w21870.htm

Events in THE WEST—1880-1890 @ http://www3.pbs.org/weta/thewest/wpages/wpgs200/w21880.htm

HarpWeek @ http://thewest.harpweek.com/

Freedom: A History of US @ http://www.pbs.org/wnet/historyofus/menu.html

Vocabulary

Words to Remember

*reservation — land set aside for Native American tribes when settlers took their ancestral lands

"final solution" — eliminating a problem by destroying a group of people

*"buffalo soldiers" — black cavalry troopers, so-called by the Indians because of their black, curly hair

*caricature — the exaggeration of personal characteristics

*symbol — something that stands for or suggests something else

*stereotype — hurtful symbols or descriptions used to describe or attack a group of people

compatible — in agreement

People to Remember

*Ohiyesa (Charles Eastman) — Sioux Indian (grandson of the great American painter Seth Eastman) who became a doctor, lawyer and writer

*Crazy Horse — Sioux Indian who won the battle of Greasy Grass River (Little Big Horn)

*General George Custer — army cavalryman whose troop was destroyed by the Sioux at the battle of Little Big Horn

*Sitting Bull — last of the Indians to engage in armed resistance

General William Tecumseh Sherman — top military commander who supported extermination of the fighting Indian tribes

Places to Remember

*Battle of Greasy Grass River or **Little Big Horn** — last major victory of the Sioux against the United States cavalry; Sitting Bull completely destroyed Custer and his troops

*Wounded Knee — last major armed encounter between the Indians and whites; a massacre of Indian men, women, and children

Lesson 11   The Indians

The Lesson

Focus Activity – 5 minutes

Notes

1. Read Abraham Lincoln's words about the Indian's warlike behavior in the first paragraph on page 80, Chapter 17 of *Reconstructing America*. Ask the students to react to the quotation.

   Ask the students:

   - How would you characterize Lincoln's perception of the Indians? (Help the students identify the perception as a stereotype.)

   - Do you think that many of his fellow Americans shared Lincoln's viewpoint? Why or why not?

2. Use the transparencies of the cartoons from Lesson 7 to review the following concepts with the students:

   - *Stereotypes* are hurtful *symbols* used to describe or attack people.

   - Many Americans in the 1800s used *stereotypes* to characterize Native Americans.

   - Using *stereotypes* reveals ignorance, fear, and dislike. Discuss: What fears or dislikes did whites have concerning the Indians?

   - People use hurtful *symbols* and words to attack persons who are unlike themselves or have a different viewpoint. Even historians sometimes allow bias or their own viewpoint to influence the way they report the stories of the past.

   - Discuss: What are the dangers of *stereotypes*? (Racism, hatred, injustice, and discrimination result when people misunderstand each other or mistreat a group of people because they are different.)

Teaching Activity – 25 minutes

1. Introduce Chapter 17, "The Trail Ends on a Reservation" by helping the students interpret the map on page 83 in

Reconstructing America. Guide the map study with the following questions:

- What is the primary dispute between the settlers and the Native Americans?

- In the 1860s through 1880s, why was Indian land taken?

- Find and describe the land held by the Indians in 1850. In 1890. What is the trend in land ownership from the 1850s to the 1890s?

- Compare the buffalo range of 1850 with that of 1890. What happened to the buffalo? What impact did the extinction of the buffalo have on the Plains Indians?

2. Explain to the students that the lifestyles of the Native Americans and the white settlers were not compatible in many ways. The two cultures directly conflicted with each other in many ways. Remind the students of the two disastrous situations that they identified earlier: the desire of both whites and Indians for the same land and the use of stereotype to characterize Indians and their culture.

3. Introduce the Vocabulary *Words, People, and Places to Remember* before the students read Chapter 17.

4. **Reading for a Purpose:** Students read silently or **Partner Read** Chapter 17 and work with teammates to define the sources of contention between the two cultures. Teams record this information on the Team Sheet: *Cultures in Conflict*. Each team member should be involved in discussing and recording information.

5. **Circulate and Monitor**: Visit each team to help the students read the chapter, describe the points of conflict between the whites and the Indians, and record that information on the Team Sheet: *Cultures in Conflict*. Check that the information is accurate and complete and that each team member is involved in the assignment.

6. Use **Numbered Heads** for teams to report the points of conflict. Engage the students in a discussion of the "Indian problem," the role and attitude of the United States government toward the Native Americans, the action of the United States Army against the tribes, and the humanitarian attempt to Americanize the Indians. Incorporate information from the Overview and Chapter 17 in the discussion.

Lesson 11   The Indians

7. Continue the discussion by examining the questions on pages 85 and 86 of *Reconstructing America*. Encourage the students to explain their responses to the questions and support their opinions with evidence.

Student Team Learning Activity – 25 minutes

Using primary sources

1. Distribute a Document Packet: *Visions and Voices* to each team.

   Explain the Student Team Learning Activity. The students read the quotations (*Voices*) of Indians who lived in the late 1800s and analyze the photographs (*Visions*).

   Based on these documents, each team lists the ways in which westward expansion affected the Native Americans.

2. **Circulate and Monitor**: Visit each team to assist with the interpretation of the quotations and the photographs. Check that all team members are involved with the research and are creating the list.

3. Teams use **Numbered Heads** to share their findings with the class. Facilitate a discussion of the impact of westward expansion on the Native Americans based on the packet materials. Also include timeline information, "From Jamestown to Wounded Knee" on page 88 of *Reconstructing America* in your discussion.

   Include the following impacts of westward expansion on the Native Americans in the discussion:

   - Loss of natural resources, including the buffalo
   - Loss of homelands, hunting grounds, and sacred land
   - Confinement on reservations
   - Forbidden to practice their religions
   - Spread of disease
   - Loss of traditional dress and customs
   - Hunger and starvation
   - Violence and death

Reflection and Review Activity – 5 minutes

1. Use the Transparency: *General Store*. Students examine the photograph closely and use **Think-Team-Share** to discuss the following questions.

   - What benefits do these people of both cultures enjoy from their close association?
   - What problems or difficulties might arise?

2. Use **Numbered Heads** for the teams to share their responses.

   Note to the Teacher: An additional resource for this lesson is the video series *Freedom: A History of US,* Episode Eight—Part One, Meanwhile, Out West, Kunhardt Productions and Thirteen/WNET for PBS. Also explore the accompanying PBS Website: Freedom: A History of US @ http://www.pbs.org/wnet/historyofus/menu.html, especially the section for teachers.

Homework

Write your personal reaction to the cultural conflicts between the whites and the Indians in the late 1800s. Do you think that cultural conflict exists in America today? In your opinion, what lessons from the past will help us solve cultural conflicts today?

Library/Media Resources

Fiction
Death of the Iron Horse by Paul Goble, Aladdin Library
Brother Eagle Sister Sky by Susan Jeffers, Dutton Books
Keeper of Fire by Jim Magorian, Council for Indian Education

Nonfiction
The Indians by Benjamin Capps, Time-Life Books of the Old West
If You Lived with the Sioux Indians by Ann McGovern, Scholastic, Inc.
Bury My Heart at Wounded Knee by Dee Brown, Holt

Dancing Colors: Paths of Native American Women by C. J. Brafford and Laine Thom, Chronicle Books

Becoming Brave: The Path to Native American Manhood by Laine Thom, Chronicle Books

What Do We Know About the Plains Indians? by Dr. Colin Taylor, Peter Bedrick Books

Cobblestone Magazine

The Buffalo

Who Were the First Americans?

Battle of Little Big Horn

Buffalo Soldiers

Plains Indians

Sioux

CD Rom

The Story of America 1: The Western Movement; Native Americans 1 and 2, National Geographic Society

Video

Freedom: A History of US, Episode Eight—Part One, Kunhardt Productions and Thirteen/WNET for PBS

The West by Ken Burns, Video series, book, and music CD

Dances with Wolves, MGM

Connections

Science/Geography — The United States government promised land west of the 95th meridian to the American Indians. Students review longitude and latitude and use a map to locate the 95th meridian and the areas promised to the Native Americans.

Library — Students research the leaders, traditions, and customs of the Plains Indians, especially the Sioux. Students might wish to do a comparative study of a Plains tribe and another Native American or ethnic culture.

Technology/Library — Students research the modern Native American and his or her lifestyle today. What connections can they identify between past events and present circumstances?

Language Arts — Students write brief essays to answer one or more of the following questions:

- What if Custer had won at Little Big Horn?
- What if the Indians had not been forced onto reservations and had kept their lands in the Plains States?

Art/Library — Students view the works of artists such as Tompkins Harrison Matteson, and the Native American portraits of George Catlin.

Local History — What Indian reservation or reservations exist in your state? Students find out about life on that reservation today.

Lesson 12
Chief Joseph
Chapter 18

Theme

In a desperate bid for freedom, Chief Joseph led his people on a brave but doomed odyssey to escape the United States Army and find safety in Canada. Chief Joseph's words remain an eloquent statement of justice for people of all races and backgrounds.

Overview

In the autumn of 1877, a missionary-reared Nez Percé chief called Joseph emerged as the tragic hero of a national morality play. The drama began twenty-two years earlier, when the tribe ceded a small portion of its ancestral range to the federal government. This concession only whetted the whites' land hunger. By the time Joseph became a chief, the United States government claimed ninety percent of the original tribal domain and was trying to evict the Nez Percé band and four others from the contested land and resettle them on the Lapwai Creek reservation.

A pacifist, Joseph politely but fearlessly and adamantly opposed both the white officials and the Nez Percé hotheads who called for war—that is until the United States Army attacked his people to force them onto the reservation. At that point, Chief Joseph took up arms. Joseph was not a war chief but a civil chief, and while he helped plan the Nez Percé's brilliant strategy and earned the sobriquet, "the Red Napoleon," his authority was subtler and more durable than a war chief's power. It rested on his rocklike dignity and calm, and his unswerving devotion to duty and principle.

The resulting battle for freedom is one of history's greatest epics of group courage and endurance, and was a most brilliantly executed retreat. About 700 men, women, and children fled their homeland and tried to find a refuge from the United States Army. During their three-month, 1,700 mile odyssey, they were constantly pursued and attacked, fighting always against great odds and superior numbers. Although fewer than 200 of the band were warriors, they repeatedly defeated, fought off, or somehow outwitted their foe and earned universal admiration for their courage, endurance, and bravery in the face of severe hardships. Even the unsympathetic General William Sherman was impressed: "The Indians throughout displayed a courage and skill that elicited universal praise . . . [they] fought with almost scientific skill, using advance and rear guards, skirmish lines, and field fortifications."

But it was to no avail. Eventually surrounded by soldiers and exhausted by their flight over rugged terrain in the beginning of winter, the band of expatriate refugees were stalemated on the first of October. For the sake of his dying people, Joseph stepped out into the blood-splattered snow, surrendered his rifle, and spoke words that touched the heart:

It is cold and we have no blankets. The little children are freezing to death. My people, some of them, have run away to the hills and have no blankets, no food;

no one knows where they are—perhaps freezing to death. I want time to look for my children and see how many of them I can find. Maybe I shall find them among the dead. Hear me, my chiefs, I am tired; my heart is sick and sad. From where the sun now stands, I will fight no more forever.

When the soldiers took a count of their prisoners of war, they found that the 700 Nez Percé who had fled had been reduced to little more than 400 and only 79 of them were men. The war for freedom was over but not the sorrow and suffering of the Nez Percé people.

Half-starved and in tatters, they were transported to Fort Leavenworth, Kansas under the orders of General Sherman, who vowed that they be treated with severity and must never be allowed to return to their homelands.

To improve the lot of his people, Joseph traveled to Washington to meet with government officials. He spoke without rancor, dwelling on the great principles that have always concerned moral men:

We only ask an even chance to live as other men live. . . . We ask that the same law shall work alike on all men. . . . Let me be a free man—free to travel, free to stop, free to work, free to trade where I choose, free to choose my own teachers, free to follow the religion of my fathers, free to think and talk and act for myself.

By 1883, the plight of the Nez Percé had become a national issue, and the following year Congress, bowing to a sympathetic press and people, dealt leniently with the surviving 268 out of the original seven hundred. Only 118 were permitted to rejoin their tribe on the reservation; the other 150, including Joseph, who was considered too dangerous to be with his own people, were exiled to the Colville reservation in Washington Territory.

In his last years, Joseph spoke eloquently against the injustice of United States policy toward his people and held out the hope that America's promise of freedom and equality might one day be fulfilled for Native Americans as well. In 1901, Joseph traveled to Washington to ask President Theodore Roosevelt for a small piece of land in the Wallowa Valley to live out his days next to the graves of his parents. The United States government did not oblige him, and still in exile from his homeland on September 21, 1904, while he sat by the fire in his tipi, he suddenly pitched forward. The reservation doctor commented, "Joseph died of a broken heart."

References

Black Elk Speaks: Being the Life Story of a Holy Man of the Ogalala Sioux. 1961 Reprint. As told to John G. Neihardt. New York: MJF Books.

Brash, Sarah. ed. 1997. *Defiant Chiefs: The American Story.* Alexandria, Virginia: Time-Life Books.

Brown, Dee. 1994. *The American West.* New York: Simon & Schuster.

Capps, Benjamin and the Editors of Time-Life. 1975. *The Great Chiefs: The Old West.* New York: Time Life Books.

"Chief Joseph Speaks: Selected Statements and Speeches by the Nez Percé Chief." *PBS.* http://www.pbs.org/weta/thewest/resources/archives/ six/jospeak.htm. Access date October 1998.

Fleet, Cameron. ed. 1997. *First Nations—Firsthand.* Edison, New Jersey: Chartwell Books, Inc.

Hoxie, Frederick E. ed. 1996. *Encyclopedia of North American Indians: Native American History, Culture, and Life from Paleo-Indians to the Present.* New York: Houghton Mifflin.

Mails, Thomas E. 1991. *The Mystic Warriors of the Plains.* New York: Barnes and Noble Books.

Milner, Clyde A., II, Carol A. O'Connor, and Martha A. Sandweiss. eds. 1994. *The*

American West. New York: Oxford University Press.

Moeller, Bill and Jan. 1995. *Chief Joseph and the Nez Percés: A Photographic History.* Missoula, Montana: Mountain Press Publishing Company.

Nevin, David and the Editors of Time-Life. 1974. *The Soldiers: The Old West.* New York: Time Life Books.

Pritzker, Barry M. 2000. *A Native American Encyclopedia: History, Culture, and Peoples.* New York: Oxford University Press.

Ward, Geoffrey C. 1996. *The West: An Illustrated History.* Boston: Little, Brown and Company.

Wheeler, Keith and the Editors of Time-Life. 1976. *The Chroniclers: The Old West.* New York: Time Life Books.

Standards

Historical Thinking

The student will

Historical Comprehension

- read historical narratives imaginatively
- evidence historical perspectives
- draw upon data in historical maps
- draw upon visual, literary, and musical sources

Historical Analysis and Interpretation

- consider multiple perspectives
- analyze cause and effect relationships and multiple causation, including the importance of the individual, the influence of ideas, and the role of chance

Historical Research Capabilities

- obtain historical data

Analysis and Decision-Making

- identify issues and problems in the past

Content

The student will demonstrate understanding of

Federal Indian policy and United States foreign policy after the Civil War

- Various perspectives on federal Indian policy, westward expansion, and the resulting struggles
    - identify and compare the attitudes and policies toward Native Americans by government officials, the U.S. Army, missionaries, and settlers
    - compare survival strategies of different Native American societies in this era
    - evaluate the legacy of nineteenth century federal Indian policy

Resources

For each student

Reconstructing America by Joy Hakim: Chapter 18, "The People of the Pierced Noses"

Notebook

For each team

Document Packet: *Chief Joseph Speaks*

For the teacher

Transparency: *Quotations*

Markers

For the classroom

Discussion questions written on chart paper

Overhead Projector

Web sites

America's West – Development and History @ http://www.americanwest.com/index.htm#post

People in the WEST – Chief Joseph @ http://www3.pbs.org/weta/thewest/wpages/wpgs400/w4joseph.html

Sayings of Chief Joseph @ http://www3.pbs.org/weta/thewest/wpages/wpgs660/jospeak.html

Freedom: A History of US @ http://www.pbs.org/wnet/historyofus/menu.html

HarpWeek @ http://thewest.harpweek.com/

Vocabulary

Words to Remember

Nez Percé — peaceful Native American tribe that refused to settle on a reservation and fled their ancestral land to seek safety from United States soldiers

travois — vehicle made from two shafts and a platform that is pulled by a dog or horse

rendezvous — to meet at an designated place

***treaty** — contract between two political authorities

***reservation** — tract of public land set aside for the use of an Indian tribe

People to Remember

*Chief Joseph — civil chief of the Nez Percé who led his people on a 1,700 mile journey to escape federal soldiers and find freedom in Canada

Ollokot — Chief Joseph's younger brother, who commanded the Nez Percé warriors

Lesson 12   Chief Joseph

The Lesson

Focus Activity – 5 minutes

1. Show the Transparency: *Quotations*

2. Students **Think-Team-Share**:

   - What do these two quotations have in common?

   Help students interpret the quotations and identify their sources.

Teaching Activity – 25 minutes

1. Introduce Chapter 18, "The People of the Pierced Noses" in *Reconstructing America* by reviewing the United States government policy toward Native Americans in the late 1800s. Incorporate information from the Overview and include the following topics in the discussion.

   - the resettlement of tribes on reservations

   - the attempt to Americanize, including the suppression of Indian culture, lifestyles, and religions

   - the annihilation of the Indian people by the United States Army

2. Use information in the Overview to provide some background information about Chief Joseph and the Nez Percé tribe.

   Students examine the photographs in Chapter 18, especially those of Chief Joseph. Ask:

   - What can they infer about Chief Joseph and his people from the photographs?

3. Introduce the Vocabulary *Words, People, and Places to Remember.*

4. **Reading for a Purpose:** Students **Partner Read** pages 89 to 93 of Chapter 18 in *Reconstructing America*. Working with their partners, the students answer the following questions written on chart paper.

Notes

- What were the characteristics of the Nez Percé tribe? (pages 89 through 90)

- Describe the early relationship between the Nez Percé and the whites. (pages 90 through 91)

- What event created a major problem between the whites and the Nez Percé? (page 91)

- How did the United States government seek to solve the problem? (page 91)

- What incident resulted in the flight of the Nez Percé? (page 92)

- Use the map and the reading to trace the flight and defeat of the Nez Percé. (pages 92 and 93)

5. Use the map on page 93 and the "Happenings Along the Way" section to discuss the tragic journey of the Nez Percé.

6. Read page 94 of Chapter 18 to the students. Assign volunteers to read Chief Joseph's words as you read the text.

   - Help the students interpret the words of Chief Joseph and discuss the following questions with the students.

   - How do Chief Joseph's words express the concept of justice?

   - How do Chief Joseph's words express the concept of equal protection under the law?

   - How do Chief Joseph's words reflect the meaning of the Declaration of Independence:

     We hold these truths to be self-evident, that all Men are created equal, that they are endowed by their Creator with certain unalienable Rights, that among these are Life, Liberty, and the Pursuit of Happiness.

   - Who else in our history has been denied justice, equal protection under the law, or their unalienable rights?

   - What are your reactions to the plight of Chief Joseph and the Nez Percé Indians?

7. **Reading for a Purpose:** Read the poem by Steven Vincent Benét on page 90 of *Reconstructing America* to the students. Help the students interpret the poem. Ask: Despite the Indians' struggle to keep their land and customs, what was the final outcome?

Lesson 12　Chief Joseph

Student Team Learning Activity – 25 minutes

Interviewing Chief Joseph

1. Explain the Student Team Learning Activity:

   Imagine you are a television reporter and have the opportunity to interview Chief Joseph.

   - What questions would you ask him?
   - Would you want to hear about his strategy or tactics?
   - Would you want to ask him how he defines justice?

   Students work with their teammates to develop a list of possible interview questions. If necessary, students refer to Chapter 18 in *Reconstructing America* to review the flight of the Nez Percé and to stimulate questions.

2. **Circulate and Monitor**: Visit each team to help the students develop interesting, thought-provoking interview questions. Check that all students are involved in the activity.

   Teams use **Numbered Heads** to briefly share some questions with the class.

3. Using the team's questions as a guide, each student works with a team partner to develop an interview. The students should strive for an accurate, realistic interview that makes use of Chief Joseph's actual words. Distribute to each team a copy of the Document Packet: *Chief Joseph Speaks,* which along with Chapter 18 in *Reconstructing America,* provides a resource of quotations.

   Circulate and Monitor: Visit each team as the partners develop their interviews. Assist students who are having difficulty with the assignment. Check that each partnership is using appropriate and accurate information and completing the task.

4. Partners decide which student will be the reporter and which will be Chief Joseph. Each partnership shares its interview with teammates.

   Circulate and Monitor: Visit each team as the students conduct their interviews. Check for accuracy and, if necessary, correct any misinformation.

5. If time permits, a number of volunteers can share their interviews with the class.

Reflection and Review Activity – 5 minutes

1. Teams use **Think-Team-Share** to discuss the following questions.

   - What do you think would have happened if the Nez Percé had reached Canada?
   - How might the problem have been resolved without violence?

2. Use **Numbered Heads** for the teams to share their responses.

   Note to the Teacher: An additional resource for this lesson is the video series *Freedom: A History of US,* Episode Eight—Part Two, The Final Confrontation, Kunhardt Productions and Thirteen/WNET for PBS. Also explore the accompanying PBS Website: Freedom: A History of US @ http://www.pbs.org/wnet/historyofus/menu.html, especially the section for teachers.

Homework

Write your personal reaction to the treatment of the Nez Percé by the United States government.

- Do you think the Native Americans should have fought for their land regardless of the consequences?
- Do you think the government was unjust in its treatment of the Nez Percé? Explain your position.

Library/Media Resources

Fiction
Keeper of Fire by Jim Magorian, Council for Indian Education

Nonfiction
The Great Chiefs by Benjamin Capps, Time-Life Books

The Indians by Benjamin Capps, Time-Life Books

If You Lived with the Sioux Indians by Ann McGovern, Scholastic, Inc.

Bury My Heart at Wounded Knee by Dee Brown, Holt

Chief Joseph: Chief of the Nez Percé by Robert B. Noyed and Cynthia Fitterer Klingel, Childs World

Chief Joseph of the Nez Percé (Photo-Illustrated Biographies) by Bill McAuliffe and Lucile Davis, Bridgestone Books

That All People May Be One People, Send Rain to Wash the Face of the Earth by Chief Joseph, Mountain Meadow Press

Cobblestone Magazine

Chief Joseph

Sioux

The Buffalo

Who Were the First Americans?

Battle of Little Big Horn

Buffalo Soldiers

Plains Indians

CD Rom

The Story of America 1: The Western Movement and *Native Americans 1 and 2*, National Geographic Society

Video

Freedom: A History of US, Episode Eight—Part Two, Kunhardt Productions and Thirteen/WNET for PBS

The West by Ken Burns, PBS (Video series, book, and music CD)

Connections

Math — Students determine the percentage of Nez Percé who survived the odyssey, the percentage who were women and children, and the percentage who accompanied Chief Joseph to Colville Reservation.

Geography/Library — Students research the physical terrain and weather conditions encountered by the Nez Percé on their odyssey. Students create a map that displays this information.

Music — Students listen to some Native American music. What part did music play in the life of the Native Americans? How were music and dance related?

Art/Library — Students use web sites or library resources to find examples of Native American drawing and decoration. What do some of the picture symbols represent?

Lesson 13
Tweed, Beach, and Nast
Chapter 19

Theme

Although the years from the Civil War to the turn of the century appeared prosperous for the reunited nation, the industrial growth of the cities created a poor working class, pollution, traffic congestion, and political corruption.

Overview

Otto L. Bettmann makes the argument in his book, *The Good Old Days—They Were Terrible*, that the years after the Civil War through the turn of the century were quite different from the popular image of an effervescent, carefree America filled with the fun and charm of the Gilded Age. Bettmann maintains that "we have to revise the idealized picture of the past and turn the spotlight on its grimmer aspects."

Indeed, the aura of well-being, gaiety, and charm was only a brittle veneer that covered widespread turmoil and suffering. The good old days were only good for a privileged few. For most people—especially farmers, laborers, freedmen, Indians, and immigrants—life was unremitting hardship. This mass of working-poor Americans (particularly the youth, who had no voice) were exploited or lived in total neglect. Problems that we consider purely of our generation—pollution, addiction, urban plight, and educational turmoil—were also problems in that gilded age.

When the Civil War ended, the American North was fully mobilized for industry. With confidence, the reunited nation set out to boldly shape a new destiny. The smoke that billowed from the masses of industrial smokestacks was considered a good omen—it meant prosperity. The resulting pollution was rationalized as a sign of progress, and few realized the effect of smoke, carbon, sulfur, and iodine on the human body. Smog (a term for fog and smoke coined in 1905) composed of acrid, industrial vapors and coal smoke smothered the cities. Nowhere was it worse than in New York City, where the filthy air of industrial Hunter's Point produced "sickness and depression, irritations of lungs and throats, and an inclination to vomit." Inquiry by the state board of health revealed that New York City owed its rich air to "sulfur, ammonia gases, offal rendering, bone boiling, manure heaps, putrid animal wastes, fish scrap, kerosene, acid fumes, phosphate fertilizer, and sludge." Most other cities suffered similar industry-polluted atmospheres.

But the air was not the only pollution problem. Pigs roamed freely in the streets, parks, and squares of the cities—the paradox of a rural resident in the urban streets. Because they ate the garbage that littered the streets—another problem due to the absence of adequate sanitation services—the porkers were tolerated. But the stench of patrolling hogs was so penetrating that (in the words of Oscar Wilde) it "made granite eyes weep."

Then there is the nostalgia of the horse and carriage. At the end of the century, over three million horses lived in American cities, one hundred fifty thousand in New York City alone. Each of these horses produced twenty to twenty-five pounds of manure a day that attracted swarms of flies and emitted a powerful stench; and in addition stables filled with urine-soaked hay stood on every block. The wind carried the dried septic muck everywhere. *Leslie's Weekly,* a popular newspaper of the time, complained about the filthy air and commented, "No barrier can shut it out, no social distinction can save us from it . . ."

Man, surrounded by his own garbage, created the most refuse in the cities. At best, nineteenth century garbage collection was capricious and inept. The "Golden Age" of garbage included kitchen slops, cinders, coal dust, horse manure, and dumped or stored merchandise pilled high in streets and on sidewalks. Pedestrians climbed over heaps of trash and waded through a bed of slime. Overcrowding, the cross-purposes of domestic and commercial needs, and the lack of regulation caused the tumbling disorder.

Amid all this mess was the traffic jam: the press of man, beast, and wagon. Although considered a modern phenomenon, the traffic jam reached hideous proportions before the turn of the century. A traffic report in 1872 from Lower Broadway broadcasted: "What a jam! Stages, carriages, cartmen, expressmen, pedestrians all melted together in one agglomerate mess!" Chaos ruled as reckless drivers and terrified horses maneuvered amid refuse, trash, and junk. Frightened New York pedestrians would agree that "It takes more skill to cross Broadway . . . than to cross the Atlantic in a clamboat." And in fact, according to the National Safety Council, the horse-associated fatality rate was ten times the car-associated rate of modern times.

But pollution and traffic jams were not the only problems of the Gilded Age. For the most part, the political system, individual politicians, and government itself were rife with corruption; nowhere was this more evident than in New York City. Here William Marcy Tweed and his cohorts kept the city under his thumb. As a volunteer fireman, Tweed had built a strong power base in his political ward, progressed to alderman, and finally served in the United States Congress. As chairman of the Tammany general committee, and eventually as grand sachem, Tweed gained absolute power in the city Democratic party by controlling party nominations and party patronage. He made his fortune from the rich plums plucked through the management of city expenditures. The Tweed Ring defrauded the city of at least thirty million dollars through padded and fictitious charges and profited from tax favors. Tweed bought votes and bribed officials, such as city judges. Attempts to oust the Tweed Ring failed, and in fact, Tweed increased his power. For a time the Tweed Ring controlled the city without interference.

Tweed maintained personal popularity and political power because of his open-handedness and charity to the poor and immigrant population of the city. Tammany gained strength by bringing newly arrived immigrants into its fold. These newcomers were found jobs, naturalized, and persuaded to vote for their benefactors. The political machine provided for the poor with food, clothing, and fuel in emergencies, and aided those who ran afoul of the law. Thus the new Americans became devoted to its organization and willingly overlooked the fraudulent election practices, graft, corruption, and other abuses that characterized the Tweed political machine.

The corruption finally aroused public indignation when a new county bookkeeper, M. J. O'Rourke, published evidence of wholesale graft. Thomas Nast continued the campaign with a series of effective political cartoons that even the illiterate could understand. Tweed commented that he did not so much care what the papers printed about him because most of his constituents could not read, but they could understand "them damn pictures." Once informed, an aroused electorate swept the Tweed Ring from power. Organized political reform efforts fought Tammany and brought Tweed to trial for felony. After three trials and a one-year prison term, Tweed escaped to Cuba and later to Spain. But thanks to another Nast cartoon, Tweed was recognized and eventually extradited to the United States where he died in prison two years later.

Early in his career, Nast had been employed by *Harper's Weekly* to draw on-the-scene sketches during the Civil War. He soon expressed his personal views regarding the war by means of his allegorical cartoons. These drawings, usually large central drawings surrounded by a series of small sketches, attracted nationwide attention to the cartoonist. Even though he condemned war itself, he hated the Democratic position that favored compromise and an early end to the conflict. President Lincoln referred to him as the Union's best recruiting sergeant, and at the close of the war, General Grant said that Nast had done as much as any one man to preserve the Union and end the war. Nevertheless, the campaign that contributed most to Thomas Nast's fame was the one he carried against the corrupt Tweed Ring in 1871.

Nast left an immense legacy. To him we owe the symbols of the Democratic donkey and the Republican elephant as well as Uncle Sam, John Bull, Columbia, and perhaps his most enduring gift, his renderings of Santa Claus. In "Santa Claus in Camp," the first picture in which Santa Claus is portrayed as we recognize him today, Nast appropriated the good saint for the Northern cause as he dressed his Santa in a star-spangled coat and striped trousers. Nast went on to illustrate Santa perched atop snowy chimneys, riding in his sleigh, creating marvels in his workshop, opening his mail, and checking his list of good and bad children. It is highly likely that the image by which Thomas Nast would most like to be remembered is not his political cartoons but his Santa Claus.

References

"American Political Cartoons: An Introduction." Truman State University. http://www.truman.edu/parker/research/cartoons.html. Access date January 2003.

Bettman, Otto. L. 1974. *The Good Old Days—They Were Terrible.* New York: Random House.

Fischer, Roger A. 1996. *Them Damned Pictures: Explorations in American Political Cartoon Art.* New York: Archon Books.

Greenwood, Janette Thomas Greenwood. 2000. *The Gilded Age: A History in Documents.* New York: Oxford University Press.

Hess, Stephen and Sandy Northrop. 1996. *Drawn & Quartered: The History of American Political Cartoons.* Montgomery, Alabama: Elliott & Clark Publishing.

"The Reconstruction Era: Tweed Ring, William Marcy Tweed (1823-1878)." *U.S. History.com.* http://www.u-s-history.com/pages/h703.html. Access date November 1998.

St. Hill, Thomas Nast. 1974. *Thomas Nast—Cartoons and Illustrations.* New York: Dover Publications.

"The World of Thomas Nast." *HarpWeek.* http://www.thomasnast.com/. Access date November 1998.

Zwick, Jim. "Political Cartoons of Thomas Nast." *Boondocksnet.com.* http://www.boondocksnet.com/gallery/nast_intro.html. Access date November 1998.

Zinn, Howard. 1999. *A People's History of the United States: 1492-Present.* New York: HarperCollins Publishers.

Standards

Historical Thinking

The student will

Lesson 13   Tweed, Beach, and Nast

Historical Comprehension

- reconstruct the literal meaning of a historical passage
- draw upon visual, literary, and musical sources

Historical Analysis and Interpretation

- analyze cause and effect relationships and multiple causation, including the importance of the individual, the influence of ideas, and the role of chance

Historical Research Capabilities

- obtain historical data
- support interpretation with historical evidence

Analysis and Decision-Making

- identify issues and problems in the past

Content

The student will demonstrate understanding of

How the rise of big business, heavy industry, and mechanized farming transformed the American peoples

- How rapid industrialization affected urban politics, living standards, and opportunity at different social levels
  - analyze how urban political machines gained power and how they were viewed by immigrants, middle-class reformers, and political bosses

Resources

For each student

Reconstructing America by Joy Hakim: Chapter 19, "A Villain, a Dreamer, a Cartoonist"

Notebook

For the teacher

Transparencies:
   Gilded Age
   Santa Claus in Camp
   Series: Fighting Political Corruption with Cartoons

For the classroom

Overhead projector

Web sites

Thomas Nast Homepage @ http://www.buffnet.net/~starmist/nast/main.htm

Thomas Nast @ http://www.historybuff.com/library/refnast.html

15 cartoons of Thomas Nast @ http://lily.mip.berkeley.edu/classes/history16/pages/cat15html

William Marcy Tweed @ http://www.infoplease.com/ce5/CE053049.html

Tammany @http://www.infoplease.com/ce5/CE050739.html

Gilded Age and Progressive Era Resources @ http://www.tntech.edu/www/acad/hist/gilprog.html

American History Sources for Students: Important Topics 1870s-1930s @ http://www.cl.ais.net/jkasper/1870.html

America in the Gilded Age @ http://www.pbs.org/wgbh/pages/amex/carnegie/gildedage,html

Vocabulary

Words to Remember

*Gilded Age — era from the end of the Civil War to the turn of the century, so called because its attractive image covered up problems, poverty, and inequality

villain — scoundrel or criminal

political boss — person who controls a political party or a political machine

political machine — powerful unofficial government that operates alongside real city government

political cartoon — humorous way to present news or a viewpoint about a political figure or event

pneumatic — air-powered

hydraulic — water-powered

alderman — member of a city legislative body

*constituents — people a politician represents

*graft — money gained in a dishonest way

*fraud — deception and swindling

patent — legal registration of an invention to protect it against theft

People to Remember

*William Marcy Tweed — political boss of New York City who became rich by fraud and graft

*Alfred Ely Beach — inventor, publisher, and patent lawyer who fought Boss Tweed and built a subway in New York City to ease the traffic congestion

*Thomas Nast — political cartoonist who exposed Boss Tweed and destroyed his power

Lesson 13   Tweed, Beach, and Nast

The Lesson

Focus Activity – 5 minutes

Notes

1. Show the Transparency: *"Gilded Age."*

2. Students **Think-Team-Share**:

   - What do these two illustrations tell about the era after the Civil War?

   Expand on the students' responses by explaining the great difference between the rich privileged class (many of whom made their money in new urban industries) and the poor working class (immigrants and freed slaves who came north following the Civil War).

   Explain that the years after the Civil War until the turn of the century are often called the Gilded Age because the wealth and privilege of a few people covered up the poverty and problems of most Americans. The wealthy were more interested in making money and spending it in showy, frivolous ways than in helping the less fortunate or promoting the ideals of America. Define *gild* as a way to cover or hide poor quality underneath a thin coating of gold.

Teaching Activity – 25 minutes

1. Introduce Chapter 19, "A Villain, a Dreamer, a Cartoonist" in *Reconstructing America* by asking the students to consider the question that begins the chapter:

   - Do you ever worry about air pollution or about dishonest politicians?
   - What problems do you see in today's cities?

   Help students connect the problems of today with those in the cities in the late 1800s. Use information from the Overview when appropriate to the discussion.

2. Introduce and define the Vocabulary *Words and People to Remember* as the students met the terms when reading the chapter.

3. **Reading for a Purpose:** Students read silently or **Partner Read** pages 95 through 96 in *Reconstructing America* to identify the problems of the big cities in the late 1800s (air pollution, garbage in the streets, pigs, flies, disease, manure, burning of coal, oil refineries, traffic congestion). List the problems on the chalkboard as the students identify them.

4. Ask the students for their reactions to the problems of the cities in the late 1800s:

   - Were you surprised to discover that some of our modern problems also existed over 100 years ago?

   - Why do you think some people consider the past a better or less complicated time than modern times?

   - What do people mean when they talk about the "good old days"?

   - Would you have liked to live in the "good old days" of the Gilded Age? Why or why not?

   Read the comment of Otto L. Bettmann about the "good old days" in the Overview to the students. Ask the students:

   - What did Bettmann mean? Do you agree? Why or why not?

5. Introduce the *villain* of Chapter 19: Boss Tweed.

   Reading for a Purpose: Students silently read or **Partner Read** the sidebars "Who's the Boss" on page 95 and "Machinery of Government" on page 97 of *Reconstructing America*. Ask:

   - What is a political machine? A political boss?

   - How does a political machine or a political boss gain and keep power?

   Reading for a Purpose: Students read the paragraph that begins at the bottom of page 96 to describe Boss Tweed. Discuss with the students:

   - Who was Boss Tweed? How did he gain power? How did he keep his power?

   - What are graft and fraud? How did Boss Tweed use graft and fraud?

   During the discussion, share additional information from the Overview about Boss Tweed and his ring with the students.

Lesson 13 Tweed, Beach, and Nast   139

6. Help the students define the terms reform and reformer and name some modern reformers. Continue the discussion by asking:

   - Can a dreamer be a reformer?

   - What modern reformer had a dream and what reform came from his dream?

   Introduce the *dreamer* of Chapter 19: Alfred Ely Beach, and his stand against the *villain*, Boss Tweed.

   Reading for a Purpose: Students read silently or **Partner Read** page 97 from the second paragraph to the end of Chapter 19 in *Reconstructing America*.

   Discuss Beach and his stand against Tweed with the students. Ask them to explain how Beach was a dreamer and a reformer.

7. Introduce the *cartoonist* of Chapter 19: Thomas Nast.

   Help the students interpret the meaning of Nast's cartoons in Chapter 19. Assist students with locating other Nast cartoons in *Reconstructing America* by using the book's index to find page numbers on which his cartoons appear.

   Share information from the Overview about Nast's early career as an on-the-scene Civil War artist for *Harper's Weekly*—the 1800s version of a news magazine like *Time* or *Newsweek*. Show and briefly discuss the Transparency: *Santa Claus in Camp*.

8. Read "George Washington *What*?" on page 99 of *Reconstructing America* to the students. Ask the students to define honest and dishonest graft, according to George Washington Plunkitt.

   Ask students for their opinions:

   - Is all graft dishonest? Why or why not?

   - Why is it wrong for public officials to take advantage of their knowledge of government business to make a profit?

Student Team Learning Activity – 25 minutes

Interpreting political cartoons

1. If necessary, very briefly review the purpose and techniques of political cartoons.

2. Use the Transparency Series: *Fighting Political Corruption with Cartoons* for students to analyze Nast's cartoons. Use the following procedure for analyzing each of the cartoons in the series.
   - Show the cartoon transparency.
   - Share the information about the cartoon with the students.
   - Students use **Think-Team-Share** to identify the *symbols* that Nast used and the *message* of his cartoon.
   - Use **Numbered Heads** for teams to share the cartoon's *symbols* and *meaning*.
   - Ask the students to determine: Why is the cartoon effective?

   Note to the Teacher: If time limits discussing the entire transparency series, choose a few of the cartoons for the activity.

Reflection and Review Activity – 5 minutes

1. Teams use **Think-Team-Share** to discuss these questions.
   - Are political cartoons an effective way to fight a villain?
   - What are some other effective ways to fight corruption?
2. Use **Numbered Heads** for the teams to share their responses.

Homework

Think of a problem in today's world. It can be a problem in your school, your neighborhood or community, or in the nation. Determine what you want to change or reform. Create a political cartoon to get your message to others. Decide on the overall message of your cartoon and the symbols to carry your meaning. Draw your cartoon.

Library/Media Resources

Nonfiction
The Good Old Days—They Were Terrible by Otto L. Bettmann, Random House

Thomas Nast's Christmas Drawings, Dover Press

Lesson 13 Tweed, Beach, and Nast

Connections

Library — Students further research the life and work of Thomas Nast. They can locate and display some of Nast's other political cartoons or his Civil War illustrations for *Harper's Weekly*.

Art — Students, after studying the techniques of engraving and woodblock printing, create an engraving or etching of their political cartoons that they designed for homework.

Math/Library — Students create a bar or line graph that shows the rural and urban population figures in the United States from 1870-1890. Graphs must include a title, labeled axis, and a key.

Math/Library — Students research the populations of major United States cities in 1870 and at the turn of the century. Students determine which were the most populated in each decade, which grew the fastest, what factors might account for this growth, what geographic characteristics they have in common, and what part of the country experienced the most growth. Students plan a way to display the results of their research.

Science — Students experiment with hydraulic and pneumatic power and build demonstration models.

Science/Library — Students investigate and then create a demonstration model of how the pneumatic subway invented by Alfred Ely Beach worked. They compare how that subway worked to how subways work today.

Writing — Students imagine that they are citizens of New York City in the 1870s and write a letter to the editor of a newspaper that published Nast's cartoon of Boss Tweed (page 95 of *Reconstructing America*). In their letters, the students answer the question posed in the caption and tell why they support or oppose Tweed and his political machine.

Fighting Political Corruption with Cartoons

Introduction to the Cartoon Series

The campaign that made Thomas Nast famous was the one he carried out against the corrupt Tweed Ring of New York in 1871. The target of his attacks was William Marcy "Boss" Tweed, leader of Tammany Hall. Tweed had worked his way upward to become the most powerful person in the government of the city and the state of New York. Nast's cartoon "Under the Thumb" demonstrates this because New York really was under the thumb of Tweed.

Cartoon 1: *"Under the Thumb"*

As head of the Cities Commission of Public Works, Tweed gave out contracts to his cronies, who then gave him and The Ring kickback money. By appointing his handpicked men to public offices, Tweed could prevent others from learning about his dishonest activities.

The Tweed Ring reached its peak of fraudulence in 1871 with the remodeling of the City Court House. The following "costs" show how Tweed padded the expenses and violated the public's trust.

- Forty old chairs and three tables: $179,792.60
- Repairing fixtures: $1,149,874.50
- A plasterer's wages during a nine month period: $2,870,464.06 including wages of $50,000 a day for a whole month

Thirty months of advertising paid to a Tweed-controlled printing company: $7,168,212.23.

Cartoon 2: *"Let us prey"*

After the public found out about the Court House scandal, Tweed and his gang hoped that things would calm down. Nast made sure this would not happen when he drew "A Group of Vultures Waiting For The Storm to 'Blow Over'."

Cartoon 3: *"Who Stole the People's Money?"*

Next, Nast drew the very effective "Who Stole the People's Money?" in which each character points to the man on his right, forming a circle of liars.

All of this was too much for Tweed, and he decided to buy off the artist. Tweed sent one of his henchmen to tell Nast that a group of public-spirited citizens, admirers of his work, wanted to send him to Europe to study art. Nast became suspicious, and he replied that he could not possibly afford to leave his work at *Harper's Weekly*. The man replied that one hundred thousand dollars was set aside for the purpose. Nast responded that it would take more than that to make it worth his while. When the amount was raised to half a million dollars, Nast ended the interview by saying he'd rather see Tweed and his gang in jail first.

"Be careful, Mr. Nast," his caller replied in parting, "that you do not find yourself in a coffin first." Not long after that, when Nast saw suspicious looking characters loitering outside of his home, he moved his family out of town.

Cartoon 4: *"The New Board of Education"*

Next Tweed tried to intimidate Nast's publishers, the Harper Brothers Company, by threatening to have the Board of Education throw out all Harper textbooks and eliminate the firm from future bidding. This would be a severe blow to the publisher. But the board of directors voted to stand by their artist and the battle with Tweed continued. Nast followed up the incident with "The New Board of Education."

Cartoon 5: *"Wholesale and Retail Thievery"*

Then Nast followed with a series of cartoons depicting Tweed and his gang as thieves. One cartoon emphasized the difference between "Wholesale and Retail Thievery."

On the eve of the elections in New York City in November 1871, *Harper's Weekly* published "The Tammany Tiger Loose—What Are You Going to Do About It?" This cartoon is considered one of the most powerful political cartoons of all time. A few days later angry voters swept the Tweed Ring from power. The young artist received the major credit.

Cartoon 6: *"Tweed-Le-Dee And Tilden-dum"*

All of the Tammany Ring were tried and sentenced to prison, but Tweed himself escaped to Spain. Someone recognized Tweed five years later, thanks to a Nast cartoon depicting Tweed in prison garb and catching two small culprits while his crimes went unpunished. The Spanish police thought the cartoon meant that Tweed was wanted for kidnapping and the word "REWARD" caught their eye. Tweed was extradited to the United States and sent to prison. He died in a New York jail in 1878.

From *Thomas Nast-Cartoons and Illustrations*,
Dover Publications, Inc. New York 1974 by Thomas Nast St. Hill.

Lesson 14
Barnum and Twain
Chapters 20 and 21

Theme

Both master showman P. T. Barnum and literary genius Mark Twain understood the excesses and opportunities of their times. And each, in his own way, used the power of entertainment and humor to create a personal fortune and promote civic reform.

Overview

No proof exists that Phineaus Taylor Barnum ever said, "There's a sucker born every minute." He did, however, believe that "every *crowd* has a silver lining," and acknowledged that "the public is wiser than many imagine." Throughout his life Barnum gave the public shameless hucksterism, peerless spectacle, and everything in between. He was truly a master showman. In choosing Barnum as one of the hundred most important people of the millennium, *Life* magazine dubbed him "the patron saint of promoters."

Barnum's flair for salesmanship became apparent when at age twenty-five he paid one thousand dollars to obtain Joice Heth, who claimed to be 161 years old and the nurse of George Washington. Barnum made fifteen hundred dollars a week exhibiting her in New York City. A shrewd businessman, Barnum purchased Scudder's American Museum in 1841, where he presented "500,000 natural and artificial curiosities from every corner of the globe." A year later he showed the "Feejee Mermaid," purported to be an embalmed mermaid from Calcutta. Although belief in her authenticity was mixed, no one doubted Barnum's ability to capture the imagination of the public.

In 1842, Barnum hired Charles Statton, who became the world famous Tom Thumb and Barnum's close friend. Barnum created another entertainment sensation when in 1850 he presented Jenny Lind, the European opera star, to the American public. "The Swedish Nightingale" sang ninety-five concerts in nineteen cities in less than a year under his sponsorship.

But the enterprise forever linked to his name—"P.T. Barnum's Grand Traveling Museum, Menagerie, Caravan, and Circus"— made its debut when Barnum was sixty years old and, at that time, was the largest circus venture in American history. Barnum's opinion that "We ought to have a big show. The public expects it, and will appreciate it," certainly proved true: his circus grossed $400,000 in its first year of operation (and that in the currency of the 1870s).

During the next twenty years, Barnum's circus expanded as he joined with other promoters. Transferred by special railway cars over the entire country, his circus covered five acres and seated 10,000 patrons at a time. In an age when story-tellers and church socials provided the only excitement in many a small town, the arrival of Barnum's circus was cataclysmic. For many westerners, especially children, the biggest event of the year occurred when "The Greatest Show on Earth" came to town.

One of Barnum's biggest successes—literally and financially—was his acquisition of "The Towering Monarch of His Mighty Race, Whose Like the World Will Never See

Again." Jumbo the elephant made history and became the darling of the American people even as his name became part of the language. In 1883, Barnum scored a dramatic promotional coup when he and Jumbo walked across the Brooklyn Bridge to test the strength of that new engineering marvel.

It is less well known that Barnum took on an active role in civic affairs. He served in the Connecticut State Legislature and as mayor of his hometown of Bridgeport. There Barnum provided funding for local schools; developed city property; donated land for Seaside Park and money for the Barnum Museum and the Mountain Grove Cemetery; and served as president of the local hospital, water company, and bank.

Even though his final words before he died in his sleep on April 7, 1891, concerned the gate receipts for his show at Madison Square Garden, his last letter to his partner better sums up his philosophy:

"Never cater to the baser instincts of humanity, strive as I have always done to elevate the moral tone of amusement, and always remember that the children have ever been our best patrons. I would rather hear the pleased laugh of a child over some feature of my exhibition than receive as I did the flatter compliments of the Prince of Wales."

Samuel Clemens would most likely have agreed with Barnum's advice, for the great humorist and writer spoke with truth and insight through his youthful characters. Clemens' adventurous life and imaginative mind enriched and deepened his humor, making it an unparalleled force in American culture and literature for more than one hundred years. Writing under the pen name Mark Twain, Clemens was no ordinary humorist. Self-proclaimed as "a preacher-humorist, a moralist-humorist, and a critic-humorist," Clemens remained constantly active throughout his life as a lecturer, writer, philosopher, traveler, and scholar.

Like Barnum with his audience, Twain loved to entertain by amusing his readers and making people laugh. Often his humor would soar in flights of pure genius and wit for its own sake. But always beneath the wit was wisdom—and a lesson to be learned—for Twain realized early in life that humor had to preach and teach in order to survive. In fact, Twain equated being a humorist with a calling to preach and explained that it was his vocation to "excite laughter in God's creatures" and to be "the week-day preacher."

Many scholars consider *Huckleberry Finn*, Twain's antislavery, antiracist classic, to be the greatest American novel. In it he attacked the Sunday morning preaching that supported slavery—a prevalent practice in the antebellum South. But even more powerfully, *Huckleberry Finn* censured Gilded Age racism. Although slavery had been abolished for twenty years when the book was published, widespread racial prejudice and oppression still flourished. In many ways the plight of black Americans during the decades following emancipation was worse than during slavery. The nation, like Twain's characters, did not know what to do with the freedman.

Huckleberry Finn was not Twain's only humorous criticism of his era. His first novel—*The Gilded Age, A Tale of Today*—was in Twain's words: "a pretty broad satire on politicians, capitalists, and Western land speculators." The book attacked the spirit of the age—a time when men worshipped the dollar. Twain disagreed with the wealthy who believed their riches were signs of their virtue. Twain also rejected the idea—held by many moralists and writers of children's books in his day—that the virtuous prosper and the wicked suffer.

Twain lampooned that philosophy by creating Tom Sawyer and Huckleberry Finn, classic bad boys who escaped punishment for all the trouble and mischief they produced. Instead, Tom and Huck found a fortune—a reward supposedly reserved for only the best of good lads. Although Twain maintained *Huckleberry Finn* was only a "hymn to boyhood," it was a realistic work about youths who lived life with greater truth and insight than their elders.

In his life and his writings, Twain criticized conventional pieties and opinions; he thought such thinking wrong and that it should be laughed out of existence. Believing that "Irreverence is the champion of liberty," he maintained that "Our race has only one effective weapon and that is laughter." And so he attacked the evils of simplistic piety and racism with humor.

Twain traveled widely in the United States and throughout the world. Through these cosmopolitan experiences, his genius gained a wider perspective of issues, people, and events than was common in nineteenth century America. Likewise, he read broadly, more so than most of his countrymen. Twain's clear vision of the evidence obtained by his extensive travel and reading made him a humorist who was also a scholar. Although not academically trained—in fact he did not even graduate from grammar school—he was a scholar nevertheless who said, "I never let my schooling interfere with my education."

Barnum and Twain were men both of and beyond their times. Each made a fortune from entertainment, laughter, and wit. But each also had a clear—if somewhat atypical—vision that he could improve his flawed Gilded Age through humor and laughter.

References

Barnum, Phineas. T. 1855. 2000 Reprint. *Life of P.T. Barnum Written by Himself.* Urbana and Chicago: University of Illinois.

Fishkin, Shelley Fisher. 1998. *Lighting Out for the Territory: Reflections on Mark Twain and American Culture.* New York: Oxford University Press.

Friedman, Robert, ed. 1997. "The 100 People." *Life: The Millennium Special Double Issue* (Fall): 135-167.

Kunhardt, Philip B. Jr. 1995. *P. T. Barnum: America's Greatest Showman.* New York: Knopf.

"P. T. Barnum: History and Tradition." *Ringling Brothers, Barnum, and Bailey.* http://www.ringling.com/history/barnum. Access date November 1998.

Railton, Stephen. "Mark Twain in His Times." *University of Virginia.* Access date November 1998.

Twain, Mark. 1999. *The Wit and Wisdom of Mark Twain: A Book of Quotations.* Dover Books.

Standards

Historical Thinking

The student will

Historical Comprehension

- read historical narratives imaginatively
- evidence historical perspectives
- draw upon visual, literary, and musical sources

Historical Analysis and Interpretation

- consider multiple perspectives

Historical Research Capabilities

- obtain historical data

Analysis and Decision-Making

- identify issues and problems in the past

Content

The student will demonstrate understanding of

Lesson 14 Barnum and Twain

Massive immigration after 1870 and new social patterns, conflicts, and ideas of national unity developed amid growing cultural diversity

- How new cultural movements at different social levels affected American life
  - describe how regional artists and writers portrayed American life in this period
  - investigate mass entertainment and leisure activities at different levels of American society

Resources

For each student
Reconstructing America by Joy Hakim: Chapter 20, "Phineas Taylor Barnum" and Chapter 21, "Huck, Tom, and Friends"

Two 5" by 7" unlined index cards

Notebook

For each team
Two sheets of chart paper

Markers or crayons

For the teacher
Examples of business cards

Web sites
Mining Co. Guide to Mark Twain @ http://www.marktwain.miningco.com

Mark Twain Quotations @ http://www.tarleton.edu/activities/pages/facultypages/schmidt/Mark_Twain.html

Mark Twain in His Times @ http://etext.virginia.edu/railton/index.html

Lycos U. S. History Guide: P.T. Barnum @ http//www-expressnet.lycos.com/guide/wire/wire_17451768_97076_3_1.html

RBBB: History: Tradition – P. T. Barnum @ www.ringling.com

P. T. Barnum @ www.historybuff.com

Vocabulary

Words to Remember
*Gilded Age — era from the end of the Civil War to the turn of the century so called because its attractive image covered up problems, poverty, and inequality

robber barons — big businessmen who used unscrupulous business practices to become wealthy, usually at the expense of their workers

reformer — person who works to improve conditions

jumbo — very large

prohibition — outlawing the sale of liquor

People to Remember
*Phineas Taylor Barnum — showman and promoter of popular entertainment who was known for his museum of oddities, traveling circus, and Jumbo, the elephant

*Samuel Clemens/Mark Twain — humorist, writer, and literary genius who captured the American scene and made Americans think about who they were and what they wanted to be

The Lesson

Focus Activity – 5 minutes

1. Write the following on the blackboard: *jumbo, the circus, Tom Thumb, Tom Sawyer, Huckleberry Finn, P.T. Barnum, Mark Twain*.

   Ask the students to **Think-Team-Share** what they know about these words and how they might be connected.

2. Students seek information about the words by examining the sidebar illustrations and comments for Chapters 20 and 21 of *Reconstructing America*.

3. Explain that the lesson concerns two men who used entertainment, humor, laughter, and showmanship to get people to laugh at themselves and others. Both men fit the Gilded Age in which they lived: both made money and enjoyed spending, and both desired to do good.

Teaching Activity – 35 minutes

1. Briefly review the characteristics of the Gilded Age with the students.

   - Great difference between a rich, privileged class and the poor, working class

   - Immense wealth of a few people masked the poverty and problems of most people

   - Wealthy were more interested in making money and spending it in showy, frivolous ways than in helping the less fortunate or promoting the ideals of America

   Reading for a Purpose: Read the two paragraphs and the Shakespeare verse on page 108 of *Reconstructing America* to the students. Help them interpret the verse and define and understand the term Gilded Age.

2. Ask the students to **Think-Team-Share**: How were the following men (which they learned about in Chapter 19 of *Reconstructing America*) typical of the times in which they lived?

Notes

- William Marcy Tweed (political boss who made a fortune from graft and fraud)

- Alfred Ely Beach (reformer who fought Boss Tweed and solved the problem of traffic congestion by building a subway under the streets of New York City)

- Thomas Nast (political cartoonist who fought the graft and corruption of Boss Tweed)

3. Introduce Chapter 20, "Phineas Taylor Barnum" in *Reconstructing America* by explaining that Barnum although quite unlike Tweed, Beach, or Nast was also typical of his time.

4. **Reading for a Purpose:** Students read silently or **Partner Read** Chapter 20 in *Reconstructing America* to describe P.T. Barnum and his amazing entertainments and to identify how he fit the age in which he lived.

   Circulate and Monitor: Visit each team to help students with vocabulary and the reading.

5. Distribute a sheet of chart paper and markers or crayons to each team. Following the reading, the teams write Barnum's name at the top of the paper and use **Roundtable** to record words and phases that describe Barnum, his great showmanship, his accomplishments, and how he fit the Gilded Age.

6. The teams use **Numbered Heads** to share their descriptions of Barnum.

   Explain that in 2000 along with such greats as Christopher Columbus, Abraham Lincoln, Frederick Douglass, and Joan of Arc, *Life* magazine choose Barnum as one of the hundred most important people of the millennium. Ask the students to **Speculate:**

   - In your opinion, why did *Life* choose Barnum? (*Life* magazine dubbed him "the patron saint of promoters" and the "consummate showman.")

   Ask the students to consider:

   - How do entertainers today promote themselves and their acts, music, or films? (For example, many producers bring out a line of toys before the release of a movie; fast food places offer a free toy or meals around movie themes; personalities and entertainers appear on talk shows; sports figures market shoes and other merchandise.)

Discuss Barnum's use of technology—the railroads—to bring his circus to the people of the West.

As you read the description of the circus coming to town (the last paragraph on page 102, the first paragraph on page 103, and the quotation in the middle of page 103 in *Reconstructing America*), have the students study the photograph of the children on the plains (pages 70 and 71 of Chapter 15). Then ask the students to imagine the impact of the circus on those children.

7. Introduce Chapter 21, "Huck, Tom and Friends" in *Reconstructing America* by introducing Mark Twain, perhaps America's greatest and most profound humorist.

8. **Reading for a Purpose:** Read Chapter 21 in *Reconstructing America* to the students, stopping to discuss Twain's accomplishments as a humorist and author. Include the following points about the importance of Twain's writing:

   - Used humor to express important and serious ideas
   - Celebrated American life but reminded readers that the promises of America (like freedom and opportunity to all) were not being met
   - Wrote about unfairness in America (such as segregation and child labor)
   - Believed that Americans were too concerned with making money and spending it in foolish ways instead of helping others
   - Felt the nation was forgetting its ideals
   - Coined the term the Gilded Age to explain the ridiculous excess of his times
   - Wrote honestly, truthfully, and directly with humor
   - Reminded Americans to think about who they were and for what they stood.

9. Distribute a sheet of chart paper and markers or crayons to each team. Following the reading, the teams write Twain's name at the top of the paper and use **Roundtable** to record words and phases that describe Twain, his accomplishments as a writer and humorist, and how he fit the Gilded Age.

   The teams use **Numbered Heads** to share their descriptions of Twain.

Student Team Learning Activity – 15 minutes

Evaluating information about historical figures

1. Explain the Student Team Learning Activity:

   Each student designs a business card for P. T. Barnum and one for Mark Twain. The students design one of the cards during class and the other card for homework.

   Distribute two unlined 5"x7" index cards to each student.

2. Help the students decide what information might appear on a business card. Show some actual business cards as examples.

   With the students make a list of possible information that might appear on a business card. Write the list on the chalkboard. For example, the business card might include:

   - The name of the person and his or her career or business
   - Accomplishments or facts about the person and his or her career or business
   - Logo or slogan
   - Quotation about the person or the business (We do the job right the first time!)

3. Students determine the most important facts from their reading and discussion to include on Barnum's and Twain's business cards.

4. Each student creates a business card for Barnum or Twain (a card for the other man will be designed for homework).

5. **Circulate and Monitor:** Visit the teams as the students design the business cards. Assist students who need help with the assignment and check that all students are engaged in the activity.

6. If time permits, students share their cards with the class or display the cards on a bulletin board.

Reflection and Review Activity – 5 minutes

1. Teams use **Think-Team-Share** to determine

- How did Barnum and Twain reflect the Gilded Age?

Teams share their responses using **Numbered Heads.** Some possible responses include:

- Both men reflected a desire to make money and reform the society of their day.
- Barnum made a fortune as a businessman and promoter.
- Twain became wealthy from his writings and humorous lectures.
- Barnum was reform and civic minded and served his community.
- Twain wrote about the good and bad aspects of the Gilded Age to encourage reform.
- Barnum entertained people and made them laugh in the years following the Civil War.
- Twain gave humorous lectures, and his humorous writings encouraged reform.

2. Ask the students to **Speculate**:
   - Which man—Barnum or Twain—will have a more lasting impact on society? Why?

Homework

Design the other business card for Twain or Barnum.

Library/Media Resources

Fiction
The Celebrated Jumping Frog of Calaveras County, and Other Sketches by Mark Twain, Filter Press
The Prince and the Pauper by Mark Twain, Puffin
The Gilded Age by Mark Twain, Bobbs-Merrill
The Adventures of Tom Sawyer by Mark Twain, Dover
Adventures of Huckleberry Finn by Mark Twain, Dover
A Connecticut Yankee in King Arthur's Court by Mark Twain, Bantam

Nonfiction
The Wit and Wisdom of Mark Twain by Alex Ayers, New American Library

Mark Twain Himself by Milton Meltzer, Random House

P.T. Barnum by David Wright, Gini Holland, and Mike White, Raintree Books

Prince of Humbugs: A Life of P.T. Barnum by Catherine M. Andronik, Atheneum

Cobblestone Magazine

Mark Twain

Connections

Art — Students design a poster advertising the arrival of Barnum's "Greatest Show on Earth" in a small prairie town in the turn-of-the-century Midwest.

Art — Students design an advertisement for one of Mark Twain's books.

Writing/Library — Students imagine they are reporters for a newspaper and are assigned to write an obituary for either Mark Twain or P. T. Barnum. They should profile his lifetime achievements, including his reform efforts.

Science/Library — Students research how the large tent is erected for a traveling three-ring circus. What tools and principles of physical science are utilized?

Geography/Library — What were America's fifteen largest cities in 1870? In 1890? Students map out a circus tour that will visit each of these cities.

Language Arts/Library — Students read a book by Mark Twain.

Review Lesson II
Lessons 7 through 14
Chapters 11 through 21

In the Review Lesson, students revisit essential ideas and vocabulary from lessons 7 through 14 to prepare for the Assessment Lesson. The Review Lesson is in the form of a card game.

If time allows, the teams may play more than one round of *Reconstructing America Review*. Even though one team member will win each round, all students win by reviewing ideas, facts, and vocabulary from the previous lessons. The goal of the game is to successfully prepare *each* member of the team for the assessment.

Reconstructing America Review II: The West

1. To ensure that each student has a chance to play, students remain in their cooperative learning teams of four or five.

2. Each team receives a set of game cards and the answer sheet.

3. Cards are shuffled, separated into their respective piles (The Cowboys, The Railroads, The Homesteaders, etc.), and placed face down in the center of the table.

4. One team member is designated as the first player (i.e. the student whose name is last in the alphabet). The student to his or her right has the answer sheet, keeping it face down on the desk. This person is the fact checker.

5. The first player chooses a card, reads the number and the question aloud, and attempts to answer it. The fact checker turns the answer sheet over, finds the correct question number, and checks the first player's response. If the student answers correctly, he or she keeps the card. If the answer is wrong, the card is placed at the bottom of the pile. The fact checker quickly turns the answer sheet face down again.

6. Play passes to the left, and the student who was the first player is now the fact checker.

7. The game ends when all the cards are gone. The student with the most cards wins.

Reconstructing America Review II: The West
Questions and Answers

The Cowboys

1. What was the job of the cowboy? To drive longhorn cattle along the Western trails to railroad centers

Review Lesson II Lessons 7 through 14

2. If you were in charge of the chuck wagon, what would your job be? To cook for the cowboys on the cattle drive

3. Why was the Chisholm Trail important? It was one of the greatest cattle drive trails from Texas to the Kansas railroad lines

4. What was the most common danger on a cattle drive? Cattle stampedes

5. Who were Calamity Jane and Nat Love? She was a famous cowgirl who also claimed to be a gold miner, nurse, pony express rider, army scout, Indian fighter, and cattle hand. He was a famous black cowboy known as Deadwood Dick who took part in many cattle drives.

6. What's a "little dogie"? A stray calf

The Railroads

7. Why was the transcontinental railroad important? Connected the eastern United States with the Pacific coast and opened the West to settlement

8. Why was Promontory Point, Utah significant? The Union Pacific and Central Pacific railroads joined there and created the first transcontinental railroad.

9. What did the Plains Indians think of the railroad? They called it the Iron Horse and hated it because it went through their hunting grounds and sacred lands.

10. What was the difference between emigrant cars and Pullman cars? Emigrant cars were an inexpensive way to travel by train, whereas Pullman cars were luxurious and more expensive.

11. What government subsidy did the railroad companies earn by laying track? Money and grants of land, which they sold to settlers

12. What did the railroad tycoons do that created a scandal? They cheated the government, gave the business of building the railroad to their own companies, and kept their investors' dividends.

The Homesteaders

13. What was the Homestead Act? Congressional act that provided government land for settlers to own by living on it and cultivating it for five years

14. How did the McCormick reaper change the West? The mechanized farm machine enabled farmers to cut and havest grain more quickly and with less labor.

15. What invention permitted farmers to protect their farmland? Barbed wire

16. What did John Deere and Cyrus McCormick have in common? Both invented farm machinery that made it possible and profitable to farm the prairie; Deere invented the steel plow and McCormick invented the reaper.

17. What was the Grange? A social and political organization (like a worker's union) for farmers

18. Name two problems that prairie homesteaders faced. Breaking the sod, harvesting large grain fields, lack of water, natural disasters, extreme temperatures, threat of Indians, loneliness, lack of building materials

The Indians and a Great Chief

19. What is a reservation? Land given to Native Americans in exchange for their ancestral lands that were taken by settlers

20. What happened at the Greasy Grass (Little Bighorn) River? Crazy Horse and his warriors destroyed General George Custer and his soldiers.

21. What caused major conflict between the settlers and the Indians? They both claimed the same land and did not tolerate each other's cultural differences.

22. Who was Chief Joseph? A civil chief of the Nez Percé tribe who led his people on a flight to escape United States soldiers and reach freedom in Canada

23. What problem drove the Nez Percé Indians from their homeland? The U.S. army tried to force the tribe to return to a reservation.

24. Who said, ". . . I will fight no more forever"? Chief Joseph

Schemers and Dreamers

25. How did William M. Tweed reflect the Gilded Age? Tweed was a political boss who became wealthy by fraud and graft.

26. How did Alfred Ely Beach reflect the Gilded Age? Beach fought political corruption and solved a traffic problem by building a secret subway.

27. How did Thomas Nast reflect the Gilded Age? Nast drew political cartoons that let citizens know how corrupt Boss Tweed was and brought him to justice.

28. How did P.T. Barnum reflect the Gilded Age? Barnum made a fortune by entertaining and amusing people, but he also served his home community.

29. How did Twain reflect the Gilded Age? Twain made a fortune from his writings, which were humorous and entertaining but highlighted the problems of his time.

30. How did the Gilded Age get its name? Mark Twain named it that because the era was one of great wealth and privilege for a few people that hid the problems and poverty of many Americans.

Lesson 15
Immigrant Voices
Chapter 22

Theme

In the nineteenth century, the rush of immigrants—who sought economic, political, and religious freedom and a better life—fed the growing needs of a burgeoning industrial nation and propelled the United States into the modern era.

Overview

Beginning with the ancient peoples who migrated to North America over the Bering Strait in the mists of prehistory to the newcomers of today, America was and continues to be the land of immigrants. From the time of the initial colonial settlements in the sixteenth century, some fifty million people have made the journey seeking a better life and the promise of freedom—economic, political, or religious. The early immigrants (mostly farmers and tradesmen) were quite similar to and thus readily accepted by those already in the New World.

The nineteenth century witnessed an unprecedented immigration of more culturally diverse peoples who were indispensable to the rapid industrial expansion and urbanization of the United States. By the turn of the century, the pattern of immigration had changed—a reflection of the nation's need for industrial workers, not farmers. Factories were springing up everywhere, and jobless Europeans came by the millions to operate the new machines and to work in the mills.

Soon, the foreign-born and their children composed nearly half of the United States population. These new immigrants came from places that seemed increasingly foreign to established Americans. Whereas earlier immigrants had been largely from northern and western Europe, now they came from the south and east. Large groups of Jews left Russia to escape religious persecution. Poles, Czechs, Hungarians, and Italians came to find relief from poverty. These new arrivals spoke little, if any, English and were mostly unskilled laborers.

The American mosaic changed as each new wave arrived: first from Germany and Ireland, then from southern and eastern Europe, and finally from Asia, Mexico, and Central America. Four out of five immigrants settled in industrial cities in the Northeast or in the rich farmland of the Midwest. Eager for jobs, they worked for a pittance. The match was perfect: their desire for economic opportunity met the nation's demand for a cheap labor force. These new "Americans" toiled before steel furnaces, in front of textile looms, along dusty railroad lines, beside long rows of crops, and inside dark, dingy mines. Without their labor, America could never have evolved into the most productive nation in the world.

America's acceptance of immigrants was and remains, above all, an economic issue. By the 1920s, the need for unskilled labor had diminished, so the United States passed laws to restrict immigration. Today, almost half of the population can trace their roots back to that great rush of people who came to the United States between 1880 and 1920. Regardless of our ambivalence concerning each new wave of immigrants, we are a nation of diversity that—however reluctantly—still offers the promise of freedom to the world's poor, homeless, and persecuted.

In 1883 a poem was engraved on the pedestal of the Statue of Liberty—that "Mother of Exiles" who already stood as a symbol of hope to ever-increasing numbers of immigrants. Emma Lazarus, an immigrant and young poet from New York, was asked to compose a poem to welcome people seeking freedom. Her poem, "The New Colossus," became—and continues to be—a welcoming anthem for generations of immigrants.

References

"Angel Island: Immigration Station." *Angel Island Association*. http://www.angelisland.org/immigr02.html. Access date January 1999.

Bettman, Otto. L. 1974. *The Good Old Days—They Were Terrible*. New York: Random House.

Daniels, Roger. 2001. *American Immigration*. New York: Oxford University Press.

"Ellis Island History." *Ellis Island Immigration Museum*. http://www.ellisisland.com/indexHistory.html. Access date January 1999.

Fleming, Maria. ed. 2000. *A Place at the Table: Struggles for Equality in America*. New York: Oxford University Press.

Greenwood, Janette Thomas. 2000. *The Gilded Age: A History in Documents*. New York: Oxford University Press.

Hoff, Rhoda. 1986. *America's Immigrants: Adventures in Eyewitness History*. New York: Henry Z. Walck.

Holt, Hamilton. ed. 1990. *The Life Stories of Undistinguished Americans*. New York: Routledge.

Marzio, Peter C. 1976. *A Nation of Nations: The People Who Came to America as Seen Through Objects and Documents at the Smithsonian Institution*. New York: Harper & Row, Publishers.

Muggamin, Howard. 1988. *The Jewish American*. New York: Chelsea House Publishers.

Perl, Lila. 1989. *The Great Ancestor Hunt: The Fun of Finding Out Who You Are*. New York: Clarion Books.

Perrin, Linda. 1980. *Coming to America: Immigrants from the Far East*. New York: Dell Publishing Co. Inc.

Rips, Gladys Nadler. 1981. *Coming to America: Immigrants from Southern Europe*. New York: Delacorte Press.

Riis, Jacob A. 1890. 1997 Reprint. *How the Other Half Lives*. New York: Penguin Classics.

Robbins, Albert. 1981. *Coming to America: Immigrants from Northern Europe*. New York: Delacorte Press.

Zinn, Howard. 1999. *A People's History of the United States: 1492-Present*. New York: HarperCollins Publishers.

Standards

Historical Thinking

The student will

Historical Comprehension

- reconstruct the literal meaning of a historical passage
- read historical narratives imaginatively
- evidence historical perspectives
- draw upon visual, literary, and musical sources

Historical Analysis and Interpretation

- identify the author or source of the historical document or narrative
- consider multiple perspectives
- analyze cause and effect relationships and multiple causation, including the importance of the individual, the influence of ideas, and the role of chance
- hypothesize the influence of the past

Lesson 15 Immigrant Voices

Historical Research Capabilities
- obtain historical data

Analysis and Decision-Making
- identify issues and problems in the past

Content

The student will demonstrate understanding of

Massive immigration after 1870 and new social patterns, conflicts, and ideas of national unity developed amid growing cultural diversity

- The sources and experiences of the new immigrants
  - distinguish between the "old" and "new" immigration in terms of its volume and the newcomers' ethnicity, religion, language, and place of origin
  - analyze the obstacles, opportunities, and contributions of different immigrant groups

Resources

For each student
Reconstructing America by Joy Hakim: Chapter 22, "Immigrants Speak"
Notebook
Student Sheet: *Coming to America*

For each team
Document Packet: *Immigrant Voices*

For the teacher
Transparency: *Statue of Liberty*
Chart paper
Markers

For the classroom
Overhead projector

Web sites
Immigration, Ellis Island @ http://cmp1.ucr.edu/exhibitions/immigration_id.html

Statue of Liberty Facts, News and Information @ http://www.endex.com/gf/buildings/liberty/liberty.html

How the Other Half Lives @ http://www.cis.yale.edu/amstud/inforev/riis/title.html

Chronology of Asian American History @ http://web.mit.edu/21h.153j/www/chrono.html

The Immigration Station at Angel Island @ http://www.angelisland.org/immig01.html

Freedom: A History of US @ http://www.pbs.org/wnet/historyofus/menu.html

The Lower East Side Tenement Museum Virtual Tour @ http://www.tenement.org/Virtual_Tour/index_virtual.html

Vocabulary

Words to Remember
*immigrant — person who comes to a new country to live

emigrant — person who leaves his or her home-land to settle elsewhere

tenement — overcrowded city apartment buildings where many immigrants lived

People to Remember
*Jacob Riis — immigrant from Denmark in 1870 whose photographs of immigrant life brought social and political reforms that helped the poor

*Carl Schurz — German immigrant who fought for freedom by speaking against slavery and the treatment of Native Americans

The Lesson

Focus Activity – 5 minutes

1. Introduce immigration in the mid-1800s by reading a portion of "The New Colossus" by Emma Lazarus as you display the Transparency: *Statue of Liberty*. Tell the students that the poem appears on the base of the statue.

Not like the brazen giant of Greek fame,
With conquering limbs astride from land to land;
Here at our sea-washed, sunset gates shall stand
A mighty woman with a torch, whose flame
Is the imprisoned lightning, and her name
Mother of Exiles. From her beacon-hand
Glows world-wide welcome; her mild eyes command
The air-bridged harbor that twin cities frame.
"Keep, ancient lands, your storied pomp!" cries she
With silent lips. "Give me your tired, your poor,
Your huddled masses yearning to breathe free,
The wretched refuse of your teeming shore.
Send these, the homeless, tempest-tost to me.
I lift my lamp beside the golden door!"

2. Ask the students to **Think-Team-Share:**

   - What is the United States' position concerning immigration as depicted in Lazarus' poem? (One of warm welcome to the world's poor and homeless who seek freedom and a better life)

3. Teams use **Numbered Heads** to share their responses with the class.

Teaching Activity – 25 minutes

1. Provide background information about the Statue of Liberty, Emma Lazarus' poem, and the mass immigration of the mid-1800s (see Overview).

   Invite the students to share their countries of ancestry.

2. Introduce the Vocabulary *Words and People to Remember.*

   Note to the Teacher: Write all the discussion questions for this lesson on chart paper, the chalkboard, or a transparency so students can refer to them as they read.

Notes

Lesson 15   Immigrant Voices

3. **Reading for a Purpose:** Students **Partner Read** the first three paragraphs on page 111 of Chapter 22, "Immigrants Speak" in *Reconstructing America* and discuss the following questions with their partners:

   - What kind of immigrants did America need in the 1800s? (Laborers and workers who could invent, farm, build, and contribute to a growing industrialized nation.)

   - According to the Lazarus' poem, what kind of immigrants did the "Lady of Exiles" welcome? (The world's poor workers who sought liberty, freedom, and a better life, and not the well-to-do, upper class of Europe)

4. **Reading for a Purpose:** Students continue to **Partner Read** through the first paragraph on page 115 of *Reconstructing America*. Students discuss the following questions with their partners.

   - In what ways did the immigrant Carl Schurz continue to fight for freedom in America? (He spoke against slavery and the treatment of the Native Americans.)

   - Explain what Schurz meant when he said: "If you want to be free, there is but one way. It is to guarantee an equally full measure of liberty to all your neighbors." (Our country is not a free country until all our people are free. Slavery jeopardizes the freedom of every person, not just the enslaved.)

   - According to Schurz, who did not have a "full measure of liberty" in America? (Blacks, especially those in slavery, and Native Americans)

   - In what ways did Schurz make full use of his opportunities in America? (He studied law and rose to prominence as American minister to Spain, general in the Union army, newspaper reporter and editor, U.S. senator, secretary of the interior.)

   - What were the two largest immigrant groups to come to the United States? (Germans and Irish)

   - What role did free public schools play in the lives of immigrant children? (Children learned to speak and write English and were Americanized in the schools.)

5. Use the map and illustration on page 114 of *Reconstructing America*. Help the students identify the countries from which immigrants came and interpret immigration patterns. **Note to the Teacher:** It may be helpful to make and use an overhead of page 114 during the discussion.

   Ask students to **Speculate:**

   - What caused the dips and peaks in the immigration patterns?

   Describe the relationships between the numbers of immigrants and their countries of origin.

6. Students divide a sheet of paper into two columns, labeling one column *Push* and the other *Pull*.

   Reading for a Purpose: Students finish reading the chapter in order to list:

   - What *pushed* immigrants from their homelands?
   - What *pulled* immigrants to the United States?

   Students use **Numbered Heads** to share their lists as you record their responses on chart paper.

Push	Pull
Rapid population growth in Europe	U.S. needed settlers and workers
No jobs	Opportunities to work
Famine	Plentiful food
Religious persecution	Freedom of religion
Political persecution	Political freedom
Closed society	Move upward in open society

Student Team Learning Activity – 25 minutes

Using primary documents to investigate the immigrant experience

1. Ask the students to imagine that they are newly arrived immigrants. Using **Roundtable**, teams create a list of difficulties to answer the following question.

Lesson 15   Immigrant Voice

- As immigrants, what difficulties might we have to overcome in America? (Different language, overcrowding, strangeness of food and customs, tenement life, large cities, little or no money, poorly paying jobs, frightened by the newness, homesickness, and so on)

2. Introduce the Student Team Learning Activity by sharing the following information about Mary Antin.

   Mary Antin, a thirteen-year-old Russian Jew, immigrated to the United States in 1894. She worked for women's rights and became a poet and an author. In 1911, she wrote an autobiography describing her immigration experiences. She called it *The Promised Land*. She remembered her parents' decision to go to America in the following way:

   > *So at last I was going to America! The boundaries burst. The arch of heaven soared. A million suns shone out for every star. The winds rushed in from outer space, roaring in my ears, "America! America!"*

   Explain to students that many immigrants thought that America was the Promised Land with streets paved with gold and cities filled with glorious opportunities. Refer to the line in the Lazarus' poem: "I lift my lamp beside the golden door . . ." For many immigrants their American dream came true, but not without hard work and sacrifice.

3. Distribute the Document Packet: *Immigrant Voices*. Teams divide the readings among their members and then share information from their individual readings with each other.

   Using the primary sources in the packet, teams further explore these questions:

   - What *pushed* immigrants from their homelands?

   - What *pulled* them to the United States?

   - Students add this information to their *Push-Pull* charts, and then discuss:

   - What did the immigrants expect to find in the United States? Describe some of their American Dreams.

   - How did the realities differ from the dreams?

   Circulate and Monitor: Visit each team as students use the Document Packet, discuss and answer the questions, and complete their charts.

4. Following their research, teams use **Numbered Heads** to share their responses to the questions with the class.

Discuss with students the reasons why the immigrants left their home countries and came to America according to the accounts in the Document Packet: *Immigrant Voices*:

> **Rene Dubos:** Unlimited possibilities in America
>
> **Swedish minister:** Poor can own their own homes, work their way up, and provide food for their families
>
> **Chinese Advertisement:** Great pay, large houses, fine food and clothing, money
>
> **Greek Advertisement:** Opportunity to send money home
>
> **Russian Jews:** Flee political terrorism and the massacre of Jewish people
>
> **Swede:** Escape poverty, find prosperity as a worker
>
> **Italian boy:** Adventure in an amazing land, money and life like the gentry, equality of opportunity to work way up in life, citizenship of common people, "In America everything was possible."
>
> **Englishman:** Escape poverty and hunger, find equality and liberty in a land where "no man is your superior"

Reflection and Review Activity – 5 minutes

1. The teams use **Think-Team-Share** to consider

   - What did the immigrants have in common with each other? With established Americans?

   - How did the immigrants differ from each other? From established Americans?

2. Use **Numbered Heads** for the teams to share their responses.

   Note to the Teacher: An additional resource for this lesson is the video series *Freedom: A History of US,* Episode Eight—Part Three: Freedom Seekers, Kunhardt Productions and Thirteen/WNET for PBS. Also explore the accompanying PBS Website: Freedom: A History of US @ http://www.pbs.org/wnet/historyofus/menu.html, especially the section for teachers.

Lesson 15   Immigrant Voice

Homework

Complete the Student Sheet: *Coming to America* and bring a small photograph or drawing of yourself to use during the Focus Activity in the next lesson.

Library/Media Resouces

Nonfiction

Immigrant Kids by Russell Freedman, Puffin Books

How the Other Half Lives by Jacob Riis, Penguin Classics

The Great Ancestor Hunt by Lila Pearl, Clarion Books

My Backyard History Book by David Weitzman, Brown Paper School Book Series

Laborers for Liberty: American Women 1865-1890 by Harriet Sigerman, Oxford University Press

Cobblestone Magazine

Chinese Americans

Greek Americans

Hispanic Americans

Irish Americans

Italian Americans

Japanese Americans

Jewish Americans

Polish Americans

Immigrants: Part I

Immigrants: Part II

CD Rom

Story of America 2: Immigration, National Geographic Society

Video

Celebrating Our Differences Video Series: Language, Race, and Religion, National Geographic Society

Freedom: A History of US, Episode Eight—Part Three, Kunhardt Productions and Thirteen/WNET for PBS

Connections

Math/Library — Students research and interpret statistics about immigration today and in the past and display that information on charts and graphs.

Research/Writing/Library — Students research the life and work of photographer Jacob Riis. Students write a biography of Riis or create a display of his photographs.

Language Arts — Students read excerpts from *How the Other Half Lives* by Jacob Riis. See the Web site for an online copy of the book.

Science — Students research the advances in transportation that shortened the length of the ocean voyage from Europe to America.

Library — Students search for the histories of other immigrants who contributed to American life (such as entertainers Harry Houdini, Irving Berlin, and Charles Chaplain). Many sports figures, artists, musicians, and actors were immigrants or came from immigrant families.

Lesson 16
Backlash
Chapter 23

Theme

Although most immigrants shared a common belief system and work ethic with established Americans, the newcomers faced strong anti-immigrant sentiment and prejudice and were on the bottom of the socio-economic scale.

Overview

Immigrants arrived in the United States through many different ports including Angel Island in San Francisco Bay, Galveston, New Orleans, Boston, Seattle, Detroit, and other cities. Nevertheless, one port of entry became synonymous with immigration: Ellis Island. As immigration burgeoned, Ellis Island became a small city complete with thirty-three buildings including a chapel, hospital, laundry room, waiting room, dormitory, money exchange office, and restaurants.

From the first immigrant to set foot on Ellis Island (a fifteen-year-old girl named Annie Moore from Ireland in 1892) until its closing in 1954, this small patch of land in New York Harbor was the main station through which hopeful newcomers were filtered. During its first thirty years of operation, ninety per cent of all immigrants came through Ellis Island—over sixteen million people. They came from over fifty countries, traveling in the packed, overcrowded holds of ships. Upon arrival, each passenger received a numbered tag, and then walked through the immigration station where officials with lists waited, watched, and judged.

Hopeful of admittance, the newcomers underwent scrutiny as inspectors looked for signs of contagious diseases and other health problems. After waiting in long lines, each immigrant faced authorities who asked approximately thirty questions in a two-minute period. Not only was the questioning fast and furious, but for many, the questions were in an unknown language—English. They were asked about job prospects, money, and their ultimate destinations.

This process intimidated most immigrants, many of whom had just survived a horrible journey packed together in the claustrophobic holds of ships. Unable to wash or properly take care of bodily needs, deprived of fresh air and exercise, and provided with poor food, many immigrants became seriously ill. During the 1800s, as many as one in ten passengers died during these nightmarish journeys. At the least, they suffered intense seasickness, as Leon Charles recounted in his journal:

> *At last the stairs were empty and I started up. At the same time a sick man started down. The poor fellow could not control his stomach and out and down it came . . . right down on me. . . .*

Although those who survived the journey then had to endure the intimidating inspection process at Ellis Island, most stood a good chance of entering the United States. Over ninety-eight percent of all applicants were ultimately admitted. Many newcomers left the inspection station bound for large cities such as Chicago or for farming communities in the Midwest, where other recent immigrants had settled. But almost a third of the immigrants stayed in New York City, packed into tenements and neighborhoods where foreign languages were more common than English.

Sometimes known as the "Ellis Island of the West," Angel Island, off the coast of San Francisco, served as the primary western point of entry for thirty years. Unlike Ellis Island, this immigration station also served as a detention center or temporary prison for thousands of Chinese immigrants.

As ships arrived in the harbor, immigration officials directed most Chinese immigrants to Angel Island. Here they were separated from their families and passed the days with enforced routines. The anxiety of waiting for the interrogation built. While they waited, many relieved their stress by writing poems on the wooden barracks walls. They carved the words or used pencils, paint, and brushes. In these poems, they found relief by expressing their emotions. One immigrant wrote,

> *Over a hundred poems are on the walls.*
> *Looking at them, they are all pining at the delayed process.*
> *What can one sad person say to another?*
> *Unfortunate travelers everywhere wish to commiserate. . . .*
> *Since ancient time, heroes often were the first ones to face adversity.*

In 1882—bowing to intense anti-immigration discrimination and fear, especially aimed at the Chinese—the United States passed its first immigration restriction law, the Chinese Exclusion Act, which denied entry to Chinese laborers.

Although public policy embraced the "teeming refuse" of foreign lands, the reality was somewhat more ambivalent. The strangeness of foreign customs and language, the cost of educating and Americanizing the immigrants and their children, the squalor and crime of the big city pockets of immigrants, and the willingness of the immigrant poor to work for a pittance created a serious backlash against immigration in a resurgence of nativism. Americans whose ancestors had been immigrants just generations before considered themselves the "true Americans" and treated newcomers with hostility. Although the ugliness of bigotry, racism, and anti-foreign sentiment in America has always existed paradoxically side-by-side with the promise of equality, freedom, and the opportunity to build a better life, most immigrants—through hard work and perseverance—managed to achieve that better life. Usually within a generation, each new wave of foreigners became assimilated Americans.

References

"Angel Island: Immigration Station." *Angel Island Association.* http://www.angelisland.org/immigr02.html. Access date January 1999.

Bettman, Otto. L. 1974. *The Good Old Days—They Were Terrible.* New York: Random House.

Bode, Janet. 1989. *New Kids in Town: Oral Histories of Immigrant Teens.* New York: Scholastic Inc.

Daniels, Roger. 2001. *American Immigration.* New York: Oxford University Press.

"Ellis Island History." *Ellis Island Immigration Museum.* http://www.ellisisland.com/indexHistory.htm. Access date January 1999.

Fleming, Maria. ed. 2000. *A Place at the Table: Struggles for Equality in America.* New York: Oxford University Press.

Greenwood, Janette Thomas. 2000. *The Gilded Age: A History in Documents.* New York: Oxford University Press.

Hoff, Rhoda. 1986. *America's Immigrants: Adventures in Eyewitness History.* New York: Henry Z. Walck.

Holt, Hamilton. ed. 1990. *The Life Stories of Undistinguished Americans.* New York: Routledge.

Marzio, Peter C. 1976. *A Nation of Nations: The People Who Came to America as Seen Through Objects and Documents at the Smithsonian Institution.* New York: Harper & Row, Publishers.

Muggamin, Howard. 1988. *The Jewish American.* New York: Chelsea House Publishers.

Perl, Lila. 1989. *The Great Ancestor Hunt: The Fun of Finding Out Who You Are.* New York: Clarion Books.

Perrin, Linda. 1980. *Coming to America: Immigrants from the Far East.* New York: Dell Publishing Co. Inc.

Rips, Gladys Nadler. 1981. *Coming to America: Immigrants from Southern Europe.* New York: Delacorte Press.

Riis, Jacob A. 1890. 1997 Reprint. *How the Other Half Lives.* New York: Penguin Classics.

Robbins, Albert. 1981. *Coming to America: Immigrants from Northern Europe.* New York: Delacorte Press.

Zinn, Howard. 1999. *A People's History of the United States: 1492-Present.* New York: HarperCollins Publishers.

Standards

Historical Thinking

The student will:

Historical Comprehension

- utilize visual and mathematical data presented in charts, Venn diagrams, and other graphic organizers
- draw upon visual, literary, and musical sources

Historical Analysis and Interpretation

- compare or contrast differing sets of ideas, values, personalities, behaviors, and institutions
- consider multiple perspectives
- analyze cause and effect relationships and multiple causation, including the importance of the individual, the influence of ideas, and the role of chance

Historical Research Capabilities

- obtain historical data

Analysis and Decision-Making

- identify issues and problems in the past

Content

The student will demonstrate understanding of:

Massive immigration after 1870 and new social patterns, conflicts, and ideas of national unity developed amid growing cultural diversity

- The sources and experiences of the new immigrants

  - distinguish between the "old" and "new" immigration in terms of its volume and the newcomers' ethnicity, religion, language, and place of origin
  - analyze the obstacles, opportunities, and contributions of different immigrant groups

Resources

For each student

Reconstructing America by Joy Hakim: Chapter 23, "More About Immigrants"

Homework assignment from Lesson 15

Photograph or drawing of self

Yarn

One or more pushpins or thumb tacks

Student Sheet: *Opposition to Immigration*

Notebook

For each team

Two copies of the Team Sheet: *Cartoon Analyzer*

One copy of the Team Sheets:
> *The Immigrant: The Stranger at our Gate*
>
> *Welcome*

For the teacher
Transparencies:
> *Immigrant Boy with Bundle*
>
> *Immigrants with Bundles*

For the classroom
Push-Pull chart from Lesson 15

World map

Overhead projector

Web sites
Immigration, Ellis Island @ http://cmp1.ucr.edu/exhibitions/immigration_id.html

Statue of Liberty Facts, News and Information @ http://www.endex.com/gf/buildings/liberty/liberty.html

How the Other Half Lives @ http://www.cis.yale.edu/amstud/inforev/riis/title.html

Chronology of Asian American History @ http://web.mit.edu/21h.153j/www/chrono.html

The Immigration Station at Angel Island @ http://www.angelisland.org/immig01.html

Freedom: A History of US @ The Lower East Side Tenement Museum

Virtual Tour @ The Immigrant Experience as Seen through the Eyes of NYC Youth @ http://www.tenement.org/immigrantexperience/

Vocabulary

Words to Remember
*immigrant — person who comes to a new country to live

*prejudice — opinion for or against someone without adequate reason

*discrimination — unjust treatment based on prejudice

*racism — prejudice against those who are of a different race

Know-Nothing Party — political party that was against Catholics and foreigners

Ku Klux Klan — anti-black and anti-Semitic hate group

Working Men's Party — anti-Asian hate group

exploit — to take advantage of

*Chinese Exclusion Act —1882 law that denied Chinese immigration to the United States

economic depression — time when a country's economy declines with widespread unemployment, low prices, and little business activity

*political cartoon — humorous way to present news or a viewpoint about a political figure or event

caricature — drawing that exaggerates personal characteristics

satire — use of sarcasm or irony to make fun of somebody or some event

People to Remember
Confucius — Chinese philosopher who taught ideas and ethics, many of which are similar to American ideals

Lesson 15   Backlash

The Lesson

Focus Activity – 10 minutes

Notes

1. Using the homework assignment from Lesson 15, the students share the contents of their immigrant bundles with their teammates and explain how they decided what items to include.

2. Show the Transparencies: *Immigrant Boy with Bundle* and *Immigrants with Bundles*. Ask the students to **Speculate**:

   - What do you think is in the bundles?

Teaching Activity – 20 minutes

Note to the Teacher: The next activity visually demonstrates the students' countries of origin. To make the best use of class time, the students do this activity, one at a time, while the class reads Chapter 23, "More About Immigrants" in *Reconstructing America*.

1. Students place their photographs (or drawings) of themselves around a world map. Then using the yarn and pushpins, they connect their photographs to the country(s) from which their ancestors originated. After students have completed the activity, the class discusses the resulting web—a graphic representation of their varied heritages—and its patterns of ancestries.

2. Using their *Push-Pull* charts from the previous lesson, the students briefly review the reasons that immigrants came to America and what they expected to find in their new homeland. Ask the students to **Speculate**:

   - Was the reality of life in America the same as the immigrants' dreams? Why or why not?

3. Briefly introduce the Vocabulary *Words and People to Remember*.

4. **Reading for a Purpose:** Students read silently or **Partner Read** Chapter 23, "More About Immigrants" in *Reconstructing America* in order to identify the reasons for

America's opposition to immigration in the late 1800s. As they read, the students record these reasons on their Student Sheets: *Opposition to Immigration*.

Opposition To Immigration

- Economic depression of the 1860s and 1870s
- Competition for jobs – immigrants willing to work for less pay
- Prejudice, racism, and discrimination
- Police and city services cost tax money
- Schools cost tax money
- Ku Klux Klan – anti-black, anti-Semitic hate group
- Chinese Exclusion Act of 1882
- Political Parties:

    Know Nothing – anti-Catholic, anti-foreign
    Workingman's Party – anti-Asian

Note to the Teacher: Individual students, one at a time, connect their pictures to the world map during this reading activity.

5. **Circulate and Monitor:** Visit each team as students read the chapter, identify the reasons for opposition to immigration, and complete their Student Sheets.

6. Use **Numbered Heads** to discuss the information on the Student Sheets: *Opposition to Immigration*. Ask the students to consider each opposition and decide

    - Is this particular objection to immigration still present in the United States today?

Student Team Learning Activity – 25 minutes

Analyzing a political cartoon

1. Distribute two copies of the Team Sheet: *Cartoon Analyzer* and a copy of each cartoon: *The Immigrant: The Stranger at our Gate* and *Welcome* to each team.

2. Review the purpose of political cartoons:

Lesson 16   Backlash

Cartoons have long been a method by which newspapers present a political viewpoint. Making fun of political figures and issues helps put them in perspective, and often gives the reader a humorous way to look at controversial events and ideas. Sometimes the cartoons illustrate an editorial viewpoint and can anger the reader. Political cartoons use *caricature* and *satire* to create humor. *Caricature* is the exaggeration of personal characteristics. *Satire* is the use of sarcasm or irony to make fun of somebody or some event. To understand a political cartoon the reader must first understand what the *symbols* represent and then try to understand the cartoon's overall *meaning*.

3. Briefly review the use of the *Cartoon Analyzer*.

4. Working in pairs, team members use the *Cartoon Analyzer* to identify the symbols and the meaning of their cartoon.

   Each pair shares its cartoon and analysis with the other team partnership.

5. **Circulate and Monitor:** Visit each team to help the students use the *Cartoon Analyzer* and to interpret the symbols and meaning of the cartoons.

6. Teams share their interpretations of the two cartoons using **Numbered Heads** and discuss the following question.

   - What do the cartoons communicate about many Americans' attitudes towards immigration?

Reflection and Review Activity – 5 minutes

1. Teams **Think-Team-Share:** Students discuss the following questions and support their answers with evidence from the lesson:

   - Why do you think many Americans opposed immigration in the mid-1800s?

   - Does anti-immigration sentiment exist in America today? Explain.

   - Are the reasons for this feeling the same as in the mid-1800s? Explain.

   - Do immigrants still come to America for the same reasons as in the mid-1800s? What are those reasons?

2. The teams use **Numbered Heads** to share their responses.

   Note to the Teacher: An additional resource for this lesson is the video series *Freedom: A History of US,* Episode Eight—Part Three: Freedom Seekers, Kunhardt Productions and Thirteen/WNET for PBS. Also explore the accompanying PBS Website: *Freedom: A History of US* @ http://www.pbs.org/wnet/historyofus/menu.html, especially the section for teachers.

Homework

Draw a political cartoon expressing your point of view about immigration today. Determine the message that your cartoon will convey and then choose the symbols and write a caption that will support its overall meaning.

Library/Media Resources

Nonfiction

Tales from Gold Mountain: Stories of the Chinese in the New World by Paul Yee, Macmillan

Angel Island Prisoner: 1922 by Helen Chetin, New Seed Press

Immigrant Kids by Russell Freedman, Puffin Books

How the Other Half Lives by Jacob Riis, Penguin Classics

The Great Ancestor Hunt by Lila Pearl, Clarion Books

My Backyard History Book by David Weitzman, The Brown Paper School Book Series

New Kids in Town: Oral Histories of Immigrant Teens by Janet Bode, Scholastic

Cobblestone Magazine

Chinese Americans

Immigrants: Part I

Immigrants: Part II

CD Rom

Story of America 2: Immigration, National Geographic Society

Video

Celebrating Our Differences Video Series: Language, Race, and Religion, National Geographic Society

Lesson 16   Backlash

Freedom: A History of US, Episode Eight—Part Three, Kunhardt
   Productions and Thirteen/WNET for PBS

Connection

Language Arts — Students read *Jar of Dreams* and/or *The Invisible Thread* by Yoshiko Uchida. Partner Discussion Guides are available for both novels from Talent Development Middle Schools, Johns Hopkins University.

Math/Library — Students analyze immigration statistics to determine the effect of the Chinese Exclusion Act in 1882. Students analyze how other measures to limit immigration affected these statistics. Students chart or graph those numbers.

Science/Library — Students research the disease tuberculosis, which caused new immigrants to be rejected and sent back to their homeland. What caused tuberculosis and why it was so feared? Students note today's reemergence of TB and why it is becoming resistant to medicines. (In part, this is due to people not finishing the full course of treatment. Why is it important to take all the pills in an antibiotic series?)

Library — Students research Ellis Island and Angel Island. The stories of both immigration centers and the newcomers who passed through them are extremely interesting. Web sites and print resources are available about each.

Library — Students research Chinese immigration or more recent Asian newcomers.

Art — Students create posters about specific groups of immigrants to America, such as the Germans, Chinese, or Irish. What customs, foods, terms, and other aspects of their heritage did these newcomers bring to the United States that became part of our heritage? Students plan a cultural celebration day to share customs, foods, and information.

Technology/Library — From what countries do most immigrants come today? Students research this question and the issue of illegal immigration in the United States today.

Lesson 17
Lee Yick Goes to Court
Chapters 24 and 25

Theme

Prejudice and discrimination against the Chinese in California led to a landmark Supreme Court decision in 1886 concerning two constitutional issues: the arbitrary enforcement of the law and the rights of aliens to equal treatment under the law.

Overview

In 1886, a Chinese immigrant in California appealed a local court decision that had found him guilty of operating a laundry in a wooden building and had shut down his business. Although clearly guilty, Lee Yick appealed because authorities invoked the law only against Chinese laundries and not against those operated by whites—except in the case of one woman. Eventually the case went to the Supreme Court, which considered two basic constitutional questions: Do the police have the right to enforce a law arbitrarily? Should the law treat aliens the same way that it treats American citizens? The Supreme Court ruled no to the first question and yes to the second, and thus further defined equality under the law for all persons—citizens or aliens—under the jurisdiction of the United States.

When America's founding fathers wrote the Constitution as the supreme law of the land, they knew the United States would change through the years. With this in mind, they created a government that could respond to change and a Supreme Court to interpret and uphold the rights and liberties guaranteed by the Constitution.

Underlying the difficult decisions made by the justices throughout the years is the Supreme Court's most important function—acting as the guardian of the Constitution. The justices must interpret the Constitution in a way that safeguards the basic rights of all Americans. The Supreme Court justices have the power to overrule an act of Congress, a presidential order, or a state law if they determine that it violates any part of the Constitution. By responding to these challenges, the Supreme Court has kept the Constitution current.

At the highest level of our judicial system, the Supreme Court hears cases from state or federal courts that have been appealed because one of the parties involved was dissatisfied with the decision, as in the case of *Yick Wo v. Hopkins*. Cases begin in the Supreme Court only if they involve ambassadors, foreign representatives, or a state government. Justices select cases that they feel deal with constitutional issues or with disputes between states or a state and the federal government.

Cases are named for the parties involved, with the name of the party that lost the case in the lower courts coming first—in this case, *Yick Wo v. Hopkins*. After hearing arguments, the justices vote on the case, and a simple majority rules. The Court's decisions can only be overruled by a vote of the American people amending the Constitution or by the court itself.

The president nominates Supreme Court justices, selecting men and women he feels are qualified and who often reflect his political and social views. The Senate questions the nominees to determine their suitability, then votes to accept or reject them. Over the years, twenty-seven nominees have been rejected. The Constitution lists no specific requirements for being a justice, but by custom, all justices to date have been United States citizens with some legal background—lawyers, judges from lower courts, governors, members of Congress, members of the president's cabinet, and even one former president—William Howard Taft.

Since the Constitution does not stipulate how many justices shall serve, the number on the Court has changed many times; but since 1869, it has remained at nine members. The president nominates the chief justice, usually from among the associate judges, and the Senate confirms him or her.

A justice serves until he or she resigns or dies but can be removed by impeachment on charges brought by the House of Representatives and convicted by a two-thirds vote of the Senate. Because the justices cannot be fired, they are not subject to pressure to agree with the president or Congress. They can be more impartial if their jobs are not threatened by their decisions.

The Supreme Court has guided the United States legal system for longer than two hundred years, and the court's decisions have been important in creating a government that could respond to changing times and expanding beliefs about Constitutional rights and liberties.

References

"About the Supreme Court." *Supreme Court of the United States.* http://www.supremecourtus.gov/about/about.html. Access date December 1998.

Foner, Eric. 1999. *The Story of American Freedom.* New York: W.W. Norton & Company.

McClenaghan, William A. 1999. *Magruder's American Government* New York: Prentice Hall.

Monk, Linda. 1995. *The Bill of Rights: A User's Guide.* Alexandria, Virginia: Close Up Publishing.

Patrick, John J. 2001. *The Supreme Court of the United States.* New York: Oxford University Press.

"Supreme Court of the United States." *Encarta.* http://encarta.msn.com/encyclopedia_761574302/Supreme_Court.html. Access date December 1998.

"Yick Wo v. Hopkins, Sheriff; Wo Lee v. Hopkins, Sheriff, Supreme Court of The United States 118 U.S. 356; 6 S. Ct. 1064; 1886." *Bills of Rights Comparative Law Materials.* http://www.hrcr.org/safrica/equality/yick_wo_hopkins.html. Access date December 1998.

"*Yick Wo* v. *Hopkins* (1886)." *Basic Readings in U.S. Democracy.* http://usinfo.state.gov/usa/infousa/facts/democrac/64.htm. Access date December 1998.

"U.S. Supreme Court: *Yick Wo* v. *Hopkins*, 118 U.S. 356 (1886)." *FindLaw.* http://caselaw.lp.findlaw.com/cgi-bin/getcase.pl?court=US&vol=118&invol=356&navby=case&linkurl=http://www.aclumontana.org/rights/yickwo.html&graphurl=http://www.aclumontana.org/rights/images/backlink.jpg. Access date December 1998.

Standards

Historical Thinking

The student will

Historical Comprehension

- identify the central question(s) the historical narrative addresses

- draw upon visual, literary, and musical sources

Historical Analysis and Interpretation

- consider multiple perspectives

- analyze cause and effect relationships and multiple causation, including the importance of the individual, the influence of ideas, and the role of chance

Historical Research Capabilities

- obtain historical data

Analysis and Decision-Making

- identify issues and problems in the past

- formulate a position or course of action on an issue

Content

The student will demonstrate understanding of

Massive immigration after 1870 and new social patterns, conflicts, and ideas of national unity developed amid growing cultural diversity

- The sources and experiences of the new immigrants

  - analyze the obstacles, opportunities, and contributions of different immigrant groups

- Social Darwinism, race relations, and the struggle for equal rights and opportunities

  - analyze political, social, and economic discrimination against African Americans, Asian Americans, and Hispanic Americans in different regions of the country

Resources

For each student

Reconstructing America by Joy Hakim: Chapter 24, "The Strange Case of the Chinese Laundry" and Chapter 25, "Going to Court"

Student Sheet: *Flowchart of the Case*

Notebook

For each team

Optional Team Sheet: *Beat the Clock*

For the teacher

Transparency: *Flowchart of the Case*

Chart paper

Markers

For the classroom

Overhead projector

Web sites

Immigration, Ellis Island @ http://cmp1.ucr.edu/exhibitions/immigration_id.html

Statue of Liberty Facts, News and Information @ http://www.endex.com/gf/buildings/liberty/liberty.html

How the Other Half Lives @ http://www.cis.yale.edu/amstud/inforev/riis/title.html

Chronology of Asian American History @ http://web.mit.edu/21h.153j/www/chrono.html

The Immigration Station at Angel Island @ http://www.angelisland.org/immig01.html

Freedom: A History of US @ http://www.pbs.org/wnet/historyofus/menu.html

Vocabulary

Words to Remember

ordinance — local law

*naturalized citizen — immigrant who becomes a United States citizen

*nativism — policy of favoring people born in the United States over immigrants

racism — prejudice or hatred against those of another race

civil court — court that tries cases in which no criminal laws have been broken

criminal court — court that tries cases in which criminal laws have been broken

local court — first lower court that tries civil and criminal cases

state court — court that listens to appeals from the local court, and where a judge determines if justice has been served

*****Supreme Court** — highest court, hears appeals from local and state courts and interprets and upholds the rights and liberties guaranteed by the Constitution

*****jury** — group of citizens who listens to the evidence and decides guilt or innocence

*****defendant** — person on trial

*****prosecutor** — person bringing charges against the defendant

witnesses — persons who have information about the case and are called to court to testify

*****appeal** — to take a case to a higher court if not satisfied with the decision of a lower court

brief — written legal argument

*****aliens** — persons who live in the United States but are not citizens

People to Remember

*****Lee Yick** — owner of a Chinese laundry whose court case decided the issues of the rights of aliens and the arbitrary enforcement of laws

The Lesson

Focus Activity – 5 minutes

1. Students share their cartoons from their homework assignment with teammates or display them in the classroom.

2. Discuss the cartoons on page 121 and 122 of *Reconstructing America*.
   - According to the cartoons, how did some Americans feel about Chinese immigrants? (Many Americans—especially in California where most Chinese settled—opposed Chinese immigration, were racist or prejudiced against the Chinese, and would not support Chinese businesses.)

3. **Reading for a Purpose**: Read and discuss the sidebar poem on page 121 of *Reconstructing America*.
   - How did many of the Chinese feel about emigrating to the United States? (Although they were sad at leaving family and friends, many Chinese were happy to be going to America where they believed that hard work would provide them with opportunity and a better life for their families.)

4. Ask the students to **Think-Team-Share**:
   - What might happen when these two viewpoints come into contact? (Answers will vary, but students should realize that many Chinese immigrants found the reality of living in America to be different from their expectations and experienced discrimination and racism.)

   Teams use **Numbered Heads** to share their responses with the class.

Teaching Activity – 20 minutes

1. Build on the preceding discussion to introduce the "Strange Case of the Chinese Laundry," Chapter 24 of *Reconstructing America*.

Notes

2. Introduce the first four terms in the Vocabulary *Words to Remember.*

3. **Reading for a Purpose:** The students read silently or **Partner Read** Chapter 24 and use **Think-Team-Share** to discuss the "Strange Case of the Chinese Laundry." Guide the discussion with these questions written on chart paper or the chalkboard:

   > - Why was the owner of the Chinese Laundry arrested? (He was operating a laundry in a wooden building and the city ordinance stipulated that all laundries must be in brick buildings.)
   >
   > - Why were the Chinese in America not citizens? (A law passed in 1790 said that only white people could become naturalized citizens.)
   >
   > - The Chinese had clearly broken the law, so why did they feel that they were treated unfairly by the law and the courts? (The sheriff arrested almost all the Chinese but only one white owner—a woman—so the law was being applied in a discriminatory way.)

   Ask the students to **Predict:** What will the Chinese laundry owners do next? Why? (Opinions will vary.)

   Circulate and Monitor: Visit each team as the students read the chapter and discuss the questions.

4. Distribute and explain the Student Sheet: *Flowchart of the Case*.

   After the teams use **Numbered Heads** to share their answers to the preceding questions, each student completes the first section of the flowchart. Be sure the students understand the essential elements of the case: Who was Lee Yick and what was his case? Who was Hopkins and what was his case?

   Circulate and Monitor: Check the students' work as they complete the first section of the flowchart.

5. Direct the teams to read and discuss the "Exclusive Rights" sidebar on page 125 of Chapter 24 in *Reconstructing America*. Be sure the students understand the conflicting ideas concerning Chinese immigration and the roles of nativism and racism in the treatment of Chinese immigrants.

Student Team Learning Activity – 25 minutes

Identifying the importance of a Supreme Court decision

1. Introduce Chapter 25, "Going to Court" in *Reconstructing America* by having the students share their earlier predictions:

    - What will the Chinese laundry owners do next and why?

2. Teams use **Think-Team-Share** to analyze the cartoons on pages 126, 127, and 128 of *Reconstructing America:*

    - What symbols are used in each of the cartoons?

    - What is the message or meaning of each cartoon?

3. Students consider the message of the cartoons and the essential elements of *Yick Wo v. Hopkins* to identify two basic unanswered questions in the case that go beyond the question of guilt:

    - Do the police have the right to enforce a law arbitrarily?

    - Should the law treat aliens the same way that it treats American citizens?

    Students refer to these questions on the Student Sheet: *Flowchart of the Case*.

    Explain that these are *constitutional* questions about equality under the law and the rights of persons within the United States who are not citizens. Ask the students:

    - In America, who decides the answers to constitutional questions? (Supreme Court)

4. Discuss the purpose and function of the Supreme Court with the students using information in the Overview. Emphasize the role of the Supreme Court to interpret and uphold the rights and liberties guaranteed by the Constitution and to hear cases appealed from state or federal courts because one of the parties involved was dissatisfied with the decision of a lower court.

    Ask the students to **Predict:**

    - Why might the case of *Yick Wo v. Hopkins* be heard by the Supreme Court? (Dissatisfaction of the defendant with the verdict and the question of unfair application of the law)

5. **Reading for a Purpose:** Guide the students with reading Chapter 25, "Going to Court," in *Reconstructing America* by having them pause at the appropriate places to define the court-related vocabulary, identify and discuss each step of the case, and record that information on the Student Sheet: *Flowchart of the Case*.

> Arrest
>
> Trial in Local Court
>
> Appeal
>
> Trial in California Supreme Court
>
> Appeal
>
> Trial in United States Supreme Court

Note to the Teacher: Define the court-related vocabulary by discussing those words and adding their meanings to the vocabulary chart.

6. Ask the students to identify the importance of the Supreme Court decision in the case of *Yick Wo v. Hopkins* as it relates to the two constitutional issues.

   Review the following information with the students:

   - How is the purpose of the Supreme Court different from the purpose of the local court? (The local court determines guilt or innocence, whereas the Supreme Court considers the larger question of constitutionality and rights under the law.)

   - Do you agree or disagree with the ruling of the Supreme Court in the case of *Yick Wo v. Hopkins*? Why? Support your viewpoint.

   - Do you agree with the lower court that Lee Yick was guilty of breaking the law? Support your viewpoint with evidence.

   - What do you think happened to the Chinese laundries after the Supreme Court decision? What do you think happened to the non-Chinese laundries? Explain your viewpoints.

   - What do you think would be fair and equal to all owners of laundries and still protect the community against fire? Support your viewpoint with evidence.

7. **Optional Activity:** If time permits, the teams use the Team Sheet: *Beat the Clock*. Can the teams beat the clock by accurately matching the legal terms with the correct definitions within a specific time limit?

Answer Sheet

civil court — court that tries cases in which no criminal laws have been broken

criminal court — court that tries cases in which criminal laws have been broken

local court — first local (lower) court to try civil or criminal cases

state court — court that hears appeals from the local court; judge determines if justice has been served

Supreme Court — highest court, hears appeals from local and state courts and interprets and upholds the rights and liberties guaranteed by the Constitution

jury — group of citizens who listen to the evidence and decide guilt or innocence

defendant — person on trial

prosecutor — person bringing charges against the defendant

witness — person who has information about the case

appeal — to take a case to a higher court if not satisfied with the decision

brief — written legal argument

alien — person who is not a citizen

Reflection and Review Activity – 5 minutes

1. Ask the teams to consider the relationship among the following:
   - The message of the cartoon on page 126 of *Reconstructing America*

Lesson 17   Lee Yick Goes to Court

- The decision of the Supreme Court in the case of *Yick Wo v. Hopkins*

- These words of Carl Schurz: *"Equality of rights . . . is the great moral element of a true democracy."*

2. Teams **Think-Team-Share**:

   - How are the three connected?

   - How are they connected to these words of Frederick Douglass: *"No man can put a chain about the ankle of his fellow man without at last finding the other end fastened about his own neck."*

   - To what inequality was Douglass referring?

   - How might the cartoon, the Supreme Court decision, and the words of Schurz and Douglass apply to racism in any form?

   - How might the three apply to racism in the United States today?

Note to the Teacher: An additional resource for this lesson is the video series Freedom: A History of US, Episode Eight—Part Four: The Strange Case of the Chinese Laundry, Kunhardt Productions and Thirteen/WNET for PBS. Also explore the accompanying PBS Website: Freedom: A History of US @ http://www.pbs.org/wnet/historyofus/menu.html, especially the section for teachers.

Homework

What do you think?

Are immigrants or aliens today free from racism and inequality under the law in the United States? Draw a political cartoon expressing your viewpoint. Support your viewpoint with evidence.

Library/Media Resources

Nonfiction

Landmark Supreme Court Cases by Don Lawson, Enslow Publishers, Inc.

Famous Supreme Court Cases by Andrew David, Lerner Publications

The Supreme Court by Ann E. Weiss, Enslow Publishers

The Supreme Court by Leon Friedman, Chelsea House Publications

Angel Island Prisoner: 1922 by Helen Chetin, New Seed Press

New Kids in Town: Oral Histories of Immigrant Teens by Janet Bode, Scholastic

Cobblestone Magazine

Chinese Americans

Immigrants: Part I

Immigrants: Part II

CD Rom

Story of America 2: Immigration, National Geographic Society

Video

Celebrating Our Differences Video Series: Language, Race, and Religion, National Geographic Society

Freedom: A History of US, Episode Eight—Part Four, Kunhardt Productions and Thirteen/WNET for PBS

Connections

Language Arts — Students read *Jar of Dreams* and/or *The Invisible Thread* by Yoshiko Uchida or *Dragonwings* by Lawrence Yep. Partner Discussion Guides are available for all three novels from Talent Development Middle Schools, CSOS, Johns Hopkins University.

Library — Students research some other important Supreme Court Cases (such as Dred Scott, *Brown v. Board of Education*, *Miranda v. Arizona*). Were any decisions controversial? What decisions were overturned by a later Supreme Court? How does the composition of the justices and the culture of the time affect Supreme Court decisions?

Library — Students do a comparative study of the Supreme Court at its beginning and today.

Writing/Library — Students write short biographies about some famous Supreme Court justices such as Sandra Day O'Connor, Roger Taney, Oliver Wendell Holmes, Jr., William H. Taft, William Douglas, Abe Fortas, Byron White, or Thurgood Marshall.

Lesson 18
The American Dream
Chapter 28

Theme

In her autobiography *The Promised Land*, Mary Antin speaks of the hopes, hardships, and dreams shared by many immigrants in the late 1800s.

Overview

In the late 1800s and early 1900s, the massive waves of immigrants from increasingly "foreign" cultures aroused deep distrust, fear, and antagonism in many Americans. As far as they were concerned, the newcomers took jobs from natives; cost tax dollars for schools, services, and police; changed the ethnic look of America; and contributed little or nothing to the nation. Over and over as former immigrants were gradually assimilated, they in turn reacted negatively to other newcomers.

Like Mary Antin's family, most newly arrived immigrants settled in large cities where there were jobs and large numbers of other foreigners. By the turn of the century, immigrant populations concentrated in four of America's largest cities—New York, Boston, Pittsburgh, and Chicago. Once farmers in their homelands, these immigrants had little money to buy farms or expensive farming equipment, and furthermore, farming techniques in America were quite different from those in Europe. So they became city dwellers, living in tenements and working in factories. Irish Catholics and Jews preferred the city because it provided a chance to worship with others of their religion without censure. Jewish people, often fleeing centuries of oppression and persecution, also found that cities afforded them the opportunity to create a small society of their own that emphasized religion, community, and education.

Although America has always been a nation of immigrants, its comfort with newcomers has been ambiguous at best, and its actions too often racist and discriminatory. Recent immigrants still face a hundred-year movement to close America's doors perpetuated by the children and grandchildren of yesterday's immigrants. Janet Bode in *New Kids in Town* observes:

> Once inside, some people develop a kind of collective amnesia, forgetting their own immigrant roots. We forget that our country's power and beauty stems from the very fact that we are a collection of different cultures.

The United States continues to be a nation of immigrants with a national make-up that is constantly changing. For our newest wave of immigrants—as for those of the past—we offer a land of opportunity and a chance to attain their American dreams. Like their predecessors in the mid-1800s, the immigrants of today take the same gamble when they set sail for the Promised Land.

References

Antin, Mary. 1912. 1997 Reprint. *The Promised Land*. New York: Penguin USA.

Bettman, Otto. L. 1974. *The Good Old Days—They Were Terrible*. New York: Random House.

Bode, Janet. 1989. *New Kids in Town: Oral Histories of Immigrant Teens.* New York: Scholastic Inc.

Daniels, Roger. 2001. *American Immigration.* New York: Oxford University Press.

Fleming, Maria. ed. 2000. *A Place at the Table: Struggles for Equality in America.* New York: Oxford University Press.

Greenwood, Janette Thomas. 2000. *The Gilded Age: A History in Documents.* New York: Oxford University Press.

Hoff, Rhoda. 1986. *America's Immigrants: Adventures in Eyewitness History.* New York: Henry Z. Walck.

Marzio, Peter C. 1976. *A Nation of Nations: The People Who Came to America as Seen Through Objects and Documents at the Smithsonian Institution.* New York: Harper & Row, Publishers.

Muggamin, Howard. 1988. *The Jewish American.* New York: Chelsea House Publishers.

Perl, Lila. 1989. *The Great Ancestor Hunt: The Fun of Finding Out Who You Are.* New York: Clarion Books.

Reuben, Paul P. "Chapter 6: Late Nineteenth Century—Mary Antin (1881-1949)." *PAL: Perspectives in American Literature: A Research and Reference Guide.* http://www.csustan.edu/english/reuben/pal/chap6/antin.html. Access date January 1999.

Riis, Jacob A. 1890. 1997 Reprint. *How the Other Half Lives.* New York: Penguin Classics.

Standards

Historical Thinking

The student will

Historical Comprehension

- reconstruct the literal meaning of a historical passage
- identify the central question(s) the historical narrative addresses
- draw upon visual, literary, and musical sources

Historical Analysis and Interpretation

- consider multiple perspectives
- analyze cause and effect relationships and multiple causation, including the importance of the individual, the influence of ideas, and the role of chance

Historical Research Capabilities

- obtain historical data

Analysis and Decision-Making

- identify issues and problems in the past

Content

The student will demonstrate understanding of

Massive immigration after 1870 and new social patterns, conflicts, and ideas of national unity developed amid growing cultural diversity

- The sources and experiences of the new immigrants
    - distinguish between the "old" and "new" immigration in terms of its volume and the newcomers' ethnicity, religion, language, and place of origin
    - analyze the obstacles, opportunities, and contributions of different immigrant groups
    - evaluate how Catholic and Jewish newcomers responded to discrimination and internal divisions in their new soundings
- Social Darwinism, race relations, and the struggle for equal rights and opportunities
    - analyze political, social, and economic discrimination against African Americans, Asian Americans, and Hispanic Americans in different regions of the country

Lesson 18   The American Dream

Resources

For each student
Reconstructing America by Joy Hakim: Chapter 28, "Mary in the Promised Land"

Push-Pull chart from Lessons 15-16

Notebook

For each team
Document Packet: *New Kids In Town*

For the teacher
Transparency: *"The New Colossus"*

For the classroom
Overhead projector

Web sites
Immigration, Ellis Island @ http://cmp1.ucr.edu/exhibitions/immigration_id.html

Statue of Liberty Facts, News and Information @ http://www.endex.com/gf/buildings/liberty/liberty.html

How the Other Half Lives @ http://ww.cis.yale.edu/amstud/inforev/riis/title.html

Freedom: A History of US @ http://www.pbs.org/wnet/historyofus/menu.html

The Lower East Side Tenement Museum Virtual Tour @ http://www.tenement.org/Virtual_Tour/index_virtual.html

The Immigrant Experience as Seen through the Eyes of NYC Youth @ http://www.tenement.org/immigrantexperience/

Vocabulary

Words to Remember
Gentile — non-Jewish person

***Promised Land** — name given to America by immigrants

***American Dream** — goal or wish that will come true by living in America

pale — visible or invisible boundaries

People to Remember
***Mary Antin** — young Jewish girl who emigrated from Russia to the United States and whose autobiography expresses the hopes, hardships, and dreams of immigrants

The Lesson

Focus Activity – 5 minutes

1. The students read the title of Chapter 28, "Mary in the Promised Land" in *Reconstructing America*. Ask the students to **Speculate**:

   - What is a "Promised Land"?
   - Where does the term Promised Land originate?
   - What is the specific Promised Land in the title?
   - Why do you think immigrants called America the Promised Land?

2. If necessary, explain that the term "The Promised Land" originates in the Bible when Moses led the Hebrews from slavery in Egypt to a fertile land that they believed had been promised to them by God. Connect this event to the longing of immigrants for a land where they could create a good life for themselves and their families, and where they could enjoy religious, political, and economic freedom.

Teaching Activity – 25 minutes

1. Introduce Mary Antin, who emigrated from Russia to the United States in the late 1800s. Examine and discuss the photographs and illustrations in Chapter 28, "Mary in the Promised Land" in *Reconstructing America* to set the stage for reading about Mary and her writing.

2. During this introduction, invite the students to share their stories of family or friends who immigrated to the United States:

   - What was their old home country like?
   - What was their primary reason for immigrating to America?
   - Were their expectations of American life different from what they found here?
   - What was the most difficult adjustment for them?
   - What was the best thing about their new life in America?

Notes

Lesson 18   The American Dream

3. **Reading for a purpose:** The students read silently or **Partner Read** pages 140 and 141 of Chapter 28 in *Reconstructing America* to share Mary Antin's story with classmates.

   Write each question on a separate strip of paper and assign one question to each team:

   - Why did Mary Antin write of her life in Russia, "I began life in the middle ages." When were the actual Middle Ages or medieval times?

   - What impact did the *pale* have on Mary's life? What does it mean to be "beyond the pale"?

   - What does it mean to be a Jew? A Gentile? What relationship existed between the Jews and the Gentiles in Mary's village?

   - What events changed Mary's life in Russia?

   - What was school like in Mary's village? What were the educational limitations for Mary in Russia?

   - What did Mary most desire and why?

   - What is meant by the American Dream? What was Mary Antin's American Dream?

   Circulate and Monitor: Visit each team as the students read the chapter and discuss their team's question.

4. Use **Numbered Heads** for each team to report the answer to their question to the class. As the students share their answers and discuss Mary's life in Russia, use a web format to record and organize information and ideas on the chalkboard.

5. **Reading for a Purpose:** Students continue reading Mary's story on pages 142 and 143 of *Reconstructing America* in order to describe

   - What was it like for Mary, her mother, and her siblings to leave Russia?

   - What new, strange experiences did Mary and her family have when they arrived in America?

   Discuss the questions with the students and continue to add information to the web organizer.

6. **Reading for a Purpose:** Students finish reading pages 144 and 145 of *Reconstructing America* and then discuss the following questions.

- What did Mary consider the most important privilege that America offered?

- Mary says that her first day at school was so important to her because of "the years I had waited, the road I had come, and the conscious ambitions I entertained." What did Mary mean by each of those three reasons?

Continue the discussion with the students and add information to the web organizer.

7. Students use **Think-Team-Share** to ponder

   - What was Mary Antin's American Dream?

   - What other American Dreams have immigrants had? Encourage students to refer to the information on their *Push-Pull* charts from Lessons 14-16.

   - How did many immigrants make their personal American Dream a reality?

   - Do you have an American dream? What is your American Dream?

Student Team Learning Activity – 25 minutes

Using primary sources to investigate the experiences of today's teenage immigrants

1. Student use **Think-Team-Share** to **Speculate** about today's teenage immigrants:

   - Do young immigrants today have American Dreams?

   - What do you think their dreams are?

   - Do young immigrants today leave their home countries and come to America for the same reasons as in the past?

   - What are those reasons?

   - Do young immigrants today face prejudice, racism, or antagonism from established Americans?

   - What do you think are some of those experiences?

2. Introduce present day immigration and distribute a Document Packet: *New Kids In Town* to each team. Each team member reads one of the first person accounts of present-day immigrant teens.

3. Teammates share the stories of their teens with each other. Then the team decides:

   - Why did the teens or their families leave their home countries?

   - What difficulties do these new immigrants face in the United States today?

   - Do these immigrants have their own American Dreams? What are they?

   Circulate and Monitor: Visit each team to help students read and discuss the primary sources.

4. With the students, summarize the immigrant experiences of today's teens as depicted in the first person accounts and connect those with Mary Antin's experiences.

Reflection and Review Activity – 5 minutes

1. Using the Transparency: *"The New Colossus,"* ask the teams to **Think-Team-Share**:

   - How might Mary Antin react to these lines?

   - How might Lee Yick react to these lines?

   - How might each of the immigrant teens today react to these lines?

   - Do you agree or disagree that America was the Promised Land for immigrants in the 1880s? Support your opinion with evidence.

   - Do you agree or disagree that America is the Promised Land for immigrants today? Support your opinion with evidence.

   Note to the Teacher: An additional resource for this lesson is the video series Freedom: A History of US, Episode Eight—Part Five: This Land is Your Land, Kunhardt Productions and Thirteen/WNET for PBS. Also explore the accompanying PBS Website: Freedom: A History of US @ http://www.pbs.org/wnet/historyofus/menu.html, especially the section for teachers.

Homework

Are immigrants today free from racism and inequality under the law in the United States? Draw a political cartoon expressing your viewpoint. Support your viewpoint with evidence.

Or

Imagine yourself as the boy or girl in one of the photographs on pages 144 and 145 of *Reconstructing America*. Write about your experience using details from the photograph.

Library/Media Resources

Non-Fiction

Immigrant Kids by Russell Freedman, Puffin Books

How the Other Half Lives by Jacob Riis, Penguin Classics

The Great Ancestor Hunt by Lila Pearl, Clarion Books

My Backyard History Book by David Weitzman, The Brown Paper School Book Series

New Kids in Town: Oral Histories of Immigrant Teens by Janet Bode, Scholastic, Inc.

The Promised Land by Mary Antin, Penguin USA

Cobblestone Magazine

Chinese Americans

Immigrants: Part I

Immigrants: Part II

CD Rom

Story of America 2: Immigration, National Geographic Society

Video

Celebrating Our Differences Video Series: Language, Race, and Religion, National Geographic Society

Freedom: A History of US, Episode Eight—Part Five, Kunhardt Productions and Thirteen/WNET for PBS

Connections

Expressive Arts/Library — Students read *New Kids in Town: Oral Histories of Immigrant Teens* by Janet Bode and create a dramatic presentation highlighting the stories of other immigrant teens.

Music — Students explore the ethnic music and folk dances of various immigrant groups that have settled in the United States.

Local History — Students plan and sponsor a cultural heritage fair and invite the community to showcase food, customs, music, and dance of immigrant groups in the local neighborhood.

Math/Library — Students research contemporary immigration statistics and create charts and graphs to display that information

Technology — Student use the web site to take a virtual tour of a New York City tenement house.

Lesson 19
A Tea Party
Chapter 26

Theme

In 1869—before national woman suffrage—Wyoming territory granted women the right to vote and hold office. Eighteen years later Wyoming stood by that decision when the territory joined the Union, demanding that the women retain their franchise.

Overview

Today in every election from the local to the national level, women cast their votes for representatives who will make laws and run the government. Most women voters—as well as the persons for whom they vote—take the right of women to participate in the voting process for granted. But in reality, woman suffrage in the United States was a long, hard-fought battle, which began in the 1830s and ended with the ratification of the Nineteenth Amendment in 1920.

At the time of its writing, the Constitution granted the right to vote only to men who were white, over the age of twenty-one, and owned property. A lengthy, difficult struggle ensued for those who were excluded—poor whites, Native Americans, African Americans, and women—to secure voting rights and, in a larger sense, make America a more democratic nation.

Although voices for women's rights and woman suffrage spoke out—especially in connection with the abolition movement of the 1830s—voting rights for women became a significant movement in 1848 during the Seneca Falls Convention. The reality of a national amendment to grant woman suffrage took seventy years—until the ratification of the Nineteenth Amendment in 1920. As activist Carrie Chapman Catt observed,

"Young suffragists who helped forge the last links of that chain were not born when it began. Old suffragists who forged the first links were dead when it ended."

This generations-long struggle involved countless people working in many different organizations with various ideas and approaches. Men and women who believed in and worked for woman suffrage faced ridicule, hostility, and violence. At first considered a radical proposal that seemed to threaten the very foundations of family life and social order, woman suffrage moved with unsteady progress through decades of social change to become an accepted political reality.

The beginnings of woman suffrage grew out of the abolition movement of the 1830s through the 1860s. Sarah and Angelina Grimke—sisters who grew up on a South Carolina plantation—traveled north to talk with women about the evils of slavery, became Quakers, and joined Lucretia Mott (herself a Quaker minister) in eventually addressing anti-slavery rallies. Attracting the attention of the press and religious leaders, opponents harshly criticized the women for their improper conduct of speaking to audiences that included men, and blacks and whites who sat beside each other. Although they suffered indignities, harassment, threats, and danger, Mott and the

Grimke sisters continued their antislavery activities.

In 1840, Lucretia Mott was elected as one of six female delegates to the World Anti-Slavery Convention in London, where she met Elizabeth Cady Stanton. The women delegates were refused participation in the meeting because, as they were informed, it was for men only. Mott and Stanton, outraged at the unfairness of antislavery workers who, of all people, were treating women as inferior persons, vowed to hold a women's rights meeting when they returned home. Eight years later, that first women's rights convention drew an amazing three hundred women and a few dozen men. At the convention, Stanton read a "Declaration of Sentiments," which stated that women were equal to men and should have the same rights and responsibilities in society, and for the first time, officially raised the radical idea that women should have the right to vote.

From that time until the passage of the Thirteenth Amendment outlawing slavery after the Civil War, the women's rights movement allied itself closely with the abolitionist movement. The American Equal Rights Association, organized by Susan B. Anthony, worked to obtain civil rights for all women and black men. But the Fourteenth Amendment, which established citizenship for all persons born in the United States, implied that all males were citizens and could vote but that women could be denied the vote.

The Fifteenth Amendment brought a setback: it assured the right to vote for black men, but not for women—black or white. Many black men agreed with Frederick Douglass—a long time supporter of woman suffrage—who now argued for quick passage of the amendment to help protect black men from a backlash of violence, including lynching. Some black women who had worked for both the abolitionist and suffrage movements found themselves torn between loyalty to their race or to their gender. Many white women could not support a voting rights amendment that ignored women and did not extend suffrage to all adults. These differences caused a split in the American Equal Rights Association, and many black women left the women's rights movement.

In 1869, Susan B. Anthony and Elizabeth Cady Stanton organized the National Woman Suffrage Association (NWSA) to secure a constitutional amendment that would give all women the right to vote. The organization also fought for other women's issues such as property rights for women and improved working conditions.

That same year, the American Woman Suffrage Association (AWSA)—a more conservative organization led by Julia Ward Howe and Lucy Stone—chose to pursue woman suffrage through smaller, state referenda campaigns instead of a Constitutional amendment. Unlike Anthony's and Stanton's organization, the AWSA avoided involvement in other women's issues.

These two suffrage associations worked independently for the next thirty years. Both had very limited success—only Colorado and Idaho passed state referendums, and although the Woman Suffrage Amendment was introduced in every session of Congress from 1868 on, it never became a reality. In 1890 the two groups rejoined under Stanton, dropped the women's rights issues, and concentrated on securing woman suffrage through both a constitutional amendment and state campaigns for the next twenty-two years.

In the midst of this, many new territories granted women the right to vote in local elections as an encouragement for women to move west where they would have more rights than in the conservative East. When Wyoming Territory applied for statehood in

1889, Congress wanted it to discontinue female voting rights as many other territories had done. The Wyoming state legislature refused to disenfranchise its women voters, and after much debate in Congress, Wyoming was admitted into the Union—the first state to allow women to vote in federal elections. But another thirty years would pass before nationwide woman suffrage would finally become a reality with the ratification of the Nineteenth Amendment in 1920.

References

Deutsch, Sarah Jane. 1994. *From Ballots to Breadlines: American Women: 1920-1940.* New York: Oxford University Press.

Eisenberg, Bonnie. 1995. *Woman Suffrage Movement: 1848-1920.* Windsor, California: National Women's History Project.

"Esther Hobart Morris." *The Architect of the Capitol.* http://www.aoc.gov/cc/art/nsh/morris.htm. Access date January 1999.

"Esther Hobart Morris." *Women of the West Museum.* http://www.autry-museum.org/explore/exhibits/suffrage/justice_full.html. Access date January 1999.

Fleming, Maria. ed. 2000. *A Place at the Table: Struggles for Equality in America.* New York: Oxford University Press.

Gale, Thomas. "Sarah Grimké, Angelina Grimké." *Thomson Gale.* http://www.galegroup.com/free_resources/whm/bio/grimk_sisters.htm. Access date January 1999.

Garraty, John A. and Mark C. Carnes, eds. 1999. *American National Biography.* New York: Oxford University Press.

Goldberg, Michael. 1994. *Breaking New Ground.* New York: Oxford University Press.

Griffith, Elisabeth. 1984. *In Her Own Right: The Life of Elizabeth Cady Stanton.* New York: Oxford University Press.

Keenan, Sheila. 1996. *Encyclopedia of Women in the United States.* New York: Scholastic Inc.

Larson, T.A. 1978. *History of Wyoming.* Lincoln, Nebraska: University of Nebraska Press.

Matthews, Glenna. 2000. *American Women's History.* New York: Oxford University Press.

"Sarah Grimké and Angelina Grimké Weld." *Sunshine for Women.* http://www.pinn.net/~sunshine/whm2000/grimke4.html. Access date January 1999.

"The Seneca Falls Convention." *National Portrait Gallery.* http://www.npg.si.edu/col/seneca/senfalls1.htm. Access date January 1999.

Sigerman, Harriet. 2001. *Elizabeth Cady Stanton: The Right Is Ours.* New York: Oxford University Press.

Sigerman, Harriet. 1994. *An Unfinished Battle: American Women 1848-1865.* New York: Oxford University Press.

Sigerman, Harriet. 1994. *Laborers for Liberty: American Women 1865-1890.* New York: Oxford University Press.

Smith, Karen Manners. 1994. *New Paths to Power: American Women 1890-1920.* New York: Oxford University Press.

Stanton, Elizabeth C. 1979. 1882 Reprint. *History of Woman Suffrage.* New York: Ayer Company Publishing.

Wilson, Jr., Vincent. 1992. *The Book of Distinguished American Women.* Brookeville, Maryland: American History Research Associates.

"Women in America." *American Studies at the University of Virginia.* http://xroads.virginia.edu/~HYPER/DETOC/Fem/home.htm. Access date January 1999.

"Women's Rights National Historical Park." *National Park Service.* http://www.nps.gov/wori. Access date January 1999.

"Votes for Women: Selections from the National American Woman Suffrage Association Collection, 1848-1921." *American Memory at the Library of Congress.* http://memory.loc.gov/ammem/naw/nawshome.html. Access date January 2003.

"1850 Women's Rights Convention." *Worcester Woman's History Project.* http://www.assumption.edu/wwhp/historical.html. Access date January 1999.

Standards

Historical Thinking

The student will

Chronological Thinking

- identify in historical narratives the temporal structure of a historical narrative or story

Historical Comprehension

- reconstruct the literal meaning of a historical passage
- identify the central question(s) the historical narrative addresses
- draw upon visual, literary, and musical sources

Historical Analysis and Interpretation

- compare or contrast differing sets of ideas, values, personalities, behaviors, and institutions
- consider multiple perspectives
- analyze cause and effect relationships and multiple causation, including the importance of the individual, the influence of ideas, and the role of chance

Historical Research Capabilities

- obtain historical data

Analysis and Decision-Making

- identify issues and problems in the past
- formulate a position or course of action on an issue

Content

The student will demonstrate understanding of

The struggle to achieve woman suffrage in the 1800s.

- The movement to achieve woman suffrage
  - analyze the basis for woman suffrage as a constitutional right
  - recognize the commitment and specific contributions of individuals to the woman's rights and suffrage movements
  - identify the opposition arguments to woman suffrage

Resources

For each student

Reconstructing America by Joy Hakim: Chapter 26, "Tea in Wyoming"

Notebook

A copy of the script: *"Failure Is Impossible"* for each student reader

For the teacher

Chart Paper

Markers

Web sites

The Woman Suffrage Movement: Home Page @ http://www.nara.gov/education/teaching/women/home.html

NAWSA Time Line @ http://lcweb2.loc.gov/ammem/vfwhtml/vfwtl.html

The Woman Suffrage Movement: the Failure is Impossible script @ http://www.nara.gov/education/teaching/women/script.html

Links to Resources @ http://www.library.wisc.edu/libraries/WomensStudies/

African American Women On-line @ http://netdive.com/ourstory.html

National American Woman suffrage Association Collection @ http://lcweb2.loc.gov/ammem/rbnawsahtml/

Freedom: A History of US @ http://www.pbs.org/wnet/historyofus/menu.html

The Lower East Side Tenement Museum Virtual Tour @ http://www.tenement.org/Virtual_Tour/index_virtual.html

The Immigrant Experience as Seen through the Eyes of NYC Youth @ http://www.tenement.org/immigrantexperience/

Vocabulary

Words to Remember

***suffrage** — right to vote

***franchise** — constitutional right such as the right to vote

People to Remember

Esther Morris — prominent suffragist who helped secure the vote for women in the Wyoming territory

Lesson 19   A Tea Party

The Lesson

Focus Activity – 15 minutes

1. Set up a simulation in which only the girls vote on a class-wide activity or choice.

   Discuss the activity or choice with the entire class, but then allow only the girls to vote.

   The boys may attempt to influence the girls' choice, but they have no vote and cannot participate in the actual decision-making process.

2. After the vote, ask the boys to describe how it felt to be excluded in that way.

   - Why do they feel that it was basically unfair? (Because the boys are class members [*class citizens*], they should have the right to vote)

   - Why is it unfair to be excluded just because you are a boy?

3. Explain to the students that women in the United States did not always have the right to vote, that not until 1920 was the Constitution amended to grant that right, called *woman suffrage*. Many men and women actively worked for over seventy years to achieve national woman suffrage.

   Ask the students to **Think-Team-Share**:

   - Why do you think women were so committed to achieving the vote?

Teaching Activity – 20 minutes

1. Introduce Chapter 26, "Tea in Wyoming" by briefly reviewing the woman suffrage movement from the early 1830s until the late 1880s using information in the Overview.

2. Introduce the Vocabulary *Words and People to Remember*.

3. **Reading for a Purpose:** The students read silently or **Partner Read** Chapter 26, "Tea in Wyoming" in

Notes

Reconstructing America to discover why Wyoming was a milestone in woman suffrage.

Write the following questions on chart paper to guide the students' reading.

- Who was Esther Morris and what did she do to advance the cause of woman suffrage? (A resident of the Wyoming territory in the late 1800s, Morris convinced Wyoming legislators in both parties to back a women's suffrage bill.)

- Why do you think that the men in the West supported woman suffrage? (Some men believed women should have the right to vote; some men in sparsely populated western lands hoped it would encourage women to move West where they would enjoy more rights than in the established East.)

- What did many men and women fear would happen if women were permitted to vote? (Women would not make good voting choices; women would vote for issues [such as temperance] that were unpopular with men; women would negatively affect political policy and government.)

- Besides granting the vote to women, what was significant about woman suffrage in Wyoming? (In 1889, Wyoming entered the Union as a full suffrage state, the first state to allow women to vote in national elections.)

Circulate and Monitor: Visit each team to help the students read the chapter and discuss the questions.

4. Students use **Numbered Heads** to discuss what happened in Wyoming and why it was important to the woman suffrage movement.

Student Team Learning Activity – 20 minutes

Using Reader Theatre

1. **Reading for a Purpose:** Introduce the play *Failure Is Impossible* by Rosemary H. Knower. Explain that the play provides an overview of the woman suffrage movement, introduces important people in the fight for woman suffrage, and puts the Wyoming event into the broader, overall story.

2. Using the Reader Theatre technique, assign different students to read the parts of the characters in the play. Assign a part to every student, even if you must divide the role of the narrator. Allow a few minutes for the students to silently read just their parts in preparation for the Reader Theatre. If necessary, teammates can assist each other with word pronunciations.

   Circulate and Monitor: Answer questions and help students read their parts.

3. Following this short practice time, the students read the play aloud.

   Note to the Teacher: You may use the script as a radio show, have the students wear placards with the name of their characters, or just sit in a circle and read the play.

Review and Reflection Activity – 10 minutes

1. After reading the play, the students use **Think-Team-Share** to discuss the following questions.

   - Upon what democratic ideals was the woman suffrage movement based?

   - What were some of the opposition arguments to woman suffrage?

   - How did the suffrage movement use these strategies to fight for their cause?

     - State referendum
     - Public pressure
     - Silent picket
     - Hunger strike
     - Public sentiment
     - Lobby
     - Constitutional amendment

   - Why do you think women finally won the right to vote?

   Note to the Teacher: An additional resource for this lesson is the video series Freedom: *A History of US*, Episode Eight—Part Five: This Land is Your Land, Kunhardt Productions and Thirteen/WNET for PBS. Also explore the accompanying PBS Website: Freedom: A History of US @ http://www.pbs.org/wnet/historyofus/menu.html, especially the section for teachers.

Homework

You are an advocate for woman suffrage in the late 1800s. Design a sign that you might have carried during a silent picket. Remember you can't talk during the picket so the words or drawings on your sign must get your message across to others. Bring your sign to class to display.

Library/Media Resources

Nonfiction

The Book of Distinguished Women by Vincent Wilson, Jr., American History Research Associates

Women Win the Vote by Betsey Covington Smith, Silver Burdett Press

The Day the Women Got the Vote: A Photo History of the Women's Rights Movement by George Sullivan, Scholastic

An Unfinished Battle: American Women 1848-1865 by Harriet Sigerman, Oxford University Press

New Paths to Power: American Women 1890-1920 by Karen Manners Smith, Oxford University Press

Biographical Supplement and Index for the Young Oxford History of Women in the United States by Harriet Sigerman, Oxford University Press

Elizabeth Cady Stanton: The Right Is Ours by Harriet Sigerman, Oxford University Press

Susan B. Anthony: Woman Suffragist by Barbara Weisberg, Chelsea House

Sojourner Truth: Self-Made Woman by Victoria Ortiz, Lippincott

Sojourner Truth: Ain't I A Woman? by Pat McKissack, Scholastic

Cobblestone Magazine

Susan B. Anthony

Videos

The Women Get the Vote narrated by Walter Cronkite

The Susan B. Anthony Story, Grace Products

One Woman, One Vote, PBS Video

Dreams of Equality, Media Products

Freedom: A History of US, Episode Eight—Part Five, Kunhardt Productions and Thirteen/WNET for PBS

Connections

Art — Students create posters or a collage depicting the individuals and events of the woman suffrage movement.

Expressive Arts — Students stage a period debate on woman suffrage.

Math — Students develop a campaign strategy for a law they would like to have passed. How would they go about getting publicity for the idea and raising money for the campaign? Students develop a campaign timeline and a budget.

Citizenship — Students invite a representative from the League of Women voters to speak about that organization, which was founded in 1920. What kinds of issues has the LWV advocated locally in the past ten to twenty years?

Library — There are several methods by which citizens can get legislation or constitutional amendments passed. The various organizations within the suffrage movement tried all of them. Students research the methods prescribed by their own state constitution for citizen-initiated legislation.

Library — Students research and share information about a key personality, organization, or movement that helped bring about woman suffrage.

Research — Students research the first president elected after women won the right to vote. Students discuss whether the "woman's vote" played a significant role in that election.

Lesson 20
Anthony Goes to Trial
Chapter 27

Theme

Although the cause of women's rights and woman suffrage had many tireless workers during its long and difficult struggle, no one was more totally dedicated than Susan B. Anthony.

Overview

No advocate was ever more totally dedicated to a cause than Susan Brownell Anthony was to the women's rights movement. Born on February 15, 1820, in Adams, Massachusetts, Susan Anthony was raised in the Quaker tradition of equality before God. A tone of independence and moral zeal pervaded her childhood home. From her father she learned to hate slavery, and she was an ardent abolitionist. But once drawn to the women's movement she made it her principal cause and devoted herself to it unstintingly for over fifty years.

A precocious child, Susan B. Anthony learned to read early and was well educated. After teaching for ten years, she settled in her family home, now near Rochester, New York. There she met many leading abolitionists, including Frederick Douglass, Parker Pillsbury, Wendell Phillips, William Henry Channing, and William Lloyd Garrison. Soon the temperance movement enlisted her sympathy, and after meeting Amelia Bloomer and Elizabeth Cady Stanton, so did the cause of woman suffrage.

The rebuff (because she was a woman) of Anthony's attempt to speak at a temperance meeting in Albany in 1852 prompted her to organize the Woman's New York State Temperance Society, the first of its kind; and Stanton became its president. Anthony, who remained unmarried, had the freedom to travel and organize—activities that suited her talents. Lacking the personality and speaking ability of Stanton, she was most effective working behind the scenes. In a short time Anthony became known as one of the cause's most zealous, serious advocates, a dogged and tireless worker. She also became a prime target of public and newspaper abuse.

Anthony's campaign with Stanton in the 1850s led to improved laws regarding married women's property rights, and she continued to serve as chief New York agent of Garrison's American Anti-Slavery Society. During the Civil War Anthony helped organize the Women's National Loyal League, which urged the case for emancipation but did little to further the cause of women's rights. After the war she campaigned unsuccessfully to have the language of the Fourteenth Amendment altered to allow for woman as well as "Negro" suffrage. Her exhausting speaking and organizing tour of Kansas in 1867 failed to win passage of a state enfranchisement law for women.

For two years, Stanton and Anthony published a weekly newspaper, *Revolution*, which promoted women's rights with the motto: "Men Their Rights and Nothing More—Women their Rights and Nothing Less." In May 1869, the two crusaders formed the National Woman Suffrage Association (NWSA), the first national organization devoted primarily to women's

Lesson 20 Anthony Goes to Trail

suffrage and dedicated to securing a constitutional amendment for national woman suffrage. A portion of the organization deserted later in the year to join Lucy Stone's more conservative American Woman Suffrage Association (AWSA), but the NWSA remained a large and powerful group with Anthony as its principal leader and spokeswoman.

As a test of the legality of the suffrage provision of the Fourteenth Amendment, Anthony cast a vote in the 1872 presidential election in Rochester, New York. She was arrested, tried, convicted, (the judge's directed verdict of guilty had been written before the trial began) and fined. Even though she refused to pay the fine, the case was carried no further. (See "The Sentencing of Susan B. Anthony for the Crime of Voting.")

Anthony traveled constantly, often with Stanton, in support of efforts in various states to win the franchise for women. In 1890, the two rival suffrage associations merged into the National Woman Suffrage Association, and at Stanton's resignation in 1892 Anthony became president. Her principal lieutenant in later years was Carrie Chapman Catt.

By the 1890s, Anthony had largely outlived the abuse and sarcasm that had attended her early efforts, and she emerged as a national heroine. In 1900, at the age of eighty, she retired from the presidency of the National American Woman Suffrage Association, passing the leadership on to Catt. Six years later, at the last suffrage convention she would attend, Anthony delivered her final declaration: "Failure is impossible." Anthony died in Rochester, New York, on March 13, 1906—never to see the passage of the national woman suffrage amendment in 1920 although it was named in her honor. With the issue of a new dollar coin in 1979, Susan B. Anthony became the first woman depicted on United States currency.

The Sentencing of Susan B. Anthony for the Crime of Voting

Anthony's 1873 trial for voting is a bizarre incident in the history of woman suffrage. The trial judge took the decision out of the hands of the jury, pronounced her guilty, and further denied the motion for a new trial. The entire trial is recorded in *History of Woman Suffrage* by Elizabeth Cady Stanton.

The Court: The prisoner will stand up. Has the prisoner anything to say why sentence shall not be pronounced?

Miss Anthony: Yes, your honor, I have many things to say; for in your ordered verdict of guilty, you have trampled underfoot every vital principle of our government. My natural rights, my civil rights, my political rights, are all alike ignored. Robbed of the fundamental privilege of citizenship, I am degraded from the status of a citizen to that of a subject; and not only myself individually, but all of my sex, are, by your honor's verdict, doomed to political subjection under this so-called Republican government.

Judge Hunt: The Court can not listen to a rehearsal of arguments the prisoner's counsel has already consumed three hours in presenting.

Miss Anthony: May it please your honor, I am not arguing the question, I am simply stating the reasons why sentence cannot, in justice, be pronounced against me. Your denial of my citizen's right to vote is the denial of my right of consent as one of the governed, the denial of my right of representation as one of the taxed, the denial of my right to a trial by a jury of my peers as an offender against law, therefore, the denial of my sacred rights of life, liberty, property, and—

Judge Hunt: The Court cannot allow the prisoner to go on.

Miss Anthony: But your honor will not deny me this one and only poor privilege of protest against this high-handed outrage upon my citizen's rights. May it please the Court to remember that since the day of my arrest last November, this is the first time that either myself or any person of my disfranchised class has been allowed a word of defense before judge or jury—

Judge Hunt: The prisoner must sit down; the Court cannot allow it.

Miss Anthony: All my prosecutors, from the 8th Ward corner grocery politician, who entered the complaint, to the United States Marshal, Commissioner, District Attorney, District Judge, your honor on the bench, one is my peer, but each and all are my political sovereigns; and had your honor submitted my case to the jury, as was clearly your duty, even then I should have had just cause of protest, for not one of those men was my peer; but, native or foreign, white or black, rich or poor, educated or ignorant, awake or asleep, sober or drunk, each and every man of them was my political superior; hence, in no sense, my peer. Even, under such circumstances, a commoner of England, tried before a jury of lords, would have far less cause to complain than should I, a woman, tried before a jury of men. Even my counsel, the Hon. Henry R. Selden, who has argued my cause so ably, so earnestly, so unanswerably before your honor, is my political sovereign. Precisely as no disfranchised person is entitled to sit upon a jury, and no woman is entitled to the franchise, so, none but a regularly admitted lawyer is allowed to practice in the courts, and no woman can gain admission to the bar—hence, jury, judge, counsel, must all be of the superior class.

Judge Hunt: The Court must insist—the prisoner has been tried according to the established forms of law.

Miss Anthony: Yes, your honor, but by forms of law all made by men, interpreted by men, administered by men, in favor of men, and against women; and hence, your honor's ordered verdict of guilty, against a United States citizen for the exercise of "that citizen's right to vote," simply because that citizen was a woman and not a man. But, yesterday, the same man-made forms of law declared it a crime punishable with $1,000 fine and six months' imprisonment, for you, or me, or any of us, to give a cup of cold water, a crust of bread, or a night's shelter to a panting fugitive as he was tracking his way to Canada. And every man or woman in whose veins coursed a drop of human sympathy violated that wicked law, reckless of consequences, and was justified in so doing. As then the slaves who got their freedom must take it over, or under, or through the unjust forms of law, precisely so now must women, to get their right to a voice in this Government, take it; and I have taken mine, and mean to take it at every possible opportunity.

Judge Hunt: The Court orders the prisoner to sit down. It will not allow another word.

Miss Anthony: When I was brought before your honor for trial, I hoped for a broad and liberal interpretation of the Constitution and its recent amendments, that should declare all United States citizens under its protecting ægis—that should declare equality of rights the national guarantee to all persons born or naturalized in the United States. But failing to get this justice—failing, even, to get a trial by a jury not of my peers—I ask not leniency at your hands—but rather the full rigors of the law.

Judge Hunt: The Court must insist—(Here the prisoner sat down.)

Judge Hunt: The prisoner will stand up. (Here Miss Anthony arose again.) The sentence of the Court is that you pay a fine of one hundred dollars and the costs of the prosecution.

Miss Anthony: May it please your honor, I shall never pay a dollar of your unjust penalty. All the stock in trade I possess is a

$10,000 debt, incurred by publishing my paper—*The Revolution*—four years ago, the sole object of which was to educate all women to do precisely as I have done, rebel against your man-made, unjust, unconstitutional forms of law, that tax, fine, imprison, and hang women, while they deny them the right of representation in the Government; and I shall work on with might and main to pay every dollar of that honest debt, but not a penny shall go to this unjust claim. And I shall earnestly and persistently continue to urge all women to the practical recognition of the old revolutionary maxim, that "Resistance to tyranny is obedience to God."

Judge Hunt: Madam, the Court will not order you committed until the fine is paid.

From the *History of Woman Suffrage*, Elizabeth C. Stanton et al., eds., Vol. II, New York, 1882, pp. 687-689.

References

Deutsch, Sarah Jane. 1994. *From Ballots to Breadlines: American Women: 1920-1940*. New York: Oxford University Press.

Eisenberg, Bonnie. 1995. *Woman Suffrage Movement: 1848-1920*. Windsor, California: National Women's History Project.

Fleming, Maria. ed. 2000. *A Place at the Table: Struggles for Equality in America*. New York: Oxford University Press.

Goldberg, Michael. 1994. *Breaking New Ground*. New York: Oxford University Press.

Griffith, Elisabeth. 1984. *In Her Own Right: The Life of Elizabeth Cady Stanton*. New York: Oxford University Press.

Keenan, Sheila. 1996. *Encyclopedia of Women in the United States*. New York: Scholastic Inc.

Linder, Douglas. "The Trial of Susan B. Anthony for Illegal Voting." *Famous Trials HomePage*. http://www.law.umkc.edu/faculty/projects/ftrials/anthony/sbahome.html. Access date January 2003.

Matthews, Glenna. 2000. *American Women's History*. New York: Oxford University Press.

"The Seneca Falls Convention." *National Portrait Gallery*. http://www.npg.si.edu/col/seneca/senfalls1.htm. Access date January 1999.

Sigerman, Harriet. 2001. *Elizabeth Cady Stanton: The Right Is Ours*. New York: Oxford University Press.

Sigerman, Harriet. 1994. *An Unfinished Battle: American Women 1848-1865*. New York: Oxford University Press.

Sigerman, Harriet. 1994. *Laborers for Liberty: American Women 1865-1890*. New York: Oxford University Press.

Smith, Karen Manners. 1994. *New Paths to Power: American Women 1890-1920*. New York: Oxford University Press.

Stanton, Elizabeth and Susan B. Anthony. "The Papers of Elizabeth Cady Stanton and Susan B. Anthony. Travels for Reform: The Early Work of Susan B. Anthony and Elizabeth Cady Stanton, 1852-1861." *The Model Editions Partnership.* http://adh.sc.edu/sa/sa-table.html. Access date October 1999.

Stanton, Elizabeth C. 1979. 1882 Reprint. *History of Woman Suffrage*. New York: Ayer Company Publishing.

"Women in America." *American Studies at the University of Virginia*. http://xroads.virginia.edu/~HYPER/DETOC/Fem/home.htm. Access date January 1999.

"Women's Rights National Historical Park." *National Park Service*. http://www.nps.gov/wori. Access date January 1999.

"Votes for Women: Selections from the National American Woman Suffrage Association Collection, 1848-1921." *American Memory at the Library of Congress*. http://memory.loc.gov/ammem/naw/nawshome.html. Access date January 2003.

"1850 Women's Rights Convention." Worcester Woman's History Project. http://www.assumption.edu/wwhp/historical.html. Access date January 1999.

Standards

Historical Thinking

The student will

Historical Comprehension

- reconstruct the literal meaning of a historical passage
- identify the central question(s) the historical narrative addresses
- draw upon visual, literary, and musical sources

Historical Analysis and Interpretation

- compare or contrast differing sets of ideas, values, personalities, behaviors, and institutions
- consider multiple perspectives
- analyze cause and effect relationships and multiple causation, including the importance of the individual, the influence of ideas, and the role of chance

Historical Research Capabilities

- obtain historical data

Analysis and Decision-Making

- identify issues and problems in the past
- formulate a position or course of action on an issue

Content

The student will demonstrate understanding of

The struggle to achieve woman suffrage in the 1800s.

- The movement to achieve woman suffrage
  - analyze the basis for woman suffrage as a constitutional right
  - recognize the commitment and specific contributions of individuals to the woman's rights and suffrage movements
  - identify the opposition arguments to woman suffrage

Resources

For each student

Reconstructing America by Joy Hakim: Chapter 27, "Are You a Citizen If You Can't Vote?"

Notebook

Silent parade sign from Lesson 19 homework

For each team

Document Packet: *Opposition to the Vote*

For the teacher

Transparency: *Quote of Carrie Chapman Catt*

Chart paper

Markers

For the classroom

Overhead projector

Web sites

The Women Suffrage Movement: Home Page @ http://www.nara.gov/education/teaching/women/home.html

NAWSA Time Line @ http://lcweb2.loc.gov/ammem/vfwhtml/vfwtl.html

The Woman Suffrage Movement: Failure is Impossible Script @ http://www.nara.gov/education/teaching/women/script.html

Links to Resources @ http://www.library.wisc.edu/libraries/WomensStudies/

African American Women On-line @http://netdive.com/ourstory.html

National American Woman Suffrage Association Collection @ http://lcweb2.loc.gov/ammem/rbnawsahtml/

Freedom: A History of US @ http://www.pbs.org/wnet/historyofus/menu.html

Vocabulary

Words to Remember

*suffrage — right to vote

*franchise — constitutional right such as voting

temperance — social movement promoting self-moderation or abstinence in the use of alcoholic beverages

abolitionist — person who works to end slavery

Quaker — member of a religious group that is antislavery and pacifist

*citizen — person who owes allegiance to a government (country) and is entitled to that government's protection

universal suffrage — right to vote regardless of gender or race

People to Remember

*Susan B. Anthony — pioneer in the women's rights and suffrage movements

The Lesson

Focus Activity – 5 minutes

1. Write the motto of Stanton and Anthony's weekly newspaper, the *Revolution,* on the chalk board: "Men Their Rights and Nothing More—Women their Rights and Nothing Less."

2. Ask the students to **Think-Team-Share:**
   - Explain what you think Elizabeth Cady Stanton and Susan B. Anthony meant by those words.

Teaching Activity – 20 minutes

1. Introduce Chapter 27, "Are You a Citizen if You Can't Vote?" by briefly introducing Susan B. Anthony and her work for women's rights and woman suffrage. Use information from the Overview.

   Connect Anthony with the play, "Failure Is Impossible," and explain the origin of the play's title.

2. Introduce the Vocabulary *Words and People to Remember*. Be sure students understand the definition of *citizen*.

3. **Reading for a Purpose:** Students silently read or **Partner Read** Chapter 27, "Are You a Citizen if You Can't Vote?" in *Reconstructing America*. Write the following questions on chart paper to guide the students' reading.

   - How were the abolitionist, temperance, and suffrage movements connected? (Many of the individuals who worked to gain woman suffrage also worked to limit the use of liquor and to end slavery. Their affiliations with these associations often worked against the suffrage movement.)
   - How did Susan B. Anthony test the meaning of "citizen"? (If women were citizens of the United States, then they should have the right to vote. So, based on legal counsel, Anthony voted in a national election to test her right as a citizen to vote.)

Notes

Lesson 20 Anthony Goes to Trial

- What new question was raised during Anthony's trial? (The right to a fair trial in a free, democratic society.)

- How did Susan B. Anthony view liberty and justice? (Rights were unalienable, that is natural and God-given, not something that governments owned and gave to citizens. We, the people included everyone, not just men; therefore, women should have all the rights and responsibilities of citizenship, including the right to vote.)

Circulate and Monitor: Visit each team as the students read the chapter and discuss the questions.

4. Students use **Numbered Heads** to share answers to the questions and discuss the suffrage movement and the role of Susan B. Anthony.

Student Team Learning Activity – 25 minutes

Creating political cartoons

1. Introduce Carrie Chapman Catt, who was Susan B. Anthony's successor as leader of the woman's suffrage movement. Catt directed the national effort throughout the first two decades of the twentieth century and led the final drive for ratification of the federal amendment.

2. Read the words on the Transparency: *Quote of Carrie Chapman Catt*.

   "[Winning the right to vote] cost the women of the country fifty-two years of pauseless campaign ... millions of dollars were raised ... hundreds of women gave the accumulated possibilities of an entire lifetime ..., thousands gave years of their lives, and hundreds of thousands gave constant interest and such aid as they could.... Young suffragists who helped forge the last links of that chain were not born when it began. Old suffragists who forged the first links were dead when it ended."

3. Using **Think-Team-Share,** the students **Speculate**:

   - Why did the woman's suffrage movement meet such resistance?

   - Who opposed woman suffrage and why?

Be sure students realize that some women opposed woman suffrage and some men supported it.

4. Distribute the Document Packet: *Opposition to the Vote* to each team.

5. Teams use the *Cartoon Analyzer* in the packet to identify:

   - What symbols are used in the cartoon?

   - What is the overall meaning or message of the cartoon?

6. **Reading for a Purpose:** Students read the *Opposition Cards* in the packet. These cards present some common arguments against woman suffrage.

   Each student on the team chooses one of the *Opposition Cards* and creates a political cartoon based on that card. Remind the students to first identify a caption or the overall meaning of their cartoon, and then choose symbols that express that viewpoint.

   Note to the Teacher: Display these cartoons and those created for homework assignments so students have the opportunity to appreciate them.

Reflection and Review Activity – 5 minutes

1. Students **Think-Team-Share**: What's your opinion?

   - Did any of the terrible things that some people thought might happen if women voted actually occur? Support your opinion.

   - What still needs to happen in our society for all women to have equal rights under the law? Support your opinion.

2. Students use **Numbered Heads** to share their responses.

   Note to the Teacher: An additional resource for this lesson is the video series *Freedom: A History of US*, Episode Nine—Part One: Are You a Citizen if You Can't Vote?, Kunhardt Productions and Thirteen/WNET for PBS. Also explore the accompanying PBS Website: Freedom: A History of US @ http://www.pbs.org/wnet/historyofus/menu.html, especially the section for teachers.

Lesson 20   Anthony Goes to Trial

Homework

Are women today free from discrimination and inequality under the law in the United States? Draw a political cartoon expressing your viewpoint concerning this question. Write a brief explanation supporting your viewpoint.

Library/Media Resources

Nonfiction

Women Win the Vote by Betsey Covington Smith, Silver Burdett Press

The Day the Women Got the Vote: A Photo History of the Women's Rights Movement by George Sullivan, Scholastic

An Unfinished Battle: American Women 1848-1865 by Harriet Sigerman, Oxford University Press

New Paths to Power: American Women 1890-1920 by Karen Manners Smith, Oxford University Press

Biographical Supplement and Index for the Young Oxford History of Women in the United States by Harriet Sigerman, Oxford University Press

Failure Is Impossible: Susan B. Anthony in Her Own Words by Lynn Sherr, Three Rivers Press

Sojourner Truth: A Self-Made Woman by Victoria Ortiz, Lippincott Williams & Wilkins Publishers

Sojourner Truth: Antislavery Activist by Peter Krass and Heather Lehr Wagner, Chelsea House

The Book of Distinguished Women by Vincent Wilson, Jr., An American History Research Associates Publication

Cobblestone Magazine

Susan B. Anthony

Videos

The Women Get the Vote narrated by Walter Cronkite

The Susan B. Anthony Story, Grace Products

One Woman, One Vote, PBS Video

Dreams of Equality, Media Products

Freedom: A History of US, Episode Nine—Part One, Kunhardt Productions and Thirteen/WNET for PBS

Connections

Library — Students research women and men involved in the struggle for women's rights and woman suffrage such as Susan

B. Anthony, Elizabeth Cady Stanton, and Carrie Chapman Catt. Students write and illustrate a biography card or poster for each of these individuals.

Math — Students create and illustrate a timeline of woman suffrage events.

Research/Library — Students research countries where women's rights to vote or obtain an education are severely restricted.

Review Lesson III
Lessons 15 through 20
Chapters 22 through 28

In the Review Lesson, students revisit essential ideas and vocabulary from Lessons 15 through 20 to prepare for the Assessment Lesson. The Review Lesson is in the form of a card game.

If time allows, the teams may play more than one round of *Reconstructing America Review*. Even though one team member will win each round, all students win by reviewing ideas, facts, and vocabulary from the previous lessons. The goal of the game is to successfully prepare *each* member of the team for the assessment.

Reconstructing America Review III: Immigration and Suffrage

1. To ensure that each student has a chance to play, students remain in their cooperative learning teams of four or five.
2. Each team receives a set of game cards and the answer sheet.
3. Cards are shuffled, separated into their respective piles (Trials and Tribulations, Court Chat, The American Dream, etc.), and placed face down in the center of the table.
4. One team member is designated as the first player (i.e. the student whose name is last in the alphabet). The student to his or her right has the answer sheet, keeping it face down on the desk. This person is the fact checker.
5. The first player chooses a card, reads the number and the question aloud, and attempts to answer it. The fact checker turns the answer sheet over, finds the correct question number, and checks the first player's response. If the student answers correctly, he or she keeps the card. If the answer is wrong, the card is placed at the bottom of the pile. The fact checker quickly turns the answer sheet face down again.
6. Play passes to the left, and the student who was the first player is now the fact checker.
7. The game ends when all the cards are gone. The student with the most cards wins.

Reconstructing America Review III: Immigration and Suffrage Questions and Answers

Trials and Tribulations

1. What do Susan B. Anthony and Lee Yick have in common? Both were arrested and went to trial. Both of their trials tested the denial of full rights to United States residents (women and aliens).

2. Why was Susan B. Anthony on trial? She voted in a national election before the Constitution granted the right to vote to women.

3. Why was Lee Yick on trial? Against a local ordinance, he operated a Chinese laundry in a wooden building.

4. Why was the *Yick Wo v. Hopkins* case so important? The Supreme Court ruled that the police did not have the right to enforce a law arbitrarily and that aliens had the same rights as citizens.

5. What new issue did Susan B. Anthony's trial raise? The right to a fair trial in a free, democratic nation

6. What was the fundamental difference between the trials of Lee Yick and Susan B. Anthony? Lee Yick, an alien, was granted a fair trial through the appeals process, whereas Susan B. Anthony, a citizen, did not receive a fair trial.

Court Chat

7. If you are on trial, what are you called? The defendant

8. If you disagree with the decision of a local court, what can you do? Appeal your case to a higher court

9. What court decides if your constitutional rights have been violated? The United States Supreme Court

10. If you have information about a case you might be called to testify as a _____? Witness

11. If you serve on a jury, what do you do? Listen to the evidence and decide guilt or innocence

12. What is a written legal argument called? A brief

The American Dream

13. Name two reasons why immigrants came to the United States during the late 1800s. To escape political unrest and injustice, to have jobs, to provide food and a better life for themselves and their families, for political freedom

14. Why were immigrants needed in the United States during the late 1800s? To settle and farm the Western plains and provide industrial workers

15. What was Mary Antin's American Dream? To get an education

16. How are Emma Lazarus and the American Dream related? Lazarus wrote the poem on the Statue of Liberty that welcomed immigrants to America

17. How did the immigrant Carl Schurz fight for freedom? A German immigrant who fought for political freedom in his home country, Schurz fought against slavery and the unfair treatment of the Native Americans in America.

18. How did Jacob Riis help improve life for immigrants? As a photographer and reporter, Riis' work brought social reform that made life better for the immigrants.

Review Lesson III   Lessons 15 through 20

The Immigrant Experience

19. Why was Ellis Island important to immigrants? At Ellis Island—the largest inspection station—immigrants were questioned, underwent health examinations, and were rejected or accepted into the United States.

20. What was the Chinese Exclusion Act of 1882? A law that stopped Chinese laborers from immigrating to the United States

21. What did the Know-Nothing Party, the Ku Klux Klan, and the Workingmen's Party have in common? They were racist organizations that opposed immigration.

22. What is a naturalized citizen? An immigrant who becomes a citizen

23. Why did most immigrants settle in large cities? Available jobs or to live close to others who shared their national origin or religion

24. What was Angel Island? An immigrant inspection station on the West Coast that served as a detention center for many Chinese immigrants

Tea and Suffrage

25. What part did the Wyoming territory play in woman suffrage? Wyoming was the first state to grant women the right to vote

26. What is suffrage? The right to vote

27. Name at least two reasons why some people opposed woman suffrage? They believed that families would suffer; children would be neglected; morals would crumble; women should be protected from the realities of life; women might vote for the prohibition of alcohol; women would demand labor laws for women and children.

28. What was the connection between temperance, abolition of slavery, and woman suffrage? Many of the same persons supported all three movements; women's rights were involved in all three movements.

29. To what cause did Susan B. Anthony devote her life? The cause of women's rights, especially the right to vote

30. Why were women not full citizens in the 1800s? Citizens had the unalienable right to vote from birth, but women born in the United States could not vote only because they were women.

Lesson 21
Happy Birthday!
Chapters 29 and 30

Theme

During its first hundred years, the United States progressed and changed greatly. Practical inventions and innovative technology spurred rapid industrialization and altered everyday life. Although reformers made gains in securing equality and liberty for all Americans, many social, economic, and political problems still faced the growing nation.

Overview

During its first hundred years, the United States experienced profound changes in its physical and political landscape. One war had secured its freedom as a nation, and another had redefined liberty and justice for more people. The young nation grew in size and population with the opening of the West and the purchase of Alaska, and the ever-changing mosaic of immigrants brought increasing cultural diversity. As a result of a powerful industrial revolution, the nation's economy moved from farming toward industry, and its people from rural folk to urban workers. Industrial growth and production brought great wealth; the national wealth increased more than five-fold between 1860 and 1900. The middle class mushroomed, and a better life seemed within the grasp of ordinary citizens.

The great American experiment in self-government that promised liberty and justice for all had weathered a cataclysmic Civil War and survived, in some ways stronger and more dedicated to its democratic mission. A sizable portion of the population was no longer enslaved; a union of independent states became one truly indivisible nation; the rights of residents and citizens became more clearly defined; and written guarantees of life, liberty, and the pursuit of happiness were added to the Constitution.

With the end of Reconstruction, the nation entered into a period of great change, characterized by bust and boom, poverty and progress, old practices and new technology. Often called the Gilded Age, those times appeared golden on the surface, but beneath that bright veneer lurked problems, inequalities, and injustices.

For many—especially immigrants, migrant southern blacks, and the poor—life in the new urban centers meant crowded tenements, filthy and dangerous streets, hunger and disease, and unremitting toil in factories and sweatshops. Not only men but also women and children worked twelve–to fourteen–hour days in horrendous conditions for a pittance and with no means of recourse. Crime grew, and living and working conditions for industrial workers worsened.

The rise of the large company, the trust, and that new concept—the corporation—grew unchecked. Government policies supported big business and the men who owned them, often at the expense of the workers. A privileged few became wealthy, creating a small but powerful elite class and widening the distance between rich and poor.

Although the passage of the Fourteenth Amendment enfranchised all men—white and black—the vote was still denied to women. Women's rights organizations struggled not only to promote voting rights but also to safeguard women and children who had little protection under the law. Although opponents to woman suffrage argued that women must be sheltered from the harsh realities of life, many women worked in factories under terrible conditions in an effort to provide for themselves and their families. And many women—especially in large city tenements and the rural South—lived in poverty and squalor.

With the demise of congressional Reconstruction in the South, serious attempts to ensure equality for blacks ended. In the following decades, blacks suffered poverty, institutionalized segregation, prejudice, racism, inequality, and terrorism, including lynching. In the rush to tame and settle the West, the Native Americans finally lost their ancestral land, their way of life, and their proud identity, and suffered great injustice and inequality for years to come.

But always some Americans vigilantly and constantly sought ways to include the disenfranchised in the promises of the Constitution. In all walks of life these individuals never lost sight of the true purposes of America and its ongoing, noble experiment in democracy. Amid the inconsistencies, those persons labored to change the nation into a more perfect one, believing that Americans could solve the problems and that the nation could truly achieve its goals of liberty and justice for all.

References

Bettman, Otto. L. 1974. *The Good Old Days—They Were Terrible*. New York: Random House.

Crichton, Judy. 1998. *America 1900: The Turning Point*. New York: Henry Holt & Company, Inc.

Dick, Everett. 1993. 1948 Reprint. *The Dixie Frontier: A Social History*. Norman: University of Oklahoma Press.

Fleming, Maria. ed. 2000. *A Place at the Table: Struggles for Equality in America*. New York: Oxford University Press.

Foner, Eric. 1999. *The Story of American Freedom*. New York: W.W. Norton & Company.

Foner, Eric. 1988. *Reconstruction: America's Unfinished Revolution, 1863-1877*. New York: Perennial.

Greenwood, Janette Thomas. 2000. *The Gilded Age: A History in Documents*. New York: Oxford University Press.

Hoff, Rhoda. 1986. *America's Immigrants: Adventures in Eyewitness History*. New York: Henry Z. Walck.

Holt, Hamilton. ed. 1990. *The Life Stories of Undistinguished Americans*. New York: Routledge.

McCutcheon, Marc. *Everyday Life in the 1800s: A Guide for Writers, Students and Historians*. Cincinnati, Ohio: Writer's Digest Books.

Riis, Jacob A. 1890. 1997 Reprint. *How the Other Half Lives*. New York: Penguin Classics.

Rydell, Robert W. 1987. *All the World's a Fair: Visions of Empire at American International Expositions, 1876-1916*. Chicago: University of Chicago Press.

Sutherland, Daniel E. 1989. *The Expansion of Everyday Life 1860-1876*. New York: Harper & Row.

Zinn, Howard. 1999. *A People's History of the United States: 1492-Present*. New York: HarperCollins Publishers.

Standards

Historical Thinking

The student will

Chronological Thinking

- distinguish between past, present and future time

Lesson 21 Happy Birthday! 223

Historical Comprehension
- read historical narratives imaginatively
- evidence historical perspectives

Historical Analysis and Interpretation
- compare or contrast differing sets of ideas, values, personalities, behaviors, and institutions
- consider multiple perspectives
- analyze cause and effect relationships and multiple causation, including the importance of the individual, the influence of ideas, and the role of chance

Historical Research Capabilities
- obtain historical data
- support interpretations with historical evidence

Analysis and Decision-Making
- identify issues and problems in the past

Content

The student will demonstrate understanding of

How industrialization, immigration, political issues, new social patterns, conflicts, and ideas of national unity developed amid growing cultural diversity and changed the nation.

- The accomplishments of the nation during its first hundred years and the problems it faced as it entered its second hundred
  - identify important accomplishments
  - identify important problems to be solved

Resources

For each student
Reconstructing America by Joy Hakim: Chapters 29, "100 Candles" and Chapter 30, "How Were Things in 1876?"

Notebook

For each team
Team Sheets:
> *Your Time Capsule for 1876*
> *Top Ten Scroll*

For the teacher
Timer

Web sites
Gilded Age and Progressive Era History Internet Resources @ http://www.tntech.edu/www/acad/hist/gilprog.html

Freedom: A History of US @ http://www.pbs.org/wnet/historyofus/menu.html

Vocabulary

Words to Remember
*gilded — giving an attractive but deceptive outer appearance; covered with gold

*centennial — hundredth anniversary

*exposition — big public exhibition

middle class — people who are neither rich nor poor

exports — goods sent out of a country

imports — goods brought into a country

*practical scientists — inventors who turn ideas into products that improve everyday life

People to Remember
*Alexander Graham Bell — inventor of the telephone

Ulysses S. Grant — former general in charge of the Union army during the Civil War who was president of the United States in its centennial year

The Lesson

Focus Activity – 5 minutes

1. After reading the titles of Chapter 29, "100 Candles" and Chapter 30, "How Were Things in 1876?" ask the students to **Speculate**:

   - Who (or what) is 100 years old?

   Explain that in 1876, the United States was 100 years old and celebrated its achievements with a wonderful Centennial Exposition held in Philadelphia.

   Explain the words *centennial* and *exposition*.

   Ask the students.

   - Why was the exposition held in Philadelphia? (The first Continental Congress met in Philadelphia to write America's Constitution, so the anniversary party was held there.)

2. Read the following quotation from a pamphlet that advertised the exhibition:

   During the past century the progress of the nation in invention and manufacture has been wonderful. . . . To bring together all the evidences of this progress, and to combine in one location the engines of industry and their products . . . we are to have in the good city of Philadelphia an International Exhibition, to open May 10th, 1876.

3. Teams **Brainstorm**:

   - What would you include in such an exhibition?
   - What achievements in the nation's first hundred years should be celebrated?

Teaching Activity – 10 minutes

1. As students share their brainstorming ideas, write them on the chalkboard. Then ask the teams to consider the following questions.

   - In addition to manufactured products and inventions, what else might be included in the exhibition?

Notes

Lesson 21   Happy Birthday!

- What changes and progress in social reforms, equality, and justice for all Americans had occurred since 1776?
- What still needed to be improved in 1876?

Encourage the students to explain and support their answers.

2. Distribute the Team Sheets: *Your Time Capsule for 1876* and *Top Ten Scroll*. Explain the Student Team Learning Activity.

The year 1876 is drawing to a close and the exposition is over. But before the exhibition is dismantled, its organizers have asked your teams to visit the exposition and decide which items and ideas should be placed in a time capsule. Each team is to choose the *Top Ten Achievements* and changes in the United States during its first one hundred years. Be sure to consider inventions and material things, as well as the ways in which liberty has grown and justice has been secured. Take a trip through the exposition and the year 1876 by reading Chapters 29 and 30 in *Reconstructing America*. As a team, decide what to include in your time capsule. Then write a brief description or create an illustration for each of your choices on the scroll to be placed in the time capsule. Also identify and record the three most important *Problems to Solve* in the next one hundred years, and include them in the capsule.

3. Share some examples of *Top Ten Achievements* and *Problems to Solve* items:
   - the torch of the Statue of Liberty to represent the immigrants who came to America
   - a sewing machine to symbolize the change from hand-sewn to machine-sewn clothing
   - a copy of the Fourteenth Amendment that defined citizenship
   - a *Problem to Solve*—help feed hungry children in the big cities

Student Team Learning Activitu – 40 minutes

Identifying America's accomplishments and problems

1. **Reading for a Purpose:** Students read silently or **Partner Read** Chapters 29 and 30 in *Reconstructing America* and

decide with their teammates what to include in their time capsules. Use a timer to help the students stay on task and complete the assignment.

2. **Circulate and Monitor**: Visit each team to help ensure that all team members are engaged in the activity. Answer and ask questions to guide the students in their work.

3. Use **Numbered Heads** for each team to share their time capsules or display them in the classroom. If time permits, teams explain how they decided what to include in their time capsules.

4. Ask the teams
   - What might you include in a millennium time capsule today?

   Create a class list of possible *Top Ten* accomplishments of our day and three or four *Problems to Solve*. Encourage a lively discussion of the choices, always asking why the accomplishment should be included.

5. Students evaluate the accomplishments on the list and decide:
   - What is the single most important accomplishment of the United States in our time? Students support their choice.
   - What is our most important problem to solve? Students support their choice.

Reflection and Review Activity – 5 minutes

1. Ask the students to ponder:
   - Which of their Problems to Solve from 1876 are still unsolved today?

2. Then ask the students to **Speculate**:
   - Why are these problems still unsolved?
   - What solution can you suggest for each problem?
   - What is the single most important problem of our time?

   Encourage students to explain their responses.

   Note to the Teacher: An additional resource for this lesson is the video series *Freedom: A History of US*, Episode

Nine—Part One: Are You a Citizen if You Can't Vote?, Kunhardt Productions and Thirteen/WNET for PBS. Also explore the accompanying PBS Website: Freedom: A History of US @ http://www.pbs.org/wnet/historyofus/menu.html, especially the section for teachers.

Homework

Which of your accomplishments would you include in a personal time capsule? List and explain five accomplishments to include in your personal time capsule.

Library/Media Resources

Fiction

Be Ever Hopeful, Hannalee Taylor by Patricia Beatty, Troll Associates

All-of-a-Kind Family by Sydney Taylor, Taylor Productions

Nonfiction

America 1900: The Turning Point by Judy Crichton, Henry Holt & Company, Inc.

All the World's a Fair: Visions of Empire at American International expositions, 1876–1916 by Robert Rydell, University of Chicago Press

Cobblestone Magazine

Thomas Edison

Women Inventors

Video

Freedom: A History of US, Episode Nine—Part One, Kunhardt Productions and Thirteen/WNET for PBS

Connections

Language Arts — Students create word games or crossword puzzles using terms from America's first hundred years.

Social Studies — Students prepare an actual time capsule with items representing their school and community.

Expressive Arts — Students design and create shoebox floats for a Centennial parade recognizing the important events and people in America's first one hundred years.

Math/Geography — Students locate Philadelphia on a map of the United States. Students determine how far the travel distance is from various other American cities. How long would it take a person from San Francisco, Chicago, or another city to reach the Centennial Exposition in 1876? How far would they have to travel?

Lesson 22
Edison: The Wizard of Electricity
Chapter 31

Theme

Thomas Edison's genius and hard work created an "invention factory" that accelerated change in the everyday life of Americans and moved the nation into a new era of progress.

Overview

Born in 1847 in Milan, Ohio, Thomas Edison grew up in Port Huron, Michigan. From an early age Edison was curious about the world around him. Surprisingly, the young Edison was a poor student and attended school for only three months. Yet during his entire life, he taught himself through reading and experimentation.

As a boy, Edison worked as a gatekeeper at his father's observatory for tourists and sold news-papers and candy to railway passengers. As a young man, he learned Morse code and worked as a telegraph operator throughout the South and Midwest. In 1869, at the age of twenty-two, Edison patented his first invention (an electric vote recorder), and thus began his career as a full-time inventor. Throughout his eighty-four years, Edison patented 1,093 inventions.

During his most inventive years, Edison conducted experiments at his Menlo Park laboratory in New Jersey. He did not work alone, but with a team of talented personnel from all over the world who assisted him all hours of the day and night. These men—mathematicians, mechanics, carpenters, laboratory assistants, and practical scientists—had the skills to make Edison's ideas and sketches into real devices.

Edison's laboratory was an "invention factory" and a business with bookkeepers and secretaries. Patents—the exclusive rights to inventions—formed an important part of that business, proving that the inventions belonged to Edison and no one else. Edison employed Samuel Mott as a draftsman to make official drawings to be sent to the United States Patent Office or to patent offices throughout the world. Edison's lawyer, Grosvenor Lowery, had the job of promoting and raising money for the inventions, even before they were realities.

On December 31, 1879, Edison demonstrated his most famous invention: the first practical incandescent electric lamp. Although not the first to experiment with electric light, Edison began testing possibilities for the use of incandescent lamps in homes and businesses. Arc lights—already popular for lighting streets, department stores, and other large areas—were too bright for lighting small areas such as houses. Other inventors had tried to dim or "sub-divide" the arc light, but Edison finally found that filaments of carbonized cardboard in a glass bulb emptied of air would glow but not burn, creating a practical light for homes.

Part of Edison's genius entailed marketing his inventions and creating the systems needed to make them practical realities. Thus Edison and his team developed an entire system—including dynamos, switches, electric meters, fuses, distribution lines, and regulators—to make electricity and distribute it to many places at the same time. He spent years creating a successful commercial electrical system and power station that would produce electricity that ordinary people could afford. After demonstrating that his system could become a commercial success, men began laying tubes for wiring to supply electricity to streets and buildings in a small area of New York City.

In 1887, Edison moved his Menlo Park laboratory and the world's first industrial research center to West Orange, Ohio. Here—in addition to other inventions and business enterprises—he patented an improved phonograph, formed Edison General Electric, invented an early motion picture camera, and perfected the alkaline storage battery. In 1929, the Henry Ford Museum and Greenfield Village opened on the fiftieth anniversary of the electric light. On that day, Edison reenacted his invention of the light bulb at the reconstructed Menlo Park lab in Greenfield Village. Two years later in 1931, Edison, aged eighty-four, died.

In the fall of 1997, *Life* magazine published a special issue on the millennium. The magazine listed several hundred of the most influential events and people of the last one thousand years, then selected the top one hundred and ranked them according to their lasting importance. To qualify for inclusion, the event or person must have changed human history and life in some way forever. Cited among the most influential one hundred people are discovers, explorers, inventors, leaders, creators, and thinkers. And at the very pinnacle of this illustrious gathering stands Thomas Edison, the most important person of the millennium. The magazine explained its choice:

> *Because of him, the millennium will end in a wash of brilliant light rather than in torch-lit darkness as it began. In 1879, Thomas Edison gave humans the power to create light without fire, by inventing a long-lasting, affordable incandescent lamp. Among life's many conveniences we can take for granted, thanks in part to him: copiers, radio, movies, TV, phones (he improved Bell's). On the night after his funeral, Americans dimmed their lights for the man who lit up the world.*

References

Beals, Gerald. "Biography of Thomas Alva Edison." *Thomas Edison.com.* http://www.thomasedison.com/biog.htm. Access date November 1999.

Beals, Gerald. "Major Inventions and Events in the Life of Thomas Alva Edison." *Thomas Edison.com.* http://www.thomasedison.com/Inventions.htm. Access date November 1999.

"Chronology of Thomas Edison's Life." *Edison National Historic Site.* National Park Service. U.S. Department of the Interior. http://www.nps.gov/edis/home.htm. Access date November 1998.

Crichton, Judy. 1998. *America 1900: The Turning Point.* New York: Henry Holt & Company, Inc.

"Edison Inventions." *Edison National Historic Site.* National Park Service. U.S. Department of the Interior. http://www.nps.gov/edis/home.htm. Access date November 1998.

Friedman, Robert, ed. 1997. "The 100 People." *Life: The Millennium Special Double Issue* (Fall): 135-167.

Garraty, John A. and Mark C. Carnes, eds. 1999. *American National Biography.* New York: Oxford University Press.

Greenwood, Janette Thomas. 2000. *The Gilded Age: A History in Documents.* New York: Oxford University Press.

McAuliffe, Kathleen. 1995. "The Undiscovered World of Thomas Edison." *The Atlantic Monthly* (December) 80-93.

"Thomas A. Edison Papers." Rutgers University. http://edison.rutgers.edu/. Access date January 2000.

Lesson 22 Edison: The Wizard of Electricity 231

STANDARDS

Historical Thinking

The student will

Chronological Thinking

- distinguish between past, present and future time
- interpret data presented in time lines

Historical Comprehension

- reconstruct the literal meaning of a historical passage
- read historical narratives imaginatively

Historical Analysis and Interpretation

- analyze cause and effect relationships and multiple causation, including the importance of the individual, the influence of ideas, and the role of chance
- hypothesize the influence of the past

Historical Research Capabilities

- obtain historical data
- support interpretation with historical evidence

Analysis and Decision-Making

- identify issues and problems in the past
- formulate a position or course of action on an issue
- evaluate the implementation of a decision

Content

The student will demonstrate understanding of

- The importance of the individual in society
    - identify the contributions of inventor Thomas A. Edison that improved everyday life
    - explain how Thomas A. Edison's inventions continue to impact modern everyday life

Resources

For each student

Reconstructing America by Joy Hakim: Chapter 31, "The Wizard of Electricity"

Notebook

For each team

Document Packet: *Three of Edison's Inventions*

Web sites

Edison National Historic Site Home Page @ http://www.nps.gov/edis/home.htm

Thomas Edison and his Menlo Park Laboratory @ http://www.hfmgv.org/histories/edison/tae.html

Thomas A. Edison Papers @ http://edison.rutgers.edu/

Edison's Homepage Table of Contents @ http://www.tir.com/~quincy/CONTENTS.HTML

Vocabulary

Words to Remember

filament — fine thread-like object that glows but does not burn

incandescent — lamp in which an electrically heated filament glows with light

practical scientists — inventors who turn ideas into products that improve everyday life

People to Remember

*****Thomas Alva Edison** — inventor of over 1,093 practical patented inventions, three of the most important being the phonograph, electric light, and motion pictures

The Lesson

Focus Activity – 5 minutes

1. Direct the students to examine the timeline, "Some American Inventions 1830 to 1910" on pages 156 and 157 of *Reconstructing America*.

   Note to the Teacher: You may need to explain some of the inventions, such as the combine.

2. Teams use **Think-Team-Share** to decide:

   - Which invention most changed the world and why?

3. Teams use **Numbered Heads** to explain their choices. Write the choices on the chalkboard.

Teaching Activity – 25 minutes

1. Introduce Edison by asking the students what they know about Thomas Edison.

   - Who was Thomas Edison?
   - What did he do?
   - Why was he "the wizard of electricity"?

2. Read the quotation by Edison on the sidebar on page 154 of *Reconstructing America* and his observation that: "Genius is 99 percent perspiration and one percent inspiration."

   Ask the students to **Speculate**:

   - What do you think Edison meant by each of these comments?

   Direct the students to keep Edison's observations about thinking and hard work in mind as they read.

   - How were his words reflected in his own life?

3. Explain that Edison was a practical scientist. Ask the students to define the term and explain how it characterizes Edison's life and work. Read Edison's comment about his son Theodore at the bottom of page 159 in *Reconstructing America*. Ask the students:

Notes

- How does this quotation characterize Edison's life and work?

4. **Reading for a Purpose:** Students read silently or **Partner Read** Chapter 31, "The Wizard of Electricity" in *Reconstructing America* in order to develop a character profile of Edison.

    Before the students begin reading Chapter 31, help them identify general traits as categories for their character profile (such as hard-working, practical, and tenacious).

    As they read, students record information about the life and work of Edison that illustrates those character traits.

5. **Circulate and Monitor** As students read and develop the character profiles, help them locate and record pertinent information.

6. Students share their character profiles of Edison.

Student Team Learning Activity – 20 minutes

Evaluating the impact of Edison's inventions

1. **Reading for a Purpose:** Distribute the Document Packet: *Three of Edison's Inventions* to each team, and explain that the packet is a portfolio that describes Edison's work. Each team is a panel of judges for the prestigious Millennium Prize.

    After reading about Edison's work in the portfolio, each team must decide which of Edison's three featured inventions is the most important of the millennium and why.

    Each team needs to make a good case for its choice. In doing so, the team should consider the past, present, and future impact of the invention on ordinary life.

2. **Circulate and Monitor**: Visit each team as the students read document materials and choose the most important invention. Answer and ask questions to guide the students in their work.

3. Use **Numbered Heads** for each team to share its decision and the reasons for its choice. Keep a tally for each of the inventions to determine which one is chosen as the most influential by the majority of the teams. Students award the Millennium Prize to that invention.

Reflection and Review Activity – 10 minutes

1. Share the following information with the students:

   In the fall of 1997, *Life* magazine published a special issue on the millennium. The magazine listed several hundred of the most influential events and people of the last one thousand years, then selected the top one hundred and ranked them according to their lasting importance. To qualify for inclusion, the event or person must have changed human history and life in some way forever. Cited among the most influential one hundred people are discovers, explorers, inventors, leaders, creators, and thinkers. And at the very pinnacle of this illustrious gathering stands the most important person of the millennium—Thomas Edison.

2. Ask the students to decide

   - Why would Thomas Edison be considered the most important person of the last one thousand years?

   - Do you agree with *Life* magazine's choice? Why or why not?

   Encourage students to explain and support their responses.

3. Read *Life* magazine's explanation of its choice to the students.

   Because of him, the millennium will end in a wash of brilliant light rather than in torchlit darkness as it began. In 1879, Thomas Edison gave humans the power to create light without fire, by inventing a long-lasting, affordable incandescent lamp. Among life's many conveniences we can take for granted, thanks in part to him: copiers, radio, movies, TV, phones (he improved Bell's). On the night after his funeral, Americans dimmed their lights for the man who lit up the world.

4. • Ask the students:

   - Do you agree that Edison changed the world more than any other person in the last one thousand years? Why or why not?

   - Name as many ways as possible that Edison changed life with his inventions.

Homework

From the time you arrive home from school until bedtime, you and your family use many things that are only possible due to Edison's inventions. Make a list of all your modern conveniences that are possible because of Edison.

Library/Media Resources

Nonfiction

How Did We Find Out About Electricity? by Isaac Asimov, Walker
The Story of Thomas Alva Edison by Margaret Cousins, Random House
Thomas Alva Edison, Bringer of Light by Carol Greene, Children's Press
Edison at Work by David W. Hutchings, Hastings House
What Has Wild Tom Done Now? by Robert Quackenbush, Prentice-Hall
Electricity by Keith Brandt, Troll Associates
Thomas Alva Edison: Young Inventor by Sue Guthridge, Aladdin Library

Cobblestone Magazine

Thomas Edison

Connections

Science — This lesson has many possibilities for science connections including the following topics:

- Electricity, how it works and its uses
- Light and how the light bulb works
- Sound and how the phonograph works
- Vision and how moving pictures "move"
- Distinction between basic and applied science

Science — Student opportunities for hands-on science include conducting experiments and creating models based on Edison's inventions.

Science — Students consult the following books or others like them to replicate Edison's experiments:

- *Edison Experiments You Can Do* by Marjorie Van Der, Harper Collins Juvenile Books

- *Electrical and Chemical Experiments from Edison* by Robert F. Schultz, Thomas Alva Edison Foundation
- *Simple Experiments on Magnetism and Electricity from Edison* by Robert F. Schultz
- *The Thomas Edison Book of Easy and Incredible Experiments* by James G. Cook, John Wiley & Sons
- *Useful Science Experiments from Edison* by Robert F. Louis.

Language Arts — Students read a biography about Thomas Edison and his work.

Lesson 23
Jim Crow
Chapters

Theme

Based on the precursor black codes of Reconstruction, Jim Crow laws cemented the philosophy of "separate but equal," undermined and eradicated the efforts of the Radical Republicans after the Civil War, and dashed the hope of equality for generations.

Overview

The landmark legal precedent of *Plessy* v. *Ferguson* paved the way for the onslaught of racial intolerance, violence, and discrimination in America following the death of Reconstruction. Ironically, the Jim Crow character—which came to symbolize the legal segregation of the races—was originally a stage character first known in the North, where the idea of separation by habit reigned comfortably.

The Southern Jim Crow laws—many of which seem ridiculous to anyone who has not had to live under them—segregated the races in all aspects of life, from birth in separate hospitals to burial in separate cemeteries. Between life and death, laws separated blacks and whites in schools, restaurants, railway cars, and other public places.

In 1896, the Supreme Court ruled in *Plessy* v. *Ferguson* that separate accommodations for black and white races did not violate the Constitution—in essence, that segregation if coupled with equality is constitutional. The South determined that separation of the black and white races was necessary to keep order in society. The Supreme Court—and many white people—believed that "separate but equal" provided the most reasonable approach, considering the social prejudice that prevailed. The rub, however, was that nothing for blacks was equal. Housing, education, and transportation for blacks were substandard to say the least. Whites in the majority—in society, in government, and in the legal system—actively prevented blacks and other minorities from enjoying equal opportunities.

Even more appalling, terrorism gained a foothold in the South with the removal of federal military troops in 1871. Individuals and organizations (such as the Ku Klux Klan and other white supremacy groups) made post-Civil War freedom for blacks worse in some ways than slavery had ever been. Acts of terrorism—such as lynching and other forms of torturous murder—were not the only tactics used to keep blacks from their equal rights as citizens and full members of American society. "Redeemers" (racist political activists who gained control of the Southern legislatures) committed voter fraud by counting votes incorrectly to throw election results, buying votes in their favor, and instituting poll taxes, which prevented blacks and poor whites from voting.

The political and philosophical battles fought in the halls of Congress and in the media did little to remedy the horror of lives lost to sheer, premeditated violence. Southern state legislatures and Congress wrote laws and statutes—often in violation of the Constitution—to protect the white community from an integrated society.

Likewise, both the state and federal court systems upheld laws that violated the rights of blacks as guaranteed by the equal protection clause of the Fourteenth Amendment.

In 1954, almost sixty years later, the Supreme Court reversed its former *Plessy* v. *Ferguson* decision. This time the Supreme Court declared that separate is not equal. Theoretically, the decision nullified Jim Crow, but a bloody road to integration lay ahead. Not until the 1960s would ensuring the civil rights of African Americans assume its place in the forefront of the American conscience.

References

Bair, Barbara. 1997. *Though Justice Sleeps: African Americans 1880-1900*. New York: Oxford University Press.

"The Black Codes of 1865." *About.com*. http://afroamhistory.about.com/library/weekly/aa121900a.htm. Access date November 1998.

"Creation of the Jim Crow South: Segregation in the South." *About.com*. http://afroamhistory.about.com/library/weekly/aa010201a.htm. Access date November 1998.

Davis, Ronald L. F. "From Terror to Triumph: Historical Overview." *Jimcrowhistory.org*. http://www.jimcrowhistory.org/history/overview.htm. Access date November 1998.

Foner, Eric. 1999. *The Story of American Freedom*. New York: W.W. Norton & Company.

Frankel, Noralee. 1996. *Break Those Chains at Last: African Americans, 1860-1880*. New York: Oxford University Press.

Gamerman, Kenneth, ed. 1969. *Afro-American History Series. Separate and Unequal-1865-1910*. Chicago, Illinois: Encyclopedia Britannica Educational Corporation.

Grossman, James R. 1997. *A Chance to Make Good: African Americans, 1900-1929*. New York: Oxford University Press.

"Introduction to the Court Opinion on the *Plessy v. Ferguson* Case." *Basic Readings in U.S. Democracy*. http://usinfo.state.gov/usa/infousa/facts/democrac/33.htm. Access date November 1998.

"Jump, Jim Crow, or Did Emancipation Make Any Difference?" UC Berkeley. http://sunsite.berkeley.edu/calheritage/Jimcrow/. Access date November 1998.

Plessy v. Ferguson, 163 U.S. 537 (1896). *About.com*. http://usinfo.state.gov/usa/infousa/facts/democrac/33.htm. Access date November 1998.

Sandifer, Jawn A. ed. 1969. *The Afro-American in United States History*. New York: Globe Book Company.

Standards

Historical Thinking

The student will

Historical Comprehension

- reconstruct the literal meaning of a historical passage
- identify the central question(s) the historical narrative addresses
- read historical narratives imaginatively

Historical Analysis and Interpretation

- analyze cause and effect relationships and multiple causation, including the importance of the individual, the influence of ideas, and the role of chance
- hypothesize the influence of the past

Historical Research Capabilities

- obtain historical data

Analysis and Decision-Making

- identify issues and problems in the past

Content

The student will demonstrate understanding of

Lesson 23   Jim Crow

Massive immigration after 1870 and new social patterns, conflicts, and ideas of national unity developed amid growing cultural diversity

- Social Darwinism, race relations, and the struggle for equal rights and opportunities
  - explain the ideas of the Social Darwinists and their opponents
  - analyze political, social, and economic discrimination against African Americans, Asian Americans, and Hispanic Americans in different regions of the country

Resources

For each student
Reconstructing America by Joy Hakim: Chapter 32, "Jim Crow—What a Fool!"
Student Sheet: *Examples of Jim Crow Laws*
Notebook

For the teacher
Chart paper
Markers

Web sites
Civil War and Reconstruction Hot Links @ http://www.sinc.sunysb.edu/Class/his265/hotlinks.htm

Outline of the Civil War With Links to Reconstruction @ http://members.tripod.com/greatamericanhistory/gr02006.htm

Freedmen and Southern Society Project @ http://www.inform.umd.edu/ARHU/Depts/History/Freedman/ home.html

Freedom: A History of US @ http://www.pbs.org/wnet/historyofus/menu.html

Vocabulary

Words to Remember
*****Jim Crow** — originally a happy black stage character who gave no one any trouble, but the term came to mean the policy of segregation

*****segregation** — separation of the races

*****voter fraud** — illegal methods that change the outcome of a vote

*****Plessy v. Ferguson** — Supreme Court ruling that segregation did not violate the Constitution and was legal if it provided "separate but equal" accommodations for blacks

Words to Review
antebellum — before the Civil War

Radical Republicans — political party that opposed slavery and supported policies to expand the voting and civil rights of freed slaves

lynching — execution without due process of law, especially by hanging

white supremacy — belief that white people are superior to others

Ku Klux Klan — white supremacy organization that used violence to intimidate freed slaves and their white supporters

"Redeemers" — Conservative Democrats who regained control of the Southern state legislatures, drove the Republicans from power, and instituted segregation and voting requirements for freed slaves

poll tax — tax that voters must pay

People to Remember
*****Homer Plessy** — man of mixed racial descent who tested the legality of segregation by sitting in a "whites only" railway car

The Lesson

Focus Activity – 10 minutes

1. Give the following directions to the students:

   Your team is a group of "Superior Beings." It is your responsibility to create some rules that will separate "Superior Beings" from "Lesser Beings." **Think-Team-Share** a number of ways in which you can keep the "Superior Beings" separate and pure while at the same time making the "Lesser Beings" useful to you.

2. Use **Numbered Heads** for the teams to share some of their rules. Briefly record the rules on chart paper.

3. Ask the students:

   - How would you feel if you were a "Superior Being?"
   - How would you feel if you were a "Lesser Being?"

Teaching Activity – 20 minutes

1. Introduce the chapter by briefly discussing the beginnings of legal segregation after the failure of Reconstruction. Explain the concept of Jim Crow laws, and help the students to connect the Jim Crow laws with the black codes of Reconstruction.

   Preview the chapter's sidebar information and illustrations with the students.

2. Briefly introduce the Vocabulary *Words and People to Remember,* and if necessary, the *Vocabulary to Review* also.

3. **Reading for a Purpose:** The students read silently or **Partner Read** pages 160 through the first paragraph on page 163 of Chapter 32, "Jim Crow—What a Fool!" in *Reconstructing America* in order to discuss the following questions written on chart paper.

   - What were Jim Crow laws?
   - How and why did Jim Crow laws begin?

Notes

Lesson 23   Jim Crow

- What were race relations like in the North and in the South before the Civil War?
- What were race relations like in the North and in the South after the Civil War?
- What does the Fourteenth Amendment and "equal protection under the law" mean?

Circulate and Monitor: Visit each team as students read the assigned pages and prepare to discuss the questions.

4. Discuss the questions with the students. Use a chart format to summarize race relations in the North and the South.

Race Relations

	North	South
Pre-Civil War		
Post-Civil War		

Be sure the students understand the purpose of the Jim Crow laws and how the state and federal political and legal systems made such laws and their enforcement possible.

Review the Fourteenth and Fifteenth Amendments and the rights those amendments were intended to guarantee. Read and discuss "A Law Review for the Constitution" on page 164 of *Reconstructing America*.

Discuss the constitutionality of the Jim Crow laws by using the questions in the first paragraph of page 163 in *Reconstructing America* with the students.

5. Introduce the *Plessy* v. *Ferguson* case. Remind the students of other Supreme Court cases (such as the cases of Dred Scott and Yick Wo) that defined the rights of United States citizens and residents under the law.

6. **Reading for a Purpose:** Students read silently or **Partner Read** pages 163 and 164 of *Reconstructing America* in order to state the

   - **Facts** in the *Plessy* v. *Ferguson* case.
   - **Issue** in the *Plessy* v. *Ferguson* case.
   - **Opinion** of the Supreme Court in the *Plessy* v. *Ferguson* case.

Circulate and Monitor: Visit each team as students finish reading the chapter and identify the facts, the issue, and the opinion of the Supreme Court of the *Plessy* v. *Ferguson* case.

7. Discuss the *Plessy* v. *Ferguson* case and its implications with the students.

   - **Facts**
   In 1892, Homer Plessy purchased a first class ticket on the East Louisiana Railway from New Orleans to Covington, Louisiana. Plessy was a racially mixed (one-eighth black and seven-eighths white), United States citizen and a resident of the state of Louisiana. When he entered the train, Plessy took a seat in the coach where only whites were permitted to sit. The conductor told him to leave the coach and find another seat on the train where non-whites were permitted to sit. Plessy did not move and was ejected with force from the train. Plessy was sent to jail for violating the Louisiana Act of 1890, which required railway companies to provide "separate but equal" accommodations for white and black races. Plessy argued that this law was unconstitutional.

   - **Issue**
   Whether laws that provided for the separation of races violated the rights of blacks as guaranteed by the equal protection clause of the Fourteenth Amendment of the Constitution

   - **Opinion**
   The Supreme Court of the United States held that the Louisiana Act, which stated that "all railway companies were to provide equal but separate accommodations for white and black races," did not violate the Constitution. This law did not take away from the federal authority to regulate interstate commerce, nor did it violate the Thirteenth Amendment, which abolished slavery. Additionally, the law did not violate the Fourteenth Amendment, which gave all blacks their constitutional rights. The Court believed that "separate but equal" was the most reasonable approach considering the social prejudices that prevailed at the time.

Student Team Learning Activity – 25 minutes

Reacting to Jim Crow laws

1. Ask the students to read the Student Sheet: *Examples of Jim Crow Laws,* and **Think-Team-Share**:

   - What was it like for blacks to live under segregation? For whites?

   Circulate and Monitor: Visit each team as students read the examples and discuss the Jim Crow laws.

2. Lead the class in a discussion of how segregation harms both races, but especially the minority race. Use questions such as the following to spark discussion:

   - Why was it possible to pass unjust Jim Crow laws?

   - What conditions in the United States made it possible for the Supreme Court to uphold the segregationist policy in its *Plessy v. Ferguson* decision?

   - How could the racist interpretation of the Fourteenth and Fifteenth Amendments so violate their original intent?

Reflection and Review Activity – 5 minutes

1. Teams use **Think-Team-Share** to consider the following questions.

   - How did your laws as "Superior Beings" compare with the Jim Crow laws?

   - How are they similar?

   - How are they different?

   - What are your reactions to your "Superior Beings" laws?

   - What are your reactions to the Jim Crow laws and the "separate but equal" decision of the Supreme Court?

2. Use **Numbered Heads** for the teams to share their responses.

   Note to the Teacher: An additional resource for this lesson is the video series Freedom: A History of US, Episode Seven—Part Six: "Separate But Equal", Kunhardt Productions and Thirteen/WNET for PBS. Also explore the accompanying PBS Website: Freedom: A History of US @ http://www.pbs.org/wnet/historyofus/ menu.html, especially the section for teachers.

Homework

Write your personal reaction to one of the following:

- Jim Crow laws
- *Plessy* v. *Ferguson* decision
- Segregation

OR

Interview family members or friends who remember segregation. What was it like for them to live under segregation? Write or share their impressions with others.

Library/Media Resources

Fiction

Sounder by William H. Armstrong, Harper Trophy

Freedom Songs by Yvette Moore, Puffin

Nonfiction

Now Is Your Time: The African American Struggle for Freedom by Walter Dean Myers, HarperCollins Juvenile Books

Video

Skin Deep: People's Century, WGBH

Nantucket: Rock of Changes, WGBH

Celebrating Our Differences: Race, National Geographic

Freedom: A History of US, Episode Seven—Part Six, Kunhardt Productions and Thirteen/WNET for PBS

Connections

Language Arts — Students read *Circle of Fire* by William Hooks. Partner Discussion Guide is available from Talent Development Middle Schools, CSOS, Johns Hopkins University.

Technology — Students use Web sites to research Jim Crow and segregation.

Research/Library — Students seek to answer: Is segregation alive in other parts of the world today? Students conduct a comparative study of segregation in the history of the United States and South Africa.

Lesson 24
Ida B. Wells
Chapters 33 and 34

Theme

With bravery and determination—and a reporter's pen—Ida B. Wells spoke out against lynch mobs that executed blacks and their white supporters without remorse and in premeditated hatred.

Overview

Ida B. Wells was the daughter of former slaves from Mississippi. She grew up in the small town of Holly Springs, where blacks and whites made an attempt to live in harmony with one another after the Civil War. Her peaceful childhood changed with the failure of Reconstruction and the onset of the Jim Crow era. Wells, who at the age of sixteen lost her parents to a yellow fever epidemic, grew up overnight when she assumed responsibility for her younger siblings and went to work as a teacher in a country school.

During her early adulthood Wells became a political activist by standing up for her convictions and for her people. Foreshadowing Rosa Parks' refusal to give up her seat on a bus, Ida B. Wells refused to move from her seat in a car for whites to the smoking car on a train, and ultimately sued the company for forcibly removing her from her seat. She won her suit, but the Tennessee Supreme Court later reversed the verdict.

While that decision discouraged her, she soon found a formidable weapon with which to fight injustice—her pen. Wells became a renowned newspaper reporter whose writings were so effective they enraged many and elicited death threats from others. Upon the lynching of her good friend, Tom Moss, she began speaking out against murderous vigilantes in her paper *Free Speech*.

Lynching was callous, premeditated murder—that included hanging, shooting, dismemberment, and being burned alive—carried out by mobs without due process of law. Committed not just in the South but throughout the United States (often with the participation and approval of community leaders), lynching was vigilante justice by white men who took the law into their own hands and executed hated blacks, Asians, and their white supporters. These executions had nothing to do with the legal process: a person could be murdered upon mere suspicion of wrongdoing. Infrequently was anyone lynched for an actual crime, and if a victim was guilty of criminal activity, that crime certainly did not merit brutal murder. An organized, planned event, a lynching often drew an appreciative audience of spectators.

Although many Americans were ignorant of the gruesome facts behind these terrorist acts, others believed the victims of lynching deserved their fate—they had committed crimes for which their murders were an acceptable punishment. Racists and white supremacy groups believed the victims deserved lynching because they were a threat to white society and its values. During the course of a forty-year period, 4,761 people in the United States were lynched, including women and children. New

England was the only region that did not practice this particular brutality, probably due to the strong Puritan religious influence there.

Ida B. Wells had enormous influence with her readers. When the city of Memphis refused to even try to find the murderer of Tom Moss, over six thousand blacks emigrated from the city at her urging.

Wells organized a streetcar boycott that presaged the bus boycott in Montgomery, Alabama in the late 1950s. Because the ban on streetcars affected many white businesses, the superintendent and the treasurer of the City Railway Company visited Wells and urged her to use her influence with blacks to get them to patronize the streetcars once again. Wells used the meeting as an opportunity to make the men admit that their livelihood depended on black patronage. Then she encouraged blacks to continue the boycott in order to make their point.

While she was at an editor's conference in New York, Wells' office was destroyed. Although this act and continuing threats of violence persuaded her to relocate to Chicago and buy a gun, she never stopped writing.

She traveled to England to gain support for her cause and there found an audience who took her seriously. She gained a reputation as a fiery orator and courageous leader of her people. It was thirty years before Wells could return to the South without the threat of a lynching interfering with her work. Many Americans tried to ignore Ida B. Wells out of true apathy, and in some cases, because they did not know how to solve the problems to which she called attention.

Wells continued her efforts as a married woman and a mother, speaking on behalf of the suffragist movement and against terrorism. An organizer and activist, she formed clubs and associations to assist the black community and advance its causes. Equally important, her original articles about lynch mobs and murders served as a foundation of research for others to build upon in the fight against this atrocity.

Wells' forty-year career as journalist, educator, reformer, and outspoken critic of the political and economic expressions of violence toward black Americans stands as a testimony of her dedication to the black community. Her passion for equal rights makes her a hero to all. Wells' life proved that the pen really is mightier than the sword!

References

Bair, Barbara. 1997. *Though Justice Sleeps: African Americans, 1880-1900.* New York: Oxford University Press.

"Creation of the Jim Crow South: Segregation in the South." *About.com.* http://afroamhistory.about.com/library/weekly/aa010201a.htm. Access date November 1998.

Davis, Ronald L. F. "From Terror to Triumph: Historical Overview." *Jimcrowhistory.org.* http://www.jimcrowhistory.org/history/overview.htm. Access date November 1998.

Foner, Eric. 1999. *The Story of American Freedom.* New York: W.W. Norton & Company.

Frankel, Noralee. 1996. *Break Those Chains at Last: African Americans, 1860-1880.* New York: Oxford University Press.

Gamerman, Kenneth, ed. 1969. *Afro-American History Series. Separate and Unequal, 1865-1910.* Chicago, Illinois: Encyclopedia Britannica Educational Corporation.

Garraty, John A. and Mark C. Carnes, eds. 1999. *American National Biography.* New York: Oxford University Press.

Grossman, James R. 1997. *A Chance to Make Good: African Americans, 1900-1929.* New York: Oxford University Press.

"Ida B. Wells-Barnett: Crusader for Justice." Hersalon. http://www.hersalon.com/herstory/ida/ida.htm. Access date November 1998.

"Jump, Jim Crow, or Did Emancipation Make Any Difference?" UC Berkeley. http://sunsite.berkeley.edu/calheritage/Jimcrow/. Access date November 1998.

Keenan, Sheila. 1996. *Encyclopedia of Women in the United States.* New York: Oxford University Press.

"The Progress of a People: Segregation and Violence." *The Library of Congress: American Memory. African American Perspectives: Pamphlets from the Daniel A. P. Murray Collection, 1818-1907.* http://memory.loc.gov/ammem/aap/aapmob.html. Access date November 1998.

Sandifer, Jawn A. ed. 1969. *The Afro-American in United States History.* New York: Globe Book Company.

Wells-Barnett, Ida B. "Lynch law in Georgia." *The Library of Congress: American Memory.* http://memory.loc.gov/cgi-bin/query/r?ammem/murray:@field(FLD001+91898209+):@@@REF. Access date November 1998.

Wilson, Vincent, Jr. 1992. *The Book of Distinguished American Women.* Brookeville, Maryland: American History Research Associates.

"Women in History. Ida B. Wells Barnett biography." Lakewood Public Library. http://www.lkwdpl.org/wihohio/barn-ida.htm. Access date November 1998.

Standards

Historical Thinking

The student will

Historical Comprehension

- identify the central question(s) the historical narrative addresses
- read historical narratives imaginatively
- draw upon data in historical maps
- utilize visual and mathematical data presented in charts, Venn diagrams, and other graphic organizers

Historical Analysis and Interpretation

- analyze cause and effect relationships and multiple causation, including the importance of the individual, the influence of ideas, and the role of chance
- hypothesize the influence of the past

Historical Research Capabilities

- obtain historical data

Analysis and Decision-Making

- identify issues and problems in the past
- marshal evidence of antecedent circumstances and contemporary factors contributing to problems and alternative courses of action
- evaluate alternative courses of action
- evaluate the implementation of a decision

Content

The student will demonstrate understanding of

Massive immigration after 1870 and new social patterns, conflicts, and ideas of national unity developed amid growing cultural diversity

- Social Darwinism, race relations, and the struggle for equal rights and opportunities
  - explain the ideas of the Social Darwinists and their opponents
  - analyze political, social, and economic discrimination against African Americans, Asian Americans, and Hispanic Americans in different regions of the country

Resources

For each student

Reconstructing America by Joy Hakim: Chapter 33, "Ida B. Wells" and Chapter 34, "Lynching Means Killing by a Mob"

Student Sheets:
- *A Woman of Character*
- *Mob Murders*

Crayons or markers

Notebook

Web sites

Ida B. Wells Barnett @ http://www.mtsu.edu/~library/wtn/bio/wells.html

Women in History - Ida B. Wells Barnett biography @ http://www.lkwdpl.org/wihohio/barn-ida.htm

Progress of a People: Ida B. Wells-Barnett @ http://lcweb2.loc.gov/ammem/aap/idawells.html

Ida B. Wells-Barnett House @ http://www.ci.chi.il.us/Landmarks/IdaBWells.html

Ida B. Wells-Barnett @ http://www.nyu.edu/pages/projects/jhistory/jhist.96/0444.html

Note to the Teacher: The Library of Congress American Memory Web site has two primary source documents written by Ida B. Wells that describe the lynching (execution killing, shooting, burning to death, and hanging) of blacks. The descriptions are extremely graphic and troubling, and probably should not be read by young students, but teachers may wish to review them as preparation for this lesson. If so, see Ida B. Wells-Barnett from The Library of Congress American Memory.

Vocabulary

Words to Remember

*****lynching** — mob murders or executions without benefit of trial

*****vigilante** — person who takes the law into his or her own hands

*****anarchy** — no government or law and order; chaos

Freedom's Journal — first newspaper in America printed and edited by African Americans

People to Remember

*****Ida B. Wells** — black newspaper reporter who drew attention to the atrocities against African Americans, especially lynching

Charles Lynch — Revolutionary War Virginian who organized posses to terrorize and kill Tories

Lesson 24   Ida B. Wells

The Lesson

Focus Activity – 5 minutes

Notes

1. Ask the students to **Speculate**:

   • What does the statement "The pen is mightier than the sword." mean?

   • Can you think of any books, documents, or other written materials that were or are more effective than the sword? (Responses might include Harriet Beecher Stowe's *Uncle Tom's Cabin,* the Bible, the Constitution, and the Declaration of Independence.)

2. Use **Numbered Heads** for the students to share their responses.

Teaching Activity – 35 minutes

1. Introduce Chapters 33 and 34 in *Reconstructing America* by briefly discussing the situation in the United States after the failure of Reconstruction.

   Emphasize the precarious circumstances of the freedmen and women of the South as white supremacists gained control of the political and legal systems.

   Ask the students to **Speculate**:

   • Why might the years of freedom after Reconstruction be as dangerous and difficult for blacks as slavery? (As freedmen, blacks lost their economic value as slaves; no legal protection; no federal military presence in the South; white backlash; etc.)

2. Acquaint students with Ida B. Wells, a crusader for justice who used her pen to inform others about the injustice of segregation and the atrocity of lynching. Use information from the Overview and examine the illustrations and Chapters 33 and 34 in *Reconstructing America* with the students.

3. Briefly introduce the Vocabulary *Words and People to Remember.*

4. Distribute the Student Sheet: *A Woman of Character* and explain the activity.

5. **Reading for a Purpose:** Students read silently or **Partner Read** Chapter 33, "Ida B. Wells" and Chapter 34, "Lynching Means Killing by a Mob" in *Reconstructing America*.

   As they read, students identify the character traits of Ida B. Wells and her actions that illustrate those traits. For example, her character trait of bravery was illustrated by her refusal to give up her seat on a segregated train. Students may find more than one action that illustrations a particular character trait.

   Students record the character traits and the biographical information about Ida B. Wells on their Student Sheets: *A Woman of Character*.

   Note to the Teacher: Because students have much to read, it is recommended that the two chapters be read interactively with you. For example, the students read the italicized quotations and the teacher reads the text. However, if students are accomplished readers they can easily read both chapters.

6. Periodically interrupt the reading to allow the students to record character traits and biographical information that supports those traits on their student sheets and to discuss that information as a class.

   Circulate and Monitor: Visit each team to help students identify and record accurate information on their student sheets.

7. When students have completed the reading and their student sheets, lead them in a discussion of Wells and her fight against injustice. Guide the discussion to include the following topics.

   - The dangers of mob rule, anarchy, and lynching to a democracy and its citizens

   - Identifying other times in history when hatred against a race produced similar atrocities (such as Nazi Germany and the Jews, United States Army and the Native Americans, South African whites and blacks, the Serbian Slavs and Kosovo Albanians, and other recent examples).

   - Lessons we might learn by studying these darker sides of history

Lesson 24   Ida B. Wells

Student Team Learning Activity – 20 minutes

Interpreting charts and creating historical maps

1. Distribute the Student Sheet: *Mob Murders*.

   Explain to students that between the years 1882 and 1958, lynching (mob murders or executions without benefit of trial) were reported in every state except Rhode Island, Connecticut, New Hampshire, and Massachusetts. The statistics on the student sheet concern those states in which more than fifty percent of the mob murders were committed against African Americans. Be sure students understand that not only black men were lynched, but also whites and Asians, women and children.

2. Students use the figures in the chart, *Mob Murders,* to create a corresponding color key and then color code the states.

   Circulate and Monitor: Visit each team as students create a color key and code the states. If necessary, team members may help each other identify the states and their abbreviations on the student sheet.

3. Use the following questions to help students analyze and interpret the information on their maps.

   - In which region were African Americans at the greatest risk of violence?

   - Were African Americans safe from violence in the North?

   - From your map, what can you infer about violence against African Americans in the years between Reconstruction and the Civil Rights movement?

Reflection and Review Activity – 5 minutes

1. Ask a student volunteer to read the sidebar "Mob Rule" on page 172 of *Reconstructing America*.

   Students **Think-Team-Share:**

- Are there times when people should take the law into their own hands? Why or why not?
- What are alternatives to vigilante justice? (Examples include the citizen's arrest, the Good Samaritan, dialing 911, neighborhood watch programs.)

2. Use **Numbered Heads** for the teams to share their responses.

Homework

Create a way to honor or remember the work of Ida B. Wells. Some possibilities include composing a poem, an acrostic on her name, or a song; designing a mural, drawing, stamp, or commemorative plaque; or drawing a picture of an important scene in her life. Bring your creation to class for display.

Library/Media Resources

Fiction
Sounder by William H. Armstrong, Harper Trophy

Freedom Songs by Yvette Moore, Puffin

Nonfiction
The Memphis Diary of Ida B. Wells by Ida B. Wells, Beacon Press

Crusade for Justice: The Autobiography of Ida B. Wells by Ida B. Wells, University of Chicago Press

Getting the Real Story: Nellie Bly and Ida B. Wells (Women Who Dared) by Sue Davidson, Seal Press

Ida B. Wells: Antilynching Crusader (American Troublemakers) by Richard M. Haynes, Raintree/Steck-Vaughn

Ida B. Wells-Barnett: A Voice Against Violence (Great African Americans Series) by Pat McKissack, Enslow Publishers, Inc.

Princess of the Press: The Story of Ida B. Wells-Barnett (Rainbow Biography) by Angela Shelf Medearis, Lodestar Books

Connections

Language Arts — Students read *Circle of Fire* by William Hooks. Partner Discussion Guide is available from Talent Development Middle schools, CSOS, Johns Hopkins University.

Library — Students read Ida B. Wells' autobiography, Memphis diary, or anti-lynching writings.

Expressive Arts/Library — Students create a short scene, play, or one-woman show based on Ida B. Wells' writings.

Lesson 25
Booker T. and W.E.B.
Chapters 35 and 36

Theme

Although Booker T. Washington and W.E.B. DuBois entertained vastly different ideas and approaches to racial issues, both men contributed to America's quest for true equality and justice for all its people.

Overview

Booker T. Washington grew up with a very strong work ethic, intensified, no doubt, by his ten years as a slave. Born five years prior to the Civil War, he received his freedom at its conclusion. At the age of ten, he began work in a salt furnace, all the while yearning to attend school. Eventually he got that opportunity between his work shifts in the morning and evening. Washington's desire for education led him east to Hampton Institute, where he received vocational training. Having no money, he worked as a janitor to pay for his tuition and living costs. His hard work won the recognition of Hampton's president and his recommendation for Washington to preside over the Tuskegee Institute. When Washington arrived to assume his presidency, he found only a ramshackle building at the institute. Undeterred, Washington and his students rolled up their sleeves and set about constructing a complex that by the turn of the century contained over forty buildings.

Despite his willingness to work and his achievement in becoming educated in spite of great odds, Washington's contribution to his people and to American society was suspect to many black activists. Because he aimed for working compromises that could lead to change slowly but surely, he tended to submit to oppressive social and governmental systems. His seeming tolerance of racism against his people and patience with the violent practices that accompanied that racism angered many blacks, including W. E. B. DuBois. Washington believed that social and political agitation should follow—not precede—the acquisition of property and a demonstrated desire to work hard by the black community.

Washington was not weak-willed nor did he lack the mental strength to be revolutionary. Instead, he possessed certain convictions and ideas based upon his own thinking and experience. People of both races rallied to his speeches and embraced his personal platforms because Washington was a thought-provoking speaker who could raise cheers and thunderous applause from his audiences.

Booker T. Washington possessed common sense and practical learning, and he wanted the same for all blacks. He advised blacks to refrain from getting caught in the dangers of "rocking the boat" by agitating against the system. With hard work and devotion to self-improvement, he had experienced great fulfillment and success. His formula seemed to work. However, Booker T. Washington, while still important to black progress in America, may have unintentionally restricted his race by compromising too much and not addressing the racial prejudice and violence that assailed blacks in his day.

In contrast, W.E.B. DuBois was a revolutionary thinker and boat rocker who challenged the philosophy of Booker T. Washington. DuBois often debunked

Washington's platforms in essays and articles, encouraging blacks not to settle for anything less than full equality as American citizens. During his lifetime, DuBois was not as widely accepted for his ideas as Washington. Today, however, most people recognize DuBois' brilliance and agree with his statements. DuBois used his great intelligence to work for his race and for America as a country of many different ethnicities. Not only did DuBois advocate for blacks, but he also spoke out against anti-Semitism and labored to guarantee fair treatment for immigrant groups. He believed that all Americans bore the responsibilities that accompany citizenship in this country, and that each person's ethnic roots brought cultural richness to American society.

The first black to receive a doctorate from Harvard, DuBois went on to edit several magazines, and ultimately to help found the National Association for the Advancement of Colored People (N.A.A.C.P). A native of a prominent Massachusetts family, William Edward Burghardt DuBois' tendency toward social and political discourse was nurtured at annual town meetings, where his ideas about democracy were formed.

DuBois' vehement disagreement with Booker T. Washington's philosophies on the methods of advancing the cause of American black people shocked his contemporaries. He thought Washington was too conciliatory and asked too little of government and white Americans. Both of these leaders possessed invaluable talents and strengths that America needed for its betterment—and they both had weaknesses.

Booker T. Washington had the wonderful capability to facilitate understanding between people who had very significant differences, whereas W.E.B. DuBois had excellent ideas and goals for America, but was less adept at working with others. HIs inability to garner support through compromise too often cost him credibility. Although the mark of a revolutionary is to be absolutely true to one's ideals and uncompromising to the end, this stance often alienates others who might have listened under more welcoming circumstances. Although too abrasive for many of his contemporaries, DuBois is now respected for his contributions, proving himself a man ahead of his times.

References

Bair, Barbara. 1997. *Though Justice Sleeps: African Americans, 1880-1900*. New York: Oxford University Press.

Dubois, W.E.B. "'Of Mr. Booker T. Washington and Others', from *The Souls of Black Folk*. (1903)." Swarthmore University Social Science Department. http://www.swarthmore.edu/SocSci/rbannis1/Progs/Dubois.html. Access date November 1999.

Dubois, W.E.B. 1998 Reprint. *The Souls of Black Folk*. Evanston, Illinois: McDougal Littell.

Foner, Eric. 1999. *The Story of American Freedom*. New York: W.W. Norton & Company.

Gamerman, Kenneth. ed. 1969. *Afro-American History Series. Separate and Unequal, 1865-1910*. Chicago, Illinois: Encyclopedia Britannica Educational Corporation.

Garraty, John A. and Mark C. Carnes, eds. 1999. *American National Biography*. New York: Oxford University Press.

Greenwood, Janette Thomas. 2000. *The Gilded Age: A History in Documents*. New York: Oxford University Press.

Grossman, James R. 1997. *A Chance to Make Good: African Americans, 1900-1929*. New York: Oxford University Press.

Hynes, Gerald C. "A Biographical Sketch of W.E.B. DuBois. W.E.B. DuBois Learning Center. http://www.duboislc.org/html/DuBoisBio.html. Access date November 1999.

"Jump, Jim Crow, or Did Emancipation Make Any Difference?" UC Berkeley. http://sunsite.berkeley.edu/calheritage/Jimcrow/. Access date November 1998.

Kennedy, David M. and Thomas A. Bailey. 2002. *The American Spirit. Volume II: Since 1865.* Boston: Houghton Mifflin Company.

"The Progress of a People: Biography: Booker T. Washington (1856-1915)." *The Library of Congress: American Memory. African American Perspectives: Pamphlets from the Daniel A. P. Murray Collection, 1818-1907.* http://memory.loc.gov/ammem/aap/bookert.html. Access date November 1998.

"The Progress of a People: Segregation and Violence." *The Library of Congress: American Memory. African American Perspectives: Pamphlets from the Daniel A. P. Murray Collection, 1818-1907.* http://memory.loc.gov/ammem/aap/aapmob.html. Access date November 1998.

Sandifer, Jawn A. ed. 1969. *The Afro-American in United States History.* New York: Globe Book Company.

"Up From Slavery: Booker T. Washington Biography." National Park Service. *ParkNet.* http://www.nps.gov/bowa/btwbio.html. Access date November 1998.

Washington, Booker T. "An Address Delivered at the Opening of the Cotton States and International Exposition." *The Library of Congress: American Memory. African American Perspectives: Pamphlets from the Daniel A. P. Murray Collection, 1818-1907.* http://memory.loc.gov/ammem/aap/aapaddr.html. Access date November 1998.

Washington, Booker T. "The Booker T. Washington Papers." University of Illinois Press. http://www.historycooperative.org/btw/volumes.html. Access date November 2000.

Washington, Booker T. 1901. *Up from Slavery: An Autobiography.* Garden City, New York: Doubleday & Co.

Zinn, Howard. 1999. *A People's History of the United States: 1492-Present.* New York: HarperCollins Publishers.

Standards

Historical Thinking

The student will

Historical Comprehension

- identify the central question(s) the historical narrative addresses
- read historical narratives imaginatively

Historical Analysis and Interpretation

- analyze cause and effect relationships and multiple causation, including the importance of the individual, the influence of ideas, and the role of chance
- hypothesize the influence of the past

Historical Research Capabilities

- obtain historical data

Analysis and Decision-Making

- identify issues and problems in the past
- marshal evidence of antecedent circumstances and contemporary factors contributing to problems and alternative courses of action
- evaluate alternative courses of action
- evaluate the implementation of a decision

Content

The student will demonstrate understanding of

Massive immigration after 1870 and new social patterns, conflicts, and ideas of national unity developed amid growing cultural diversity

- Social Darwinism, race relations, and the struggle for equal rights and opportunities
  - explain the ideas of the Social Darwinists and their opponents
  - analyze political, social, and economic discrimination against African Americans, Asian Americans, and Hispanic Americans in different regions of the country

Resources

For each student

Reconstructing America by Joy Hakim: Chapter 35, "A Man and His Times" and Chapter 36, "A Man Ahead of His Times"

Student Sheet: Booker T., W.E.B., and Me Notebook

Web sites

Booker T. Washington National Monument Home Page @ http://www.nps.gov/bowa/home.htm

The Two Nations of Black America: Booker T & W.E.B @ http://www.pbs.org/wgbh/pages/frontline/shows/race/etc/road.html

WWW Sources for Information on DuBois @ http://www.msu.edu/course/mc/112/1920s/Garvey-DuBois/ MGLinks.html

W.E.B. DuBois links @ http://www.students.haverford.edu/cstoner/W.E.B.-DuBois-links.html

Vocabulary

Words to Remember

*anti-Semitism — hostility toward Jews

*National Association for the Advancement of Colored People (NAACP) — organization of whites and blacks formed to fight racial prejudice

*ideal — goal or standard of excellence

People to Remember

*Booker T. Washington — head of the Tuskegee Institute and African American spokesman who believed blacks should gain economic independence and education before seeking social and political equality

*W.E.B. DuBois — brilliant African American speaker and writer who agitated for full equality for all Americans

The Lesson

Focus Activity – 5 minutes

1. Ask the students to put themselves in the shoes of a black leader at the end of the 1800s.

   Think-Team-Share:

   - What would be your advice to your people? To the white community? To the nation's leaders?

2. Use **Numbered Heads** for the students to share their advice.

Teaching Activity – 35 minutes

1. Using information from the Overview, acquaint students with Booker T. Washington and W.E.B. DuBois as leaders and spokesmen for their people. Briefly explain that although both men worked for the advancement of black Americans, each man had his own distinct personality, style, and message. Ask students if they can think of other leaders who differed from each other in their ideas and methods (for example, Martin Luther King and Malcolm X).

   Help students realize that differing viewpoints, ideas, and backgrounds enrich us as Americans. The ideas and examples of both Booker T. Washington and W.E.B. DuBois are important to all Americans because each man wanted to help our country be true to its ideals and fair to all people.

2. Explain the assignment. Distribute the Student Sheet and explain the grid categories and examples.

   - **Man** — Background information about each man's life that shaped his character and point of view (For example: Booker was a freed Southern slave; W.E.B. was from a respected, educated Northern family.)

   - **Message** — Ideas and beliefs about black Americans in the nation's society and government (For example, Booker said blacks should get good jobs then fight for other freedoms; W.E.B. wanted full equality for blacks immediately.)

Notes

- **Mien** — Personality or manner (For example, Booker compromised with whites whereas W.E.B. wouldn't compromise with anyone)

- **Method** — Ways in which each man got his message across or accomplished his goals (For example, Booker was a great speaker and inspired his audiences; W.E.B. wrote brilliant books and articles.)

Students ignore the *Me* column on the grid at this time. Directions for its completion will be provided after the sections on Booker and W.E.B. are finished.

Note to the Teacher: As in the previous lesson, Chapters 35 and 36 may be read interactively— with the students reading the italicized quotations and the teacher reading the text—or silently, if students are accomplished readers.

3. Briefly introduce the Vocabulary Words to Remember.

4. **Reading for a Purpose:** Students individually read or **Partner Read** Chapter 35, "A Man and His Times" and Chapter 36, "A Man Ahead of His Times." As they read, students identify the contrasting messages, styles, and personalities of the two great leaders, Booker T. Washington and W.E.B. DuBois. Students synthesize that information on their Student Sheets: Booker T., W.E.B., and Me.

5. Periodically interrupt the reading so students can record appropriate information on their grids.

   Circulate and Monitor: Visit each team to help students identify and record accurate information on their Student Sheet grids. Ask a few volunteers to share some of their grid information as examples for the other students.

6. When students have completed the reading and their student sheets, engage them in a discussion of the two men, their personalities, methods, and messages.

   Be sure students appreciate each man's strengths and weaknesses in moving his people and all Americans toward our nation's ideals of justice and equality.

7. Discuss the following questions with the students.

   - Why do we need compromisers **and** agitators?
   - Why do we need thinkers **and** doers?
   - Why do we need inspiring messages **and** protesting actions?

Student Team Learning Activity – 20 minutes

Deciding on a course of action

1. Students will use the **Me** section on their Student Sheets: Booker T., W.E.B., and Me to consider the following topics.

    - Their own backgrounds, personalities, and beliefs

    - How they would go about changing prejudice, injustice, and inequality at school or in their own neighborhoods.

2. To prepare students for the activity, discuss each of the grid categories as it relates to the students themselves.

    - **Man** — What in your background shapes your actions and personality? For example, consider your education, the influence of your family or friends, or your admiration for a public figure.

    - **Message** — What would be your message to your own family, friends, or schoolmates? What advice would you give to your schoolmates or friends? To your neighborhood or school leaders?

    - **Mien** — Which of your personality traits would advance your cause? Are you a good listener? Are you a hard worker? Do you make friends easily? How can you bring your personality strengths to the task?

    - **Method** — How would you get your message to leaders, friends, or schoolmates—your audience?

3. After considering themselves and their messages, each student completes the *Me* section of the grid.

    Circulate and Monitor: Visit each team as students consider themselves and their messages. If necessary, help students complete the grid by answering and asking questions.

4. Depending on the time available, student volunteers share their personal *Me* information with their teams or the class.

    Ask the students to briefly evaluate the ways they are like or different from Booker and W.E.B. Students should understand that all personal qualities and strengths are needed in a democracy.

5. Engage the students in a class conversation about the message of W.E.B. DuBois.

   Begin with his quotation,

   > "We are Americans, not only by birth and by citizenship, but by our political ideals. . . . And the greatest of those ideals is that ALL MEN ARE CREATED EQUAL."

   Ask the students:

   - What are ideals?
   - How did DuBois define *Americans*?
   - Do you agree with his statement? Explain.
   - What are some other American ideals?

   Ask the students to react to DuBois' concept of the double inheritance that each American has that includes:

   - The responsibilities and rights that go with American citizenship
   - The personal richness of our own ethnic roots
   - Our diverse backgrounds which enrich us all, for it is this collection of heritages that make America special.

   Discuss the following questions with the students.

   - What are our responsibilities as American citizens? Our rights?
   - What personal richness from your ethnic roots do you bring to America?
   - How do our different heritages enrich our class or school?

Reflection and Review Activity – 5 minutes

1. Teams react to the following "supposes."
   - Suppose there were only "compromisers" in our history.
   - Suppose there were no "compromisers" in our history.
   - Suppose there was only one race or ethnic group in the United States. What would we gain? What would we lose?

2. Use **Numbered Heads** for the teams to share their responses.

Homework

Create a way to honor or remember the work of Booker T. Washington **or** W.E.B. DuBois. Some possibilities include composing a poem, an acrostic on his name, or song; or designing a mural, drawing, stamp, or commemorative plaque. Bring your creation to class for display.

Library/Media Resources

Fiction
Sounder by William H. Armstrong, Harper Trophy

Freedom Songs by Yvette Moore, Puffin

Nonfiction
Now Is Your Time: The African American Struggle for Freedom by Walter Dean Myers, Harper Collins Juvenile Books

Up from Slavery by Booker T. Washington, Penguin Classics or Dover Thrift Edition

Black Diamonds: The Wisdom of Booker T. Washington edited by Frank Hill, Health Communications

Booker T. Washington (Photo-Illustrated Biography) by Margo McLoone, Bridgestone Books

The Story of Booker T. Washington (Cornerstones of Freedom) by Pat McKissack, Children's Press

The Souls of Black Folk by W. E. B. Dubois, Bantam

Du Bois: A Pictorial Biography by Shirley Graham Dubois, Johnson Publishing Company

W.E.B. DuBois (Journey to Freedom: The African American Library) by Don Troy, Child's World

Connections

Library — Students read the autobiographies or biographies of Booker T. Washington and W.E.B. DuBois.

Writing/Library — Students create biography cards for Booker T. Washington and W.E.B. DuBois.

Expressive Arts — Students role play a dialogue between Booker T. Washington and W.E.B. DuBois in which they state each man's ideas and philosophies.

Lesson 26
End Words
Chapter 37

Theme

The post-Civil War years of Reconstruction and reform were a time of change, diversity, and striving for justice in America. Although Americans made great advances toward equality and freedom for all, poverty, racism, and injustice, especially for African Americans, Native Americans, Chinese and other immigrants, blemished the time.

Overview

So here we are at the end of another era, one that promised great things: the reconstruction of a broken nation after a terrible civil war and the reform of its inequalities. Reconstruction promised a new beginning with no slavery, with freedom for all, blacks as well as whites. America had a second chance to begin aright. The nation was, as Civil War scholar Shelby Foote said, "at the crossroads of our being."

So what direction did we take at that crossroads? Did we journey toward achieving the famous words of Jefferson and the Declaration of Independence?

We hold these truths to be self-evident, that all Men are created equal, that they are endowed by their Creator with certain unalienable Rights, that among these are Life, Liberty and the Pursuit of Happiness . . .

The road—a bumpy, twisting one from the Civil War to the turn of the century—at times headed toward the bright promise of freedom as scripted by Thomas Jefferson, John Adams, and Benjamin Franklin. But at other times, the vision was limited and the road veered sharply from the golden destination into ugly vistas of racism, hatred, and injustice. Yet, slowly and with great pain, Americans paved the way to a more inclusive society that would mean greater liberty for all citizens.

Sometimes along the journey, individuals who saw the destination clearly and fully understood the nation's mission lit the path for others:

- Thaddeus Stevens knew that the supreme power of the United States was the people—all the people—and he finished his life as he had lived it, directing that he be laid to rest in an integrated cemetery.

I repose in this quiet and secluded spot,
Not from any natural preference for
  solitude
But, finding other Cemeteries limited
  as to
Race by Charter Rules,
I have chosen this that I might illustrate
  in my death
The Principles which I advocated
Through a long life.
Equality of man before his Creator.

- Chief Joseph hauntingly echoed the ideals of the nation's founders when he asked nothing more for himself and his people than to be treated as an equal under the law:

We ask that the same law shall work alike on all men . . . Let me be a free man—free to travel, free to stop, free to work, free to trade where I choose, free to choose my own teachers, free to follow the religion of my fathers, free to think and talk and act for myself—and I will obey every law, or submit to the penalty... Whenever the white man treats the Indian as they treat each other, then we will have no more wars. We shall be alike—brother of one father and one mother, with one sky above us and one country around us, and one government for all.

- The immigrant Carl Schurz carried on the struggle for freedom in his new country and perfectly expressed the essence of liberty for all when he said,

If you want to be free, there is but one way. It is to guarantee an equally free measure of liberty to all your neighbors.

- W.E.B. DuBois refused to be limited in his thinking. He recognized that ethnic diversity enriched America, and he worked for the exercise of all civil rights without regard to color.

We are Americans, not only by birth and by citizenship, but by our political ideals... And the greatest of those ideals is that ALL MEN ARE CREATED EQUAL.

- Susan B. Anthony, whose newspaper motto avowed, *Men their rights and nothing more; women their rights and nothing less,* spoke not just for women but for all citizens. At her trial for voting illegally, she told the judge:

Your denial of my citizen's right to vote is the denial of my right of consent as one of the governed, the denial of my right of representation as one of the taxed, the denial of my right to a trial by a jury of my peers as an offender against law, therefore, the denial of my sacred rights of life, liberty, property, and—(at this point, the judge interrupted Miss Anthony and would not permit her to continue).

After the Revolutionary War, Americans began to realize a truth with which they continue to struggle: there is no such thing as a little freedom. If you begin to fight for it for one group, you must admit that all men and women have a right to the same. Freedom, by its very nature, is not exclusive. As John Adams commented in 1776,

There will be no end to it [talk of independence]. New claims will arise; women will demand a vote; lads from twelve to twenty-one will not think their rights enough attended to; and every man who has a farthing will demand an equal voice with any other, in all acts of state.

References

Bettman, Otto. L. 1974. *The Good Old Days—They Were Terrible.* New York: Random House.

Capps, Benjamin and the Editors of Time-Life. 1975. *The Great Chiefs: The Old West.* New York: Time Life Books.

"Carl Schurz." *BoondocksNet.com.* http://www.boondocksnet.com/moa/moa_schurz.html. Access date December 1999.

"Chief Joseph Speaks: Selected Statements and Speeches by the Nez Percé Chief." *PBS.* http://www.pbs.org/weta/thewest/resources/archives/six/jospeak.htm. Access date October 1998.

Dick, Everett. 1993 (1948 Reprint). *The Dixie Frontier: A Social History.* Norman: University of Oklahoma Press.

DuBois, W.E.B. 1998 Reprint. *The Souls of Black Folk.* Evanston, Illinois: McDougal Littell.

Foner, Eric. 1988. *Reconstruction: America's Unfinished Revolution, 1863-1877.* New York: Perennial.

Foner, Eric. 1999. *The Story of American Freedom.* New York: W.W. Norton & Company.

Frankel, Noralee. 1996. *Break Those Chains at Last: African Americans, 1860-1880.* New York: Oxford University Press.

Garraty, John A. and Mark C. Carnes, ed. 1999. *American National Biography*. New York: Oxford University Press.

Greenwood, Janette Thomas. 2000. *The Gilded Age: A History in Documents*. New York: Oxford University Press.

Linder, Douglas. "The Trial of Susan B. Anthony for Illegal Voting." *Famous Trials HomePage.* http://www.law.umkc.edu/faculty/projects/ftrials/anthony/sbahome.html. Access date January 2003.

McCutcheon, Marc. *Everyday Life in the 1800s: A Guide for Writers, Students & Historians.* Cincinnati, Ohio: Writer's Digest Books.

Stevens, Thaddeus. "Thaddeus Stevens Papers On-Line." *Furman University.* http://history.furman.edu/~benson/docs/stevenstmp.htm. Access date December 1999.

"Thaddeus Stevens." *Spartacus Education.* http://history.furman.edu/~benson/docs/stevenstmp.htm. Access date December 1999.

Sutherland, Daniel E. 1989. *The Expansion of Everyday Life 1860-1876.* New York: Harper & Row.

Zinn, Howard. 1999. *A People's History of the United States: 1492-Present.* New York: HarperCollins Publishers

Standards

Historical Thinking

The student will

Historical Analysis and Interpretation

- analyze cause and effect relationships and multiple causation, including the importance of the individual, the influence of ideas, and the role of chance
- hypothesize the influence of the past

Historical Research Capabilities

- obtain historical data

Analysis and Decision-Making

- identify issues and problems in the past
- marshal evidence of antecedent circumstances and contemporary factors contributing to problems and alternative courses of action
- evaluate alternative courses of action
- evaluate the implementation of a decision

Content

The student will demonstrate understanding of

The role of persons and events during Reconstruction

- The role of specific persons and events in advancing or limiting the American ideals of liberty and equal justice under the law
  - explain the impact of a particular person or event
  - explain the personal meaning of the introductory words of the Declaration of Independence
  - evaluate the advances and setbacks of the era of Reconstruction and Reform in achieving liberty and justice for all Americans

Resources

For each student

Reconstructing America by Joy Hakim: Chapter 37, "End Words"

Notebook

Student Sheets:
   Impact Arrow
   Name or Event Slip

For the teacher

Transparency: *Layers of Democracy*

Web sites

US History Sources @ http://www.cl.ais.net/jkasper/1870.html. Gilded Age and Progressive Era U.S. History

Lesson 26 End Words

Internet Resources @ http://www.tntech.edu/www/acad/hist/gilprog.html

Vocabulary

Words to Remember

*democracy — government in which the people rule themselves by law

self-evident — obvious, automatically apparent

endowed — naturally furnished

*unalienable — cannot be surrendered or taken away

*reconstruction — the act of rebuilding

*reform — to make better or improve what is corrupt or defective

*justice — fair and right treatment under the law

change — to make or become different

diversity — being different or having differences

People to Remember

*Thomas Jefferson — author of the Declaration of Independence

The Lesson

Focus Activity – 10 minutes

1. Ask the students to consider the important events and people during the time of *Reconstructing America*. If necessary, students may refresh their memories by browsing through the text.

2. Help the students identify the three themes of *Reconstructing America*.

   - What are the three themes of *Reconstructing America*? Write the themes on the chalkboard: change, diversity, and justice. Ask the students to define the terms.

3. Students review the themes of *Reconstructing America* using **Think-Team-Share**.

   - How was the period after the Civil War a time of *change*?
   - How was the era a time of *diversity*?
   - How was *justice* extended during this time?
   - What *problems or difficulties* occurred during this era that prohibited the nation from achieving full equality and justice for all Americans?

4. Use **Numbered Heads** for the students to share their opinions and insights.

Teaching Activity – 20 minutes

1. Introduce Chapter 27, "End Words" of *Reconstructing America*. Read the great words of the Declaration of Independence written by Thomas Jefferson on page 181 to the students.

   Explain that these words were both a beginning point when the new nation was created and a goal that Americans would work to achieve. The words are the foundation of our political ideals. Those ideals are still not met and the country struggles in every era to create a "more perfect union." As our nation continues to grow and

Notes

Lesson 26 End Words

develop, it is guided and evaluated using those words as a standard.

2. **Reading for a Purpose:** Students read silently or **Partner Read** Chapter 27, "End Words" in *Reconstructing America* to determine:

   - What were some of the advancements made toward full democracy during the era of Reconstruction and reform?

   Circulate and Monitor: Visit each team to help students read the chapter and identify the advancements toward full democracy.

3. Display the Transparency: *Layers of Democracy*. Explain that each generation adds to the promise of freedom by forming new layers of democracy as the nation strives to achieve liberty and justice for all.

   Guide the students in reviewing the era's achievements by discussing:

   - What new levels of democracy did the nation achieve during Reconstruction and reform?

   Write student responses on the pyramid levels of the transparency. (Some possible responses include: Fourteenth Amendment, the Freedmen's Bureau, the Fifteenth Amendment, the anti-lynching writing of Ida B. Wells, the establishment of public schools for immigrants and freed blacks, Homestead Act, the downfall of "Boss Tweed" by cartoonist Thomas Nast, and so on.)

Student Team Learning Activity – 20 minutes

Evaluating persons and events

1. Display the following passage from the Declaration of Independence on a chart:

   > *We hold these truths to be self-evident, that all Men are created equal, that they are endowed by their Creator with certain unalienable Rights, that among these are Life, Liberty and the Pursuit of Happiness...*

2. Distribute the Student Sheet: *Impact Arrow* and **one** of the *Name or Event Slips* to each student.

Each student decides

- How did this person or event advance the cause of liberty and move the nation closer to its democratic goals during the time of Reconstruction and reform?

Students use *Reconstructing America* to locate information (such as quotations) that supports their answers. Teammates assist each other with locating information or discussing the contributions of the persons and events.

3. Each student writes the name or event from his or her slip and a brief answer to the preceding question on a Student Sheet *Impact Arrow*.

   Circulate and Monitor: Visit each team. If necessary, help students locate information to complete their *Impact Arrows*.

4. Each student explains how his or her person or event moved the nation towards its democratic goals. Students display their *Impact Arrows* by clustering them around the excerpt from the Declaration of Independence.

   If necessary, add information about the persons and events to further review the era.

5. Next, review some of the events or persons who tried to divert the nation from achieving the goal of full liberty to all people (for example, the "Redeemers," Andrew Johnson, Indian reservations, William Marcy Tweed, Chinese Exclusion Act, Ku Klux Klan, Judge Ward Hunt, Jim Crow, lynching, and others).

6. Ask the students to evaluate the era.

   - Did liberty and democracy make more advances than setbacks during the time of Reconstruction and reform? Explain your opinion.

7. If time permits, share the ideas and words of Stevens, Chief Joseph, Schurz, DuBois, Anthony, and Adams from the Overview with the students.

Reflection and Review Activity – 10 minutes

1. Each student writes an explanation of what this passage from the Declaration of Independence means to him or her personally.

> *We hold these truths to be self-evident, that all Men are created equal, that they are endowed by their Creator with certain unalienable Rights, that among these are Life, Liberty and the Pursuit of Happiness . . .*

2. Each student compares this explanation with the one he or she wrote in Lesson 1.

   - How do the two interpretations compare with each other?
   - How did the study of *Reconstructing America* change or advance my understanding of the passage from the Declaration of Independence?
   - How did my understanding of America's ideals grow by studying the events and people who advanced the cause of liberty and justice in this country?

Homework

Nominate an event and a person that you think most deserves to be included in a Reconstruction and Reform Hall of Fame. Explain why the event and person should have a place in the hall of fame.

Library/Media Resources

Nonfiction

America by Alistair Cooke, Knopf

The Life Stories of Undistinguished Americans edited by Hamilton Holt, Routledge

American Childhoods edited by David Willis McCullough, Little, Brown Publishing

The Book of Distinguished American Women by Vince Wilson, Jr., Little, Brown Publishing

Connections

Library — Introduce the students to the writings of Mark Twain and Laura Ingalls Wilder. Students read one of their books, short stories, or essays.

Art/Library — Students use the web site A Portrait of History (http://www.photographymuseum.com/) to tour architecture, natural photography, features, and exhibitions. With its endless biographies and art, this on-line museum has much information on the history of reconstruction and reform.

Review Lesson IV
Lessons 21 through 26
Chapters 29 through 37

In the Review Lesson, students revisit essential ideas and vocabulary from lessons 21 through 26 to prepare for the Assessment Lesson. The Review Lesson is in the form of a card game.

If time allows, the teams may play more than one round of *Reconstructing America Review*. Even though one team member will win each round, all students win by reviewing ideas, facts, and vocabulary from the previous lessons. The goal of the game is to successfully prepare *each* member of the team for the assessment.

Reconstructing America Review IV: Unfinished Journey

1. To ensure that each student has a chance to play, students remain in their cooperative learning teams of four or five.
2. Each team receives a set of game cards and the answer sheet.
3. Cards are shuffled, separated into their respective piles (Jim Crow, Electrifying, Crusaders, etc.), and placed face down in the center of the table.
4. One team member is designated as the first player (i.e. the student whose name is last in the alphabet). The student to his or her right has the answer sheet, keeping it face down on the desk. This person is the fact checker.
5. The first player chooses a card, reads the number and the question aloud, and attempts to answer it. The fact checker turns the answer sheet over, finds the correct question number, and checks the first player's response. If the student answers correctly, he or she keeps the card. If the answer is wrong, the card is placed at the bottom of the pile. The fact checker quickly turns the answer sheet face down again.
6. Play passes to the left, and the student who was the first player is now the fact checker.
7. The game ends when all the cards are gone. The student with the most cards wins.

Reconstructing America Review IV: Unfinished Journey Questions and Answers

Jim Crow

1. What were Jim Crow laws? Laws that segregated blacks and whites after Reconstruction
2. What was the outcome of the *Plessy v. Ferguson* case? The Supreme Court ruled that segregation was legal if equal conditions were provided.

Review Lesson IV   Lessons 21 through 26

3. What did Homer Plessy do? He tested the legality of segregation by sitting in a "whites only" railway car

4. After Reconstruction, how did racists keep blacks from voting? By passing poll taxes and requiring literacy tests

5. How did segregation violate the Fourteenth Amendment? The Fourteenth Amendment gives equal protection of the law to all citizens, whereas segregation denies equal protection to an entire group of people because of their race.

6. How did Jim Crow laws violate the Fifteenth Amendment? The Fifteenth Amendment gives the right to vote to black males, whereas Jim Crow laws deny suffrage to blacks, and the poor or illiterate.

Electrifying

7. How did the nation celebrate its birthday in 1876? With a grand centennial exposition of displays and activities

8. What invention amazed visitors at the Centennial Exposition by "speaking"? Telephone

9. Which of Edison's inventions most changed the lives of ordinary people? Electric light bulb

10. Why was Edison called a practical genius? His inventions improved the everyday lives of ordinary people.

11. Name at least two of Edison's three most important inventions. Phonograph, electric light, and motion pictures

12. What handicaps did Edison overcome? He had little schooling, and he was deaf from childhood.

Crusaders

13. What newspaper reporter exposed the horrors of lynching? Ida B. Wells

14. What led Ida B. Wells to investigate mob murders? Her good friend was lynched by a mob.

15. According to Booker T. Washington, what did blacks need before seeking equality? Working skills, jobs, economic independence

16. Who was known as "the voice of his people?" Booker T. Washington

17. Who wanted full equality immediately for his people? W.E.B. DuBois

18. According to DuBois, what makes us all Americans? Our birth, our citizenship, and our political ideals

Who Said That?

19. Who said, "We are Americans, not only by birth and by citizenship, but by our political ideals?" W.E.B. DuBois

20. Who said, "... I had the feeling that to get into a schoolhouse and study ... would be about the same as getting into paradise." Booker T. Washington

21. Who said, "I have no power to describe the feeling of horror that possessed members of the race in Memphis when the truth dawned upon us that the protection of the law was no longer ours"? Ida B. Wells

22. Who said "Our Constitution is colorblind, and neither knows nor tolerates classes among citizens"? The dissenting opinion of Supreme Court Justice John Marshall Harlan in the *Plessy v. Ferguson* case

23. Who said, "Genius is 99 percent perspiration and one percent inspiration"? Thomas A. Edison

24. Who said, "separate but equal" does not violate the Constitution? The United States Supreme Court ruling in the case of *Plessy v. Ferguson*

Words! Words! Words!

25. What is a centennial? Hundredth anniversary

26. What are Jim Crow laws? Laws of segregation

27. What is lynching? Mob murders or execution without the benefit of a trial

28. What was *Plessy v. Ferguson*? Supreme Court case that permitted segregation

29. What is the N.A.A.C.P.? The National Association for the Advancement of Colored People founded by W.E.B. DuBois

30. What does the Declaration of Independence say about equality? "All men are created equal, that they are endowed by their Creator with certain unalienable rights, that among these are life, liberty, and the pursuit of happiness."

Made in the USA
Lexington, KY
01 August 2016